Creative Ecologies

Creative Ecologies
Theorizing the practice of architecture

HÉLÈNE FRICHOT

BLOOMSBURY VISUAL ARTS
LONDON · NEW YORK · OXFORD · NEW DELHI · SYDNEY

BLOOMSBURY VISUAL ARTS
Bloomsbury Publishing Plc
50 Bedford Square, London, WC1B 3DP, UK
1385 Broadway, New York, NY 10018, USA

BLOOMSBURY, BLOOMSBURY VISUAL ARTS and the Diana logo are trademarks of
Bloomsbury Publishing Plc

First published in Great Britain 2019

Copyright © Hélène Frichot, 2019

Hélène Frichot has asserted her right under the Copyright, Designs and Patents
Act, 1988, to be identified as Author of this work.

Cover design: Eleanor Rose
Cover image © Marian Goodman Gallery

All rights reserved. No part of this publication may be reproduced or
transmitted in any form or by any means, electronic or mechanical,
including photocopying, recording, or any information storage or retrieval
system, without prior permission in writing from the publishers.

Bloomsbury Publishing Plc does not have any control over, or responsibility for, any
third-party websites referred to or in this book. All internet addresses given in this
book were correct at the time of going to press. The author and publisher regret any
inconvenience caused if addresses have changed or sites have ceased to exist, but can
accept no responsibility for any such changes.

A catalogue record for this book is available from the British Library.

Library of Congress Cataloging-in-Publication Data
Names: Frichot, Hélène, author.
Title: Creative ecologies : theorizing the practice of architecture / Hélène Frichot.
Description: New York : Bloomsbury Visual Arts, 2018. |
Includes bibliographical references and index.
Identifiers: LCCN 2018030761 (print) | LCCN 2018032208 (ebook) |
ISBN 9781350036536 (ePDF) | ISBN 9781350036543 (ePub) |
ISBN 9781350036567 (hardback : alk. paper) |
ISBN 9781350042087 (pbk. : alk. paper)
Subjects: LCSH: Architecture–Philosophy. | Architectural practice.
Classification: LCC NA2500 (ebook) |
LCC NA2500 .F7375 2018 (print) | DDC720.1–dc23
LC record available at https://lccn.loc.gov/2018030761

ISBN: HB: 978-1-3500-3656-7
PB: 978-1-3500-4208-7
ePDF: 978-1-3500-3653-6
ePub: 978-1-3500-3654-3

Typeset by Newgen KnowledgeWorks Pvt. Ltd., Chennai, India
Printed and bound in Great Britain

To find out more about our authors and books visit www.bloomsbury.com.
Here you will find extracts, author interviews, details of forthcoming events
and the option to sign up for our newsletters.

Contents

List of illustrations vii
Acknowledgements ix

Prologue – Story one: Maria Reiche – Surveying 1

Introduction: Ecologies of creative practice 7

PART ONE Environment-worlds

1 Environments 17

Environments 19
Environmentalities 29
Worlds and worlding 31
Environment-worlds 36
Practice scene: tacit, taciturn, Tacita 46

2 Ecologies 55

An ecology of practices 58
Ecologies of creative practices 61
Practice scene: Katla Maríudóttir's volcano 64
Exhaustion: of environment-worlds 69

PART TWO Things

3 Object oriented 81

Story two: Agnès Varda – gleaning 81
Things 86
Rock, grotto, inscrutable thing 87
Hyperobjects 93

Object-oriented things 96
OOPs! 98
OOOh, no! 101
Practice scene: Chelle Macnaughtan's *Trottoirs* 109
Thing-power 116

4 Thing-power 119

Object-oriented democracy 119
Architectural things 121
An entangled web of things 125
Practice scene: Julieanna hauls mud 126
Onflows, through-flows and things 133
Exhaustion: of things 137

PART THREE Thinkables

5 Noology 145

Story three: Zoë Sofia (Sofoulis) – unthinkables 145
Thinkables 149
Noology 150
Noopolitics 152
Noourbanography 154
Practice scene: Michelle Hamer follows one stitch at a time 156

6 Concept-tools 165

Image of Thought 165
Thinkables 174
Concept-tools 179
Practice scene: Michael Spooner's *A Clinic for the Exhausted* 187
Exhaustion: of the concept 194

Conclusion: Exhaustion and its after-affects 205

Practice scene: Margit Brünner's joys 208
Exhaustion, beatitude 211
Practice scene: Camilla Damkjaer's handstand 214
After-affect: beatitude, joy 216

Bibliography 219
Index 239

Illustrations

Cover: Tacita Dean, *Fatigues*, 2012 (detail). Chalk on blackboard, 6 panels, 230 × 1110 cm; 230 × 557 cm; 230 × 744 cm; 230 × 1110 cm; 230 × 557 cm; 230 × 615 cm. Courtesy the artist; Marian Goodman Gallery New York/Paris and Frith Street Gallery, London

P.1 *Maria Reiche dot-to-dot* 2

P.2 Image of poster for Venice Biennale of Architecture featuring Maria Reiche, Venice 2016 4

1.1 Bridie Lunney, *Suspension Test* 18

1.2 Tacita Dean – still images from the 16 mm colour film *Boots*, 2003. Three films (English, French and German versions) 50

2.1 *Katla Maríudóttir*, Compass, *Jarðnæði: Tranquil Terra* 66

2.2 *Katla Maríudóttir*, Architectural Events, *Jarðnæði: Tranquil Terra* 67

2.3 Alex Schweder, *Your Turn*, Aldrich Contemporary Art Museum, Ridgefield, CT, 2017 75

3.1 *Agnès Varda dot-to-dot* 83

3.2 *ARCH+ Journal for Architecture and Urbanism*: Release Architecture, May 2016 89

3.3 Christian Kerez, *Incidental Space*, Swiss Pavilion, Venice Biennale of Architecture, 2016 91

3.4 Alisa Andrasek, *PROBOTICS AGENTWARE RESEARCH* 2008–9, directed by Alissa Andrasek DRL/Architectural Association London 2008–9 97

- **3.5** Alisa Andrasek and Jose Sanchez, *BLOOM*, Bloom Games, London Olympics 2012 100
- **3.6** Chelle Macnaughtan, *Les Trottoirs de Paris*, Spatial Listening Exhibition, 2011, RMIT Gallery 110
- **3.7** Chelle Macnaughtan, Spatial Listening Exhibition, 2011, RMIT Gallery 112
- **4.1** Julieanna Preston, *Moving Stuff*, 2013 128
- **4.2** Julieanna Preston, *Moving Stuff*, 2013 129
- **4.3** Julieanna Preston, *A Reconciliation of Carboniferous Accretions*, performance 130
- **5.1** Michelle Hamer, *Fatigue Kills*, tapestry thread on plastic grid, 2005 157
- **5.2** Michelle Hamer, *When War Is Over*, tapestry thread on plastic grid, 2017 160
- **6.1** Margaret and Christine Wertheim and the Institute For Figuring, *Crochet Coral Reef*, Museum of Arts and Design, New York, 2016 185
- **6.2** Michael Spooner, The Swimming Pool Library, *A Clinic for the Exhausted*, rendered image, 2010 188
- **6.3** Michael Spooner, The Landscape Room, *A Clinic for the Exhausted*, cross section, 2010 190
- **6.4** Michael Spooner, The Landscape Room, *A Clinic for the Exhausted*, model, 2010 192
- **C.1** Margit Brünner, Catcher I; Catcher II; Surveyor Metro Melbourne; Surveyor Crown Casino, *Cosmethic Space Refinements*, 2002 209
- **C.2** Margit Brünner, *Zwischen Büschl* [Among Tufts], 2005. Videostill 213
- **C.3** Camilla Damkjaer's handstand 215

Acknowledgements

Thinking does not happen alone but in the company of companion thinkers. There are many students, colleagues, friends and family I would like to thank for helping me bring this book project to realization, for giving me the courage to think and in thinking to practice further. Pedagogical relationships and responsibilities should never be underestimated, and I owe a great debt to the students who have worked with me in seminars, design studios and in the context of their own research projects at KTH, Stockholm, and at RMIT University, Melbourne. I am thankful for the conversations I have had during the early stages of preparing this book, specifically, I am grateful for the time and space allowed me during a fellowship at Architecture Theory Criticism History (ATCH), University of Queensland, between June and August 2016, and I thank Geraldine Barlow for looking after me while I was in Brisbane. More recently, I am grateful for conversations and encounters with Gail Jones and Anna Gibbs in the Writing and Society Research Centre, and Stephen Healy and Katherine Gibson in the Institute for Culture and Society, both located at Western Sydney University. I thank Zoë Sofia aka Sofoulis for letting me land on her doorstep in the Blue Mountains, Sydney, and talk to her about her work. I have presented work in progress at Manchester University, the Staedelschule Architecture Master Class (SAC) Frankfurt at the invitation of Johan Bettum, at the Graz Architecture Lectures, TU Graz (thank you Dubravka Sekulic), and at the Bartlett School of Architecture where I am especially grateful for the support and friendship of Peg Rawes and Jane Rendell. My colleagues and friends who have offered invaluable feedback on the manuscript include: Isabelle Doucet, Mattias Karrholm, Jonathan Metzger, Douglas Spencer, Karin Reisinger and Helen Runting. I thank the critical and creative practitioners whose work I have been able to discuss for trusting me: Michelle Hamer, Katla Maríudóttir, Chelle Macnaughtan, Julieanna Preston, Michael Spooner and also Alex Schweder. The architect-thinkers Alexander Müller and Mathieu Wellner kindly invited me into their temporary studio space, Argue MullerWellner during the artistic occupation of the historic Ruffinihaus in Munich for a writing retreat exactly at that desperate moment when I was attempting to finalize the manuscript, and here I also thank Eva Krauss for putting me up in Munich. In February 2017, I took up brief residence in a cottage in Coasters Retreat, New South Wales, to write and think, and I want to thank Sally McInerney and my dear friend Julia Lehman for making this possible. I thank James Thompson at Bloomsbury for his encouragement, and David Kelly for his careful copy-editing. This book was in large part funded by a generous Riksbankens Jubileumsfond sabbatical grant, which allowed me the invaluable time to dedicate myself to writing as well as paying visits to a number of institutions. Finally, my family has been suffering for way too long with my all-consuming state of distraction, and so while I suppose they will not have the patience to read this book, I dedicate it nonetheless to Rochus, and Felix and Florian.

Prologue
Story one: Maria Reiche – Surveying

> *To see a landscape as it is when I am not there … .*
> SIMONE WEIL, *Gravity and Grace* (1952: 42)

A woman stands near the top rung of an aluminium ladder and looks out across a vast desert wilderness. Her hair is held back with a scarf and her cotton skirt gently billows in a warm breeze. Her arms are afloat, which means she is balanced somewhat precariously. She is wearing flip-flops and on the ground below is a leather satchel and what looks like a bundle of rope. Perched there on her ladder it is hard to imagine what this woman could have to do with architecture, or with any kind of creative, material, space-making practice. Instead it would appear that she apprehends a tabula rasa, which begs the question: Why was this image of a lady on a ladder to be found everywhere during the 2016 Venice Biennale of Architecture? She was spotted all over Venice, on billboards, on posters at ferry stops and at Marco Polo airport. The same desert vista repeated at small and large scales, the same lady on a ladder gazing out across a vast uninhabited landscape, searching for something.

Is she looking towards the past or towards the future? She could be the last 'modest witness' of the after-effects of a devastating event of global reach, or else she could be documenting an ancient prehistoric site and its curious markings. Could she be looking for signs of architecture or purposeful design?

Her name is Maria Reiche. She is a mathematician and an anthropologist, and, like an architect, she knows how to read a complex site and then document it through drawings. The landscape vista she apprehends is the ancient *Pampas de Jumana* in the Nazca desert of southern Peru, and her project is the documentation of the 2,000-year-old large-scale land tracings

2   CREATIVE ECOLOGIES

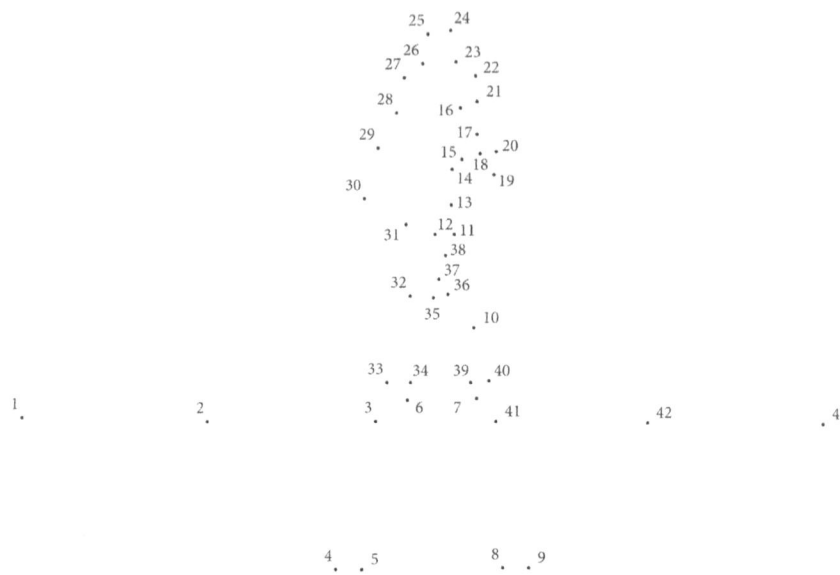

FIGURE P.1 Maria Reiche dot-to-dot. *Drawing by Hélène Frichot, 2015.*

known as the Nazca lines. These ancient landscape markings comprise geometric forms that beg decryption. They include a bestiary of animals: a guano bird, a spider monkey, a dog and a humming bird (Chatwin 1989: 89), among others. In order to bear witness to these patterns, Maria needed to achieve a slightly elevated, technologically augmented point of view on the situation before her. Through measuring and drawing the landscape markings she renders sensible a secret otherwise kept by the landscape.

Maria has been appropriated by the curator of the 2016 Venice Biennale of Architecture, Chilean architect Alejandro Aravena, as his mascot, his 'aesthetic figure', through which, I argue, he aims to produce certain effects *and* affects. She is the figure by which Aravena asks us how we (all whose practices are somehow related to architecture) might offer a 'report from the front'.

When you open the Venice Biennale of Architecture 2016 website, the title of which was *Reporting from the Front*, or when you collect your ticket, catalogue, guide and other paraphernalia, you catch sight of Maria on her ladder. Immediately on entering the Giardini Exhibition, you are in Maria Reiche's room. And Aravena has some interesting reasons for using her as his key aesthetic figure:

1 Maria demonstrates inventiveness in the face of scarcity. She has scarce resources, and must make do with her simple ladder-technology to gain a point of view over the landscape, which would otherwise remain a meaningless dry plane full of incomprehensible clusters of stone and gravel.

Challenge for architects: With scarce resources and minimal means how can we nevertheless produce valuable outcomes?

2 Maria's response to the landscape is 'pertinent', Aravena argues, challenging the abundance of technologies she *may* have used, for instance, a truck to transport her across the plain with her ladder mounted on top for an even better point of view. But, as Aravena explains, such a mode of transport would have quickly destroyed the fragile ground that she wishes to document and preserve. Pertinence means paying attention to the situation at hand, which is what Maria does.

Challenge for architects: Pay close attention to your sites of engagement and be respectful amidst your encounters. Do not destroy what is of value in your sites before you have even begun your work.

It is essayist and traveller Bruce Chatwin who introduces Maria Reiche to the world when he writes an article about his encounter with her in the *Sunday Times*, and it is Chatwin's essay that has aroused Aravena's interest. Maria had been occupying the Peruvian landscape for some forty years, since 1932, when Chatwin met her while travelling in the 1970s. She had taken it upon herself to measure and trace the ancient Nazca lines to determine whether their arrangement was coordinated with the movement of the planets, the cycle of the seasons and the winter and summer solstices. The Nazca lines are negative geoglyphs, shallow trenches dug into the ground, across an area of 450 square kilometres, by removing the reddish pebbles and uncovering the whitish earth beneath.

Chatwin explains that Maria could add up 'strings of decimals' in her head, and when these got too large, she would make a note of them in the folds of her cotton skirt (1989: 94), the one we see billowing out in a warm breeze. That is to say, she works with what she has ready-to-hand. On her aluminium ladder, which she carries around the desert landscape with her, Maria Reiche becomes technologically augmented. She achieves just the right distance above the ground, while remaining materially attached to it. Embedded in the landscape at the same time as able to achieve just the slightest of technological advantages, she manages to secure an advantageous point of view. From this technologically augmented, embodied position she is able to perform what can be called 'immanent critique' or 'critique-from-within' (Doucet 2015; Stengers 2005a). She is attached to the empirical ground, in

FIGURE P.2 *Image of poster for Venice Biennale of Architecture featuring Maria Reiche, Venice 2016. Photography by Rochus Hinkel.*

situ, but with just the right amount of distance to achieve criticality from within her local environment-world.

Again, it might seem that she has little to do with architecture. The geoglyphs can hardly be called architectural, if architecture is understood in a conventional sense. In his essay Chatwin points out that Maria in fact holds no truck with 'theory' because what she has, she explains to him, are the 'facts'. But, I want to respond to Maria, surely theory can assist in the thinking through of material facts and (architectural) theory can be put to work amidst material practices? I am interested in Maria's practice on account of her modest use of technologies, her aluminium ladder, the notes she pencils on her skirt when strings of numbers get too long, and because of the ambiguity of the vistas she gains access to. She is an important reminder of older women thinkers and their transdisciplinary work. As I have suggested, we might speculate whether in this image she is looking towards the future or the past. She stands there, for my purposes, as a figure confronting what has come to be called the 'Anthropocene', witnessing the exhaustion of worlds, past and present. Where, after all, have the ancient Peruvians gone? How, finally, will humankind disappear? And what material signs and traces will they leave in their aftermath? 'Every landscape is haunted by past ways of life' (2017: G2), Anna Tsing, Heather Swanson, Elaine Gan and Nils Bubandt argue in their beautiful book *Arts of Living on a Damaged Planet*, a book that can be read backwards and forwards, from the points of view of monsters or ghosts. How do we open our eyes to see what is to be learnt from such landscapes? How do we reinvent creative practices so they engage more responsibly, and with more care in them?

If we pause imaginatively to project into a future, what will some alien 'other' witness when humankind has been erased from the face of the earth, and the world-historical scene of the *Anthropos* has all but faded from view?

We are told, by anyone from geologists and political scientists to cultural studies theorists and philosophers of science, that an imaginary future alien other would bear witness to what has come to be called the 'Anthropocene'. In *Anthropos*-cene, the *Anthropos* draws attention to the privileged unit of 'man' and the cene both to a very long span of time and, etymologically, to the 'new'. We can also hear 'scene' in this recently coined neologism, prompting us to consider the part we play across our contemporary world-historical scene, and how the Anthropocene presents us with a novel geophilosophical event.

Anthropocene is a term you may have encountered, as it has been gaining increasing currency since being offered up for consideration by Paul Crutzen and Eugene Stoermer (2000). It is a concept and a thesis that frames a large-scale account of how the material geological constitution of the planet earth has been transformed as a result of humankind's industrial activities. How long these transformations have taken place depends on your point of view, but the largest impacts have been made since the Industrial Revolution. Built into the Anthropocene, there is a sense of something exhausted, scenes of exhaustion via resources depletion, compounded extinctions and climate change. With the designation of the Anthropocene as event and geological span of time, there is hubris mixed with shame. What have we (human creatures) achieved and at what expense to our local environment-worlds?

I am of course wilfully constructing the figure of Maria here as though she might be a witness to such scenes of worldly exhaustion. She has in fact borne witness to the aftermath of the exhaustion of at least one world, the lost civilization that artfully constructed the Nazca lines. Her landscape of engagement could be called 'posthuman' – a posthuman landscape – in that it follows after the labour of a lost civilization, about which we know little more than these stones arranged in marvellous patterns. It could be called more-than-human, in that it speaks of a future yet to come, in which we might pause to acknowledge more than simply human relations.

A posthuman landscape is composed of exhausted worlds, though not necessarily the absence of the 'human' per se. Instead, the posthuman is a speculative gesture, a figure that must radically adjust its position, be wary of assuming its place of privilege and exception, and instead understand that it is bound up and entangled with all manner of things, material and immaterial, corporeal and incorporeal worldly forces. Importantly, the 'posthuman' cannot be extricated from its location. It can claim no special vantage point or privilege. It must undertake its work from within a situation, which presents the problem of how to undertake an adequate survey from where you are. Who surveys what, and with what purpose in mind? No site can be entirely exhausted, because surveying opens up future possibilities and potentialities that must be considered with a sense of responsibility and responsiveness amidst our ecologies of creative practice.

Introduction:
Ecologies of creative practice

An orientation towards architecture is usually taken on frontally, with the architectural object in view, looming forward from an indistinct background, claiming its formal autonomy. The celebrated forms of architecture, their iconic status and their contribution to the identity formation of global cities, together with the signature architects who author world-significant projects, are generally what is assumed to properly represent architecture. An orthodox approach to architecture demands that the object that is architecture is kept in focus, and that space, form, program, typology and material distribution are prioritized. This book approaches architecture from quite another direction in order to argue that the object-hood of architecture is but a small part of what constitutes this vastly differentiated discipline. Sometimes an *indisciplined* approach reveals more about what is at stake in carving out spaces, territories and shelter and acknowledging contingent encounters that accept inconvenient relations.[1] What if a full frontal approach to architecture were turned around, and instead of an orientation towards the object of architecture carefully framed and curated, its facilitative background was allowed to emerge and the deceptively circumscribed object became near indistinguishable from these surroundings? What if the architectural object were revealed to be something closer to a thing among other things, operating necessarily in ecological relation, apt to emerge only to decay?

This would be to allow the environment-worlds of architecture to be considered, as well as the minor characters who work away quietly at the periphery, those who slowly challenge the core assumptions of the discipline so that the media-savvy monolith that is assumed to be architecture comes to be ever so slightly shifted or, better still, multiplied across a more diverse array of points of view. The minor creative practitioners who go so far as to say there is no 'core of architecture', there is rather architecture conceived as a multiplicity of diverse concerns in engagement with local environment-worlds at the threshold of exhaustion. This is an architecture in the midst of things, undergoing continuous variation, emerging from the contingency of events across complex social, political, economic, ecological, technological, material and conceptual fields. I approach architecture from the seething milieu that is the environment to better get at its ecologies of creative practice and its furious activity of making-worlds.

It should be stated promptly that this book is not interested in either the icons or the idols of architecture, which are covered copiously elsewhere. Instead, I am concerned with other ways of doing architecture, especially where architecture as a circumscribed discipline becomes muddied by alternative disciplinary influences, for the purposes of this project, specifically in relation to art, philosophy and literature, especially where these intersect with the environmental and the architectural humanities, and in light of the emergence of creative practice research.

Supporting architecture and facilitating its projects, compelling 'environmentalities' constrain possible world imaginings – and here an emphasis can be placed on the question of the environment as a complex ecological conundrum of territory and habitat, site and place, culture and nature, as well as on the 'mentalities' of environ-*mentalities*. That is to say, how subjectivities of various kinds cluster as mental and social ecologies in relation with their environment-worlds. This immediately requires that 'ecology' is cracked open and allowed a wider sense that extends beyond natural phenomena, special interest groups and the specializations of the natural sciences, towards political, social and subjective relations. To speak of 'creative ecologies' is to participate in the making of liveable environments, as distinct from the pursuit of short-term profits, a project T. J. Demos calls the decolonization of nature (2017: 20). The conjunctive resonance of environment-worlds, a term I introduce in this book, is of crucial importance in relation to creative ecologies, drawing attention to how, amidst environments, worlds of sense are carved out by specific subjectivities and social collectives based on their capacity for world-making projects and for making life liveable. While such projects might admit a troubling anthropocentric tendency towards the exhaustion of worlds, to say nothing of the extinction of worlds, the diminution of landscapes of perception and the delimitation of a capacity to produce ameliorative effects, yet, amidst the symptoms of (architectural) exhaustion, possibilities all the while emerge, possibilities we must urgently reclaim.

In undertaking the reorientation of architecture that I propose, a larger-scale and a more challenging background must be acknowledged, already introduced in my prologue: the seemingly ineluctable milieu of the so-called

Anthropocene and its associated crises and how it describes the *longue durée* of our environment-worlds entangling ecologies, economies and technologies in an all-pervasive capitalist economic logic. From geologists, atmospheric chemists (Crutzen and Stoermer 2000) and political scientists, to cultural studies theorists and philosophers of science (Haraway 2016; Stengers 2015), architectural historians (Barber 2016) and architectural theorists (Turpin 2013), speculations are ventured as to what an imaginary post-human other would bear witness to in the aftermath of a geological epoch that bears the traces of human industrial activity. As the editor of a new volume dedicated to the environmental humanities, Ursula K. Heise explains it was the ecologist Eugene Stoermer who coined the term in the 1980s, but its popularity took off in the 2000s following the reception that greeted several co-authored articles by Stoermer and the atmospheric chemist Paul Crutzen (Heise 2017: 2). Kathryn Yusoff (2015) cites Crutzen as he opens up this vision of an imagined future, speculating on the points of view of our descendants in the year 2200 or 2500: 'They might liken us to aliens who have treated the Earth as if it were a mere stopover for refueling, or even worse, characterize us as barbarians who would ransack their own home . . . Remember, in this new era, nature is us' (Crutzen and Schwagerl, cited by Yusoff, 2015). The Anthropocene thesis recognizes that the collective labours of the human species-being have become a distinguishable trace in the lithosphere, the earth's outer crust and mantle, making them the co-author of their own likely demise (Colebrook 2017; Yusoff 2015). Though even to speak of a species-being as such is to make a great many assumptions about who and what belong to this category of the human.

The Anthropocene, I argue, is already what could be identified as a near-exhausted concept, and while this is not a reason to give it up, it is a reason to treat it with the greatest critical caution. It has become the scholar's and intellectual's alternative to the more popularized threat of 'climate change' and sustainability discourse. Something is changing and we, whoever is supposed to count as this 'we', are caught up in its midst. Certainly, the question needs to be asked, as many have asked, and as Etienne Turpin does in his book of collected essays *Architecture in the Anthropocene*: 'Is the Anthropocene not just another assertion, typical of European society, of the ascendancy of man over nature?' (Turpin 2013: 3). It would seem that the denomination of the Anthropocene aims to collectivize human concerns either under a global concept of whole-world hubris or else distress.

Where the cene of the Anthropocene designates a vast geological epoch that problematically anticipates the sentient observation of some alien other who bears witness in the distant future to the residue of a natural phenomenon once called *Homo sapiens*, a scene is far more fleeting. It is a circumscribed part performed in a movie, a play or an opera, a scene across which certain actors rehearse various roles only to recede again into the shadows. This begs the question of how the scene comes to be composed, with the use of what resources and how it distributes its sensible parts and produces its affects. I pay special heed to the (s)cene where I present the scenes of practice that punctuate the three parts of this book and my conclusion. Amidst the eight practice scenes I present, ecologies of creative practice experimentally and experientially express themselves. By ecologies of practice I acknowledge my debt to the philosopher of science Stengers, who insists that no practice should be considered as just like any other, and that each practice is organized by obligations and requirements specific to its concerns and disciplinary milieu. She also points out that practices are at constant risk of exhaustion.

Across a series of practice scenes, I build relations with a number of practitioners whose creative practice troubles disciplinary boundaries and whose work might seem improper, even threatening, when viewed from the conservative core of the discipline of architecture. Where possible, my aim is to present practice works that I have encountered, by creative practitioners I have entered into dialogue with. With some of the practices discussed, I have even shared a pedagogical relationship, but here pedagogy must be understood in a specific way, as that which responds to an ethics of the encounter and in relation to the 'pedagogy of a concept', simply what we learn through the generosity of exchanging and sharing concept-tools. The eight distinct practice scenes tell of ecologies of creative practices undertaken in intimate relation with environment-worlds, things and thinkables. They are explored by subjectivities that are 'larval' in that they discover themselves and their concrete situations via their practices, and keep on discovering. One of the things they discover as they go is their intractable embroilment in post-human landscapes of change. The feminist human geographer Doreen Massey claims that the question of subjectivity has been one raised most pointedly by feminist thinkers (Massey 2005), and this is where I acknowledge that one of my primary concerns is how women practitioners, understood as a minority within architecture, work within their ecologies of creative practice. Architecture as a disciplinary framework still has much work to do in terms of acknowledging the contribution of those precarious subjectivities working at the periphery of the discipline and the profession, perhaps having had to 'exit the discipline' or else reside in its hinterlands. An argument for them is ventured, and their representation as part of a broader feminist ethos in architecture is celebrated.

There will be practice scenes, and there will be stories. Inspired by Donna Haraway and Stengers, among other feminist thinkers, I can agree that 'Each time a story helps me remember what I thought I knew, or introduces me to new knowledge, a muscle critical for caring about flourishing gets some aerobic exercise' (Haraway 2016: 29). Stengers likewise insists that we have a desperate need for other stories that are not simply fairy tales but accounts of how situations can be transformed by way of practical experimentation (2016: 132). The three stories I present offer brief visions of aesthetic figures, each one suggesting a lesson through which creative practitioners might think, and in thinking, practice, and in practising, think further. The stories, which open each part of this book, focus on sage older women, even somewhat idiosyncratic women, including the anthropologist Maria Reiche, the documentary film-maker and artist Agnès Varda and the Australian cultural theorist Zoë Sofia (Sofoulis). Each guide offers a much-needed counterbalance to the masculine heroes who are usually rolled out for demonstrations of world-making practices. There is nothing essential about the choice of these particular figures; it is not as though they are somehow exemplary. They simply open three distinct points of view to help us along. As aesthetic figures or guides, they speak in turn of activities of surveying environment-worlds, gleaning things and confronting the unthinkable.

There are three guiding concepts that organize the work: An environment-world, or *Umwelt*, is a complex and specific site composed of material and immaterial things and relations; its logic is one of a material semiotics (Barad 2007; Haraway 1991) or a mixed semiotics (Sauvagnargues 2016: 17), by which I mean materially embedded systems of signs that provide the means for the sustenance of a life and a capacity for sense-making ventures. Suffice to say, signs emerge in situ. An environment-world is an intensive zone in which the ecological registers of mentalities, socialities and environmentalities co-mingle, contravening any assumed divide between Nature and Culture and any hard-and-fast distinction between human and non-human actors, though I do not subscribe to a 'flat ontology'. The beings and becomings of things are uneven, composed of too many dominating actors and silenced minorities to be considered hierarchically indistinguishable.

Where environment-worlds organize the first part of this book, things organize the second part. The thing is a material and/or incorporeal artefact that can be passed from hand to hand, offered in exchange and presented as a provocation to thought. We glean things, we voraciously consume and exchange things and, as I will explain, a great deal of noise has been made about things in recent theoretical discourse. A great deal of intellectual labour has been exhausted, from Actor Network Theory to feminist and other New Materialisms, to Affect Theory, to Speculative Realism and Object Oriented Ontology, in asking what is a thing, or what can a thing do, or whether we can ever get at a thing without privileging the human point of view on things. I propose to reorientate these questions so that the ecology of creative practices that pertains to minor expressions of architectural thinking and doing can be examined; in the process, I will hold tight to the impossible slipperiness of things and their complex relational matrices, keeping in mind

Gregory Bateson's advice that 'We are not outside the ecology for which we plan – we are always and inevitably part of it' (2000: 512). Critical and creative practitioners have a way of 'following the material' that amounts to an ethico-aesthetics, offering important things to say about how 'things' and 'thinkables' together produce a pronounced impact on the construction and destruction of environment-worlds.

A thinkable, which is the concern that organizes the third part of this book, does not assume the pre-existence of a thinking subject in command of her cognitive powers. A thinkable is that which either constrains habits of thought or liberates them from the midst of environment-worlds. Thinking a thought is a practice most often over-coded by the habits of thinking determined by the status quo, clichés, the imposition of good sense and common sense. It is terribly hard to grab hold of a thought, and who has the time to think these days anyway? No one thinks alone, even when they appear to be sitting silently at their desk or staring out the window while riding a bus. We necessarily think collectively, with and against other thinkers, our conceptual friends and foes. Thinking happens collaboratively, and no concept arrives out of nowhere. While concepts tend to be signed by certain thinkers, this does not mean thinkers can stake out proprietorial rights. Concepts have their own journey forms and histories, but their pertinence depends on the exigency of encounters in which they erupt, where urgent work needs to be done. A concept, and more specifically what I will introduce as a concept-tool, is what makes a thinkable provisionally durable. Furthermore, I hold no truck with the announcement of the end of theory, or the death of theory as regularly advertised or lamented. Pronouncements of theory fatigue and its impending extinction must be exhausted so that we can move on with the hard work of reclaiming what theory can do in relation to our practices, and how theory-work is itself a form of practice.

Amidst the assembly of thematic concerns, stories and practice relations I have introduced earlier, an insistent undercurrent moves the work as a whole. It is the crucial question of exhaustion, the exhaustion of environment-worlds, the exhaustion of things and the exhaustion of thinkables, all of which include the exhaustion of subjectivities unfolding in process, exhaustively. Exhaustion is not simply a condition of tiredness, but a condition of having had enough. When one is tired, it is still possible to rest a while in order to recover. I rearticulate exhaustion via a methodology of exhaustion, and at the conclusion of each of the three parts of the book, I offer a discussion of exhaustion and exhaustivity that intersects with environment-worlds, things and thinkables. Exhaustion can proceed in two directions: towards out-and-out exhaustion approaching the threat of erasure, even the obliteration of modes of life, a sixth extinction event; or towards a process of gleaning, making do with what is available, collecting, considering, reclaiming, recovering and contracting encounters with others. Depletion of resources, post peak oil, species extinctions, exponentially exploding populations and aging populations, global warming, climate change, the globally generalized ubiquity of an economic rationalism financializing the world and all that is in it, the dwindling of affect, slavery, the rape of refugee girls, homelessness, the instrument of control that social media too quickly becomes: Exhaustive lists such as these bombard us on an everyday basis suggesting global exhaustion amidst our environment-worlds. Yet, sometimes, a leak, a scurrilous escape, exhaustion can move in the other direction as an expression of creative resistance. Exhaustion is a corporeal and psychic state that doggedly continues, exhausting itself, but somehow clinging to moments of exuberant joy, to visions and sonorities and other possibilities. This, I suggest, is what creative research amidst ecologies of creative practices can demonstrate.

Note

1 'Indiscipline' is a concept that is currently being explored by Jasmin Dücker in relation to her comparative reading between Deleuze and the poet Emily Dickinson. I first encountered Dücker's work at the Deleuze Studies Camp in Istanbul, Turkey, 2014. See http://anglistik1.phil-fak.uni-koeln.de/22327.html (accessed 2 August 2016).

PART ONE

Environment-worlds

1

Environments

On Tuesday much of Christchurch abruptly collapsed to the ground. The Cathedral lost its steeple. Closer to home, and all that summer, the eastern seaboard had been inundated with water. Dislodged interior furnishings were adrift down erstwhile suburban streets. Wild winds assailed coastal towns and from time to time the smaller settlements in the hills were razed by fire. Some ten years ago now the family home succumbed to wayward flames. She walks its ghostly perimeter attempting to revivify the architectural corpse. Where there was once floor, now there is ceiling and remnants of rafter. Where the roof once proudly kept at bay the forces of inclement weather, there is now only thin air. It is a radical redistribution of materials.

ADRIEN ALLEN, Hélène Frichot and Bridie Lunney (2011)

In this first chapter, I proceed from a reflection on environments and 'environmentalities' towards worlds and 'worldings' in order to arrive at the conceptual construction of environment-worlds. Environment and world are placed in disjunctive relation to create the compound environment-worlds, a literal translation of the German word *Umwelten*. From there, I circle back around in Chapter 2 to a discussion of ecologies in order to introduce what the philosopher of science Stengers calls an ecology of practices. As well as alluding to the organization of the household, ecology, *oikos* and *logos*, tells us of the intimate connection between organism and environment. More specifically for my purposes, it is a term that sends me towards the promise of ecologies of creative practice, that is to say, the practices that take place amidst environment-worlds, and what we do there as we make the places

FIGURE 1.1 *Bridie Lunney,* Suspension Test. *Research image, 2011.*

where we live and die more or less habitable. And so, in Part One, I explore an incremental additive process, overlaying one term upon the other in order to suggest a conceptual construction that sets the scene for ecologies of creative practice. It is a survey that no doubt attempts to travel too far and wide for the conceptual territory I apprehend is growing daily. I conclude with an introduction to exhaustion, understood not only as an affective demeanour, both conceptual and corporeal, but as a methodology and even a means of further creation. Exhaustion will be considered distinct though related to the extinction events we experience today as human and non-human creatures across post-human landscapes. Exhaustion, I venture, can be reconstructed as a methodology of exhaustion. It is an approach that I have learnt slowly, incrementally, iteratively, through my encounters with critically aware architects, designers and artists, whom I am calling creative practitioners. I hasten to add that this is not to exclude other kinds of practitioners from creative work, but only to allow me some specific disciplinary focus. The methodology of exhaustion, as I will progressively demonstrate, follows one slow step at a time so that connections between things and thinkables and environment-worlds can be rendered durable, even if only provisionally.

Environments

If you were to ask me I would struggle to tell you anything about my environment. Do I start, as do too many philosophers, with my desk? Do I extend outwards by way of concentric rings from a domestic or an institutional environment, depending on what day of the week it is and where I happen to be sitting? Should I speak of the woods that are accessible at the edge of town? Is *that* where the environment is to be found? Should I address the virtual environments I am plugged into on a daily basis, surfing, uploading, downloading, updating? This is what has provoked the question of environments, the recognition that I am unable to offer an adequate answer. Environments are ubiquitous, everywhere, yet I feel ill-equipped to speak of them and how they are composed. I remain wary of attempts to offer exhaustive historiographies of the concept cum material conundrum that is 'the environment'; though I admire such efforts, they inevitably leave out too many minor voices (Sörlin and Warde 2009; Warde, Robin and Sörlin 2018). From this position I am obliged to hesitate, to express my limits, which means I am also prepared to bear witness to what I encounter. What do environments do? I know in a general sort of way that environments surround all living things, offering them support and sustenance. I understand that without environments there is no life for the living creature, and that at the same time the living creature reciprocally 'environs' its local scenes through modes of action particular to its capacities. Organism and environment operate in a contrapuntal relationship, which is not to say that the power relation between them is always balanced.

When it comes to architecture, the first environment we tend to acknowledge is the built one, where environments operate as designed technological infrastructures, facilitating the presumed exceptionalism of human life and too often forgetting the profound intermingling of diverse forms of life. Architecture contributes to the manufacturing of environments across varying scales, and is in turn nested within environments, real and virtual. Our vulnerability and fragility become pronounced, as Judith Butler writes, when these designed infrastructures fail us (2014, 2015).

Environment is a word that, despite the pervasiveness of its material effects, too often recedes into the background of architectural and creative practice considerations. Environment is inescapable, despite the human creature's desire to propel itself beyond the atmosphere to secure another point of view on what it presumes to be its world, a world imagined as a blue-green Christmas bauble hanging in space (Kepes 1972: 10). It is tempting to believe that the word 'environment' names some place that is out there; and in some vague and diffuse way, we (humans) know that an environment supports us, but we rarely think of how we depend on it for our survival and for the very forms of life we express. We know that an environment supports us, but somehow to think about it renders it fragile and unstable. Neither can this 'we' that I have just now incanted be considered as without presumption, for the 'we', whoever we are, is equally at stake in rethinking architectural environment-worlds, where the complex question of what environments do is compounded with the means by which worlds are constructed.

Who are we who gather around our matters of care and concern amidst an environment-world? Many implicit assumptions are sheltered in the simple enunciation of a 'we'. Are you with me or against me? Who is this 'we' you claim to speak for? (Stengers 2012; Tsing et al. 2017: M4–M5). Gregory Bateson states it simply as: 'in the pronoun "we" I of course included starfish and the redwood forest, the segmenting egg, and the Senate of the United States' (Bateson 2002: 4) – which is to say, as Eduardo Kohn points out in *How Forests Think*: '"We" are not the only kind of *we*' (2013: 16; emphasis in original). A diverse mix of different kinds of assembly that collect not just humans and non-human creatures and life processes, but institutional arrangements and technological infrastructures, and which demand that 'we' likewise reorient our thinking about, *and* practising amidst, environments. A 'we' immediately suggests an assembly of socially conscious participants sharing some matter of concern or care. 'Who speaks and acts? It is always a multiplicity, even within the person who speaks and acts. All of us are groupuscules' (Foucault and Deleuze 1977: 206), including the fact that the greater part of our bodies is composed of 'bacteria, fungi, protists, and such' (Haraway 2007: 3; Tsing et al. 2017: M3–M5), as Haraway is fond of pointing out. This means that rather than the habitual emphasis on the sovereign human subject, we are obliged to think in terms of our species-being as humans (Barber 2016: 1167; Chakrabarty 2009) and the effects we have made at a macro-scale, and how these effects hit the ground amidst the ordinary affects and circumstances of everyday life.

Who is the Anthropos anyway? This is a question raised when environmental and ecological issues are discussed today in light of the Anthropocene thesis (Alaimo 2017: 89–120; Colebrook 2017: 10; Heise 2017: 5; LeMenager 2017; Stengers 2013: 176) and when addressing an exhausted earth. While the Anthropos, designating the human species-being en masse, is a more circumscribed part of the lively and diverse 'we' described earlier, the act of rendering it exceptional or privileged, beyond culpability, is an act likely to conclude in the diminution of its own collective well-being. Who do we think we are anyway? Should all human life and expression be collapsed under the category Anthropos if it is a more circumscribed set of human actors that have collectively brought about the earth's geological transformation? Nevertheless, 'we', in being earthbound, all seem to be in it together. Who is the Anthropos? is not a question with an adequate answer, and no doubt needs to be shifted to something like: What do we think we are doing? For the creative practitioner at least, this becomes a speculative issue of adequate ethico-aesthetic practices explored amidst situated, singular and collective experiences and experiments. Ethico-aesthetic practices pertain to ecologies of creative practice, bringing together modes of (aesthetic) expression with an awareness of the ethical implications of such expressions.

Environment is what unfurls when the architect or creative practitioner turns her back to the built object – which is an environment of a special sort, contained, 'well-tempered' (Banham 1984) and controlled – and witnesses another point of view; yet it is not a vista that can be claimed as though the architect or creative practitioner safely stands outside a situation to look out across a landscape. Position is always embedded in facilitative environments, which are the milieux that render creative projects possible. This is what Maria Reiche demonstrates from the top of her aluminium ladder, securing a technologically augmented position just above the ground, all the while embedded on the earth and deeply involved in her material practice.

Environment, when taken for granted as a given and stable condition, is that which is mapped and analysed as a site prepared to support future construction and world-making projects, but the environment is never simply a given condition; it is far more lively than that and likely to surprise. The environment is neither stable nor passive. It is not simply a natural resource to be plundered, nor simply a cultural condition to be further organized via acts of rarefication and construction. Science studies thinkers such as Donna Haraway and Bruno Latour have taken to conjoining these modifiers, natural and cultural, in order to insist on a conceptual construction: Latour's *nature-culture* (Latour 1993) or Haraway's *naturecultures* (Haraway 2007; 2016). We should be wary of the 'Nature/Culture schema' (Latour 2017: 226) where the backslash insists on absolute division, or what Latour describes as modernist purification. Andreas Malm offers warnings here, suggesting that this conceptual sleight of hand, this hybrid amalgam of society and nature (he speaks of society rather than culture), risks dissolving the two terms, rendering them indistinguishable, even eradicating them altogether (2018: 83–88). I believe something rather more complex is at work. I argue that these loaded terms maintain their distinction, and at the same time they cannot be easily disentangled. They do not collapse, but clinch together. The challenge, it would seem, is to maintain this clinch, nature-culture, in a quivering embrace, to not entirely collapse the distinction between the terms, but neither to draw them dangerously apart. It is neither a ratio that can be stabilized nor a relation that can be equalized once and for all. It is not a container in which things simply sit, but contributes to the very formation and life of things by way of a relational ontology, which is what Actor Network Theory (ANT) and Science Technology Studies (STS) teach us. And this would appear to be where environments, with an emphasis on the plural, are laid out, in this tangle, like a complex conceptual knot or a scrubby patch of weeds.

Embedded in a rhythm of embrace and withdrawal, the creative practitioner is swallowed by, and then emerges out of the background of, her environmental milieu, advancing and receding, creating as she goes so many intersecting ripples, unexpected connections, patterns of diffraction and entanglements.[1] There are foregrounds and backgrounds, depending on position and point of view, but there is no offstage to the world. When the creative practitioner goes to work, she transforms her environment-world, at the same time as transforming herself, at the same time as being transformed by her environment-world – even if, as Rachel Carson once suggested, the environment endures far longer than the human creature (Carson 2002); even if, as Stengers states, the world will continue without us and we will constitute yet 'one more "contingent event" in a long series' (Stengers 2000: 144; also cited in Colebrook 2014a: 29); even if, as Gilles Deleuze has remarked when he reads Michel Foucault, 'we must take quite literally the idea that man is a face drawn in the sand between two tides: he is a composition appearing only between two others, a classical past that never knew him and a future that will no longer know him' (Deleuze 1988a: 89). The man-form is 'destroyed by that inexhaustible force' (Foucault 1970: 278) as other formations spill in to take up his place. Yet, we must somehow find the means to persist, to extend the gesture of a creative ameliorative act amidst environment-worlds.

Environments support, but also intrude unexpectedly via environmental events, volcanic eruptions, hurricanes, tsunamis and a spot of bad weather. Environments are never simply outside or in the background, but run through and are intermingled with organisms. The intimate, entirely co-dependent and co-constitutive relation between organism and environment is resilient and fragile, now able to thrive and as quickly apt to decay. By now, we cannot but be acutely aware that the human creature has collectively wreaked an increasingly large impact on its differentiated environments. We slowly come to realize, with a mixture of horror and joy, that environments do not simply surround and support creatures, but enter and exit living creatures and their worlds of significance. Cecilia Åsberg, Kathrin Thiele and Iris van der Tuin use pollen allergy as an analogy to explain the flow-through of the environment: 'so many things remind us today of the extent of our precariously contextualized situation, from pollen allergy (the environment in the human) to climate change (the human in the environment)' (Åsberg, Thiele and van der Tuin 2015: 151). Discussing dust and exhaustion, Jussi Parikka likewise suggests: 'But something can be so near that it loses focus, falls out of view – these not-enough-to-be-things, or too-near-for-thingness (a tongue in cheek Heideggerianism) are what might enter us through our nostrils, inhaled, and cause a cough, or a rash on the skin' (2013). The organism, human or otherwise, may well inhabit an environment, but the environment likewise inhabits it, flowing through; forging constructive relations and providing the basic means of sustenance, air, food, water entering and then exiting as so much waste, or else flowing through and decomposing organisms via forms of bacterial or viral infection, poison, general malaise or some chemico-industrially composed material like plastic or asbestos. This flow-through of environment immediately indicates that more and more of the materials and information environments carry have been synthesized through human industrial prowess, arousing a growing interest in the potential of a bioeconomy (Walker 2015).

I propose no exhaustive history of the 'environment' as it pertains to architecture. While I am not an architectural historian, I am heartened by the work of a new formation called the environmental humanities and its growing influence on architectural historiography.[2] The environmental humanities is a project of building relations among humans, non-humans and environments. Stephanie LeMenager remarks on this new formation: 'The very name "the environmental humanities" indicates that the humanities have met the world and been changed by it' (LeMenager 2017: 480). For those working in the fields of architecture and design, as well as art, it might be tempting to believe that their own disciplinary fields are being territorialized. You might be surprised to witness the emergence of a disciplinary domain that so closely overlaps with your own concerns. Another approach would be to understand the importance of sharing problematic fields towards an understanding of local and global histories and theories of environments, including the traffic and utility of shared concept-tools and creative practices. While the emphasis of the environmental humanities, at least in architecture, is so far predominantly historical rather than theoretical (Barber 2016), what I take away from this promising new institutional formation is a mounting emphasis on practice and the stories we can tell each other about our ecologies of practice. It is remarkable how a concept that is also a milieu such as the environment erupts powerfully as a rallying call in response to world-historical events and their concrete, material, concatenating effects.

In response to this rallying call, at each turn we should ask: Who has access to environments and their associated goods? The management of the environment benefits the lives of some and diminishes the lives of others. The fundaments of environment and its contemporary governance is an environmental-political problem. For instance, the liberty of air, assumed to be generally accessible and even a basic (human) commons, can also become a product, as Mark Dorrian warns, 'commodified, privatised or militarised' and thereby subjugated (Dorrian 2013: 149). Much the same can be said of water, a resource steadily being corralled by multinational companies such as Nestle, who bring us our favourite bottled beverages. As for fire and earth, they have already been reined in for the ignition of industrial machines, and for large-scale agri-business and its territorializations, troubling what Maria Puig de la Bellacasa calls human–soil relations (Puig de la Bellacasa 2017: 169; see also Demos 2016; Shiva 2012; Stengers 2015). Stengers remarks: 'The privatization of resources that are simply essential to survival, such as water, is the order of the day, as well as that of those institutions which, in our countries, had been considered as ensuring a human right, like education' (Stengers 2015: 80). And these are just the basics.

As I proceed I will continue to posit environment as both material milieu and concept, that is to say, as a complex material semiotics. Donna Haraway explains that material semiotic nodes or knots are where 'diverse bodies and meanings co-shape one another' (2007: 4), and this is not about representation or being didactic. This requires undertaking a tireless conceptual category work, to sort out the terms of use – a work that can in no way be exhausted, because revised terms are required to tackle newly emerging problems.

Inevitably, when the question of the environment is raised, the exhausted concept of 'nature' likewise enters the picture. The challenge, according to Didier Debaise, Stengers and their collaborators speaking together as a collective voice, is how to situate nature without assigning it a place (2015: 169). Nature can be 'secret, hostile, nurturing, mechanical, sublime, infinite, in danger, or even capable of making humans endowed with reason agree with each other.' They explain 'what we used to call "nature" implied the association of the modern sciences with a general kind of method' (2015: 171). They make reference to A. N. Whitehead, who describes the 'bifurcation of nature', where, on one side an 'objective' nature persists blind to our human values, indifferent to our projects; and on the other side a nature that is the very stuff of our dreams, values and projects makes itself available for study and for use (see also Debaise 2017: 7–11). Debaise, Stengers and their colleagues do not want to give up on nature. They speak of those who do not believe in nature, perhaps on account of it being such an exhausted concept, and at the same time they remark that distinctions are needed, such as the one between nature and earth (Debaise et al. 2015: 173). But where and how do you draw your line? What kind of category work is required in order to get a grip on things? There is always the risk that the conceptual map you make will be misused by the person who next picks it up. Questions of the environment are also projective, asking what is to be done, and in what ways can architecture and creative practice contribute?

There are those who adamantly deny climate change, and there are those who suffer a weary exhaustion in response to environmental anxieties. All the while, unabated, a disastrous forgetfulness sinks in. A persistent distraction leads us away from thinking about the intrusion of 'nature' amidst our environment-worlds, or what Stengers instead calls the intrusion of Gaia (2015: 43–50). Stengers offers a word of caution: '*To name is not to say what is true but to confer on what is named the power to make us feel and think in the mode that the name calls for*' (2015: 43, emphasis in original). The power of naming an architecture or a city 'green' or 'sustainable', for instance, risks lulling us into the sleep of short-term reassurance.

It is evident from the current situation of exacerbated crisis, not to mention the presentiment of crises looming, that whatever might have been learnt in the age of environmentalism of the 1960s and the 1970s were lessons too easily forgotten. Even though a book such as Rachel Carson's *Silent Spring* is said to have inaugurated an environmental movement, there persists today the terrible sensation of slipping into forgetfulness or else into a melancholic malaise. To Carson's *Silent Spring* can be added other influential works, as Peg Rawes suggests, such as Arne Naess's discussion of deep ecology (1973) and Gregory Bateson's approach to an ecology of mind, specifically his discussions of the fine-tuned imbrication of nature and mind in his books *Steps to an Ecology of Mind* and *Mind and Nature* (Rawes 2013: 8, Bateson 2000, 2002). There is in addition James Lovelock's Gaïa theory of the earth, which Stengers and Latour have recently returned to (Latour 2017; Stengers 2015). All of these works with their warnings would appear to be lessons learnt previously, lessons warning human creatures how they should be conscious of their embeddedness in their environment-worlds and how far they depend on them as a matter of well-being and survival. Acts of environing are met with unexpected environmental events, but as Gyorgy Kepes, artist, theorist and educator, wrote in the early 1970s, 'without an ecological conscience, we have very little hope for change' (Kepes 1972: 9). Kepes states simply: 'We have had many warnings' (1972: 1). While T. J. Demos argues that a wholesale reorientation of our habits is still possible today (Demos 2016) and that we may yet succeed in decolonizing nature, changing our light bulbs, recycling our rubbish and riding bicycles will not have been enough, Stengers dryly notes (2015: 10). Stengers explains that we have suffered something of a missed encounter, because there have been so many impassioned pleas made well before her own.

At the opening of his essay *The Three Ecologies*, penned in the 1980s, Félix Guattari writes of how the planet Earth is undergoing an intense period of techno-scientific transformation, and if no remedy is found, 'the ecological disequilibrium this has generated will ultimately threaten the continuation of life on the planet's surface' (2000 [1989]: 27). Earlier, uttering much the same lament, Kepes writes: 'A wildly proliferating man-made environment has shrunk living space, dimmed light, bleached colour, and relentlessly expanded noise, speed and complexity' (Kepes 1972: 1).

So many thinker-practitioners are calling out to those who will listen: Pay attention!

In the 1970s, there was another trajectory, which set out a different set of tactics, strategies and practices that were underwritten by feminist concerns (Rawes 2013: 8–9). Here too the work of eco-feminists, and more recently feminist political ecologies (Harcourt and Nelson 2015), to which can be very recently added so-called Anthropocene feminism (Grusin 2017), should be acknowledged. As Leslie Kane Weisman demonstrated in the 1990s, feminist thinkers in architecture have persistently engaged with questions of space, environment and territoriality. We too easily forget or overlook feminist thinkers, much as we forget the oft-repeated warning calls: 'It is easy to accept unthinkingly the man-made landscape as a neutral background. It is not so easy to understand the environment as an active shaper of human identity and life's events' (Weisman 1992: 2). Felicity Scott makes the point that the environment in the 1970s was increasingly being understood as a 'man-made milieu' (2007), which must assume some agreement among 'men' in terms of how environmental infrastructures such as cities, towns and rural landscapes, and more recently online communities might be organized and distributed. Tendencies of thinking, acting and practising together, for better or worse, dominated by a privileged class of human creature.

While 'man-made' is supposed to be gender neutral, it should in no way be read as such, as demonstrated by feminist ecological thinkers and architectural philosophers like Peg Rawes (2013) and Elizabeth Grosz (2013) and in the recent collection *Arts of Living on a Damaged Planet* (Tsing et al. 2017). The Australian philosopher Elizabeth Grosz argues that, 'Climate change, the poisoning of the atmosphere, the extinction of countless species, has undoubtedly been effected by those who regulate large amounts of energy, something rarely accessible to most women throughout human history' (2013: 134). In being conceptualized as a man-made milieu, the environment is also being understood as a system or infrastructure that supports the flows and stoppages of information. The concerns enunciated with the rise of environmentalism in the 1960s through to the 1970s do not abruptly dissipate, but are to be found here and there, despite the indulgences of the 1980s, and the quagmire of theory for the sake of theory in the 1990s, where diverse approaches to feminist thinking are likewise too often occluded.

Acts of critical and creative reclamation and resistance are required (Doucet and Frichot 2018). Storytelling has emerged as a powerful mode of expression by which the plight of environment-worlds is told. This has to do with acknowledging the conceit of maintaining an objective position, and instead speaking from your situation, as partial and fragmentary as it may be. LeMenager observes that it is worth considering 'how life itself begins to encourage new representational regimes' (LeMenager 2017: 477). Haraway, who argued powerfully in the late 1980s for the benefits of interlacing partial and situated knowledge (1988), continues to stress the joyful usefulness of speculative fictions, speculative facts and science fictions, all of which are designated by the one acronym SF, to be deployed where it works (2016). It is important what stories we tell about our environment-worlds, and how, and 'it matters what stories tell stories', Haraway asserts (2016: 34).

Rachel Carson's *Silent Spring* is an oft-cited book that confounds easy classification on account of its storytelling poetics. It is what I would call a ficto-critical work. With its distinct voice it pre-empts some of the storytelling approaches that are currently being explored by the environmental humanities at their conference events, such as *Stories of the Anthropocene Festival* (Stockholm, October 2016)[3] and *Anthropocene Slam: A Cabinet of Curiosities* (Madison, WI, 2014).[4] How the story of the environment is told is important. In her recent work, much inspired by Carson, Karin Reisinger investigates nature reserves as institutions and delicately allows the tangled web of their mutual interferences of natural and cultural forces, humans and non-humans, to be felt (Reisinger 2018). Reisinger took part in the Anthropocene festival in Stockholm in 2016, not only to tell stories of more-than-human encounters amidst war-torn nature reserves in Africa and in Eastern Europe, but also to spatialize her work with images and projections across abandoned niches in the underground space where delegates gathered, a gathering space thirty metres underground and once the site of Sweden's first experimental nuclear reactor on the campus of KTH (Royal Institute of Technology, Stockholm). All of this is to say that from distinct disciplinary niches new kinds of storytelling emerge in different places, amidst different gatherings. They are what the political scientist Jane Bennett calls onto-stories (2010). The power of such storytelling is what I hope will animate the practice scenes and stories I present across this book.

What about practices that acknowledge their deep imbrication in environmental milieux, or what I call environment-worlds? This is not about 'saving the environment', which risks being merely an expression of inflated hubris, but about working with and alongside whatever we mean by environment. Whether we call it nature, the environment, ecology, Gaïa, or invent new concepts for it such as the hyperobject, what we must collectively acknowledge is that whatever it is, it 'is no longer the backdrop for our human projects, with no project of its own, but is intruding in our dreams, values and projects' (Debaise et al. 2015: 168).

The challenge, as Zoë Sofia (Sofoulis 2000) puts it, is how to sustain 'facilitating environments' and avoid the 'exhaustion' of the planet's supplies. This 'how' leads us to the challenge of thinking practices and practising theories. As Albena Yaneva argues, cosmopolitical thinkers like Stengers and Bruno Latour, and to this party she adds the name Peter Sloterdijk, all argue that nature no longer offers a unifying vision, a stable or stabilizing pattern for humans. Unlike a vision of a unified cosmopolis, cosmopolitical practices multiply, expressing a diversity in the world and a diversity of worlds and entities (Yaneva 2016: 2). The different definitions of environment, nature, ecology, habitat and territory we construct are very much entangled with our material relations. This requires working on a good enough definition of environment, worked out in situ in relation to a creative practitioner's practice: a concern central to this work. The environment, as many of the aforementioned thinkers stress, is not simply 'out there' playing backdrop to human activities. As Stephen Mosley argues: 'Nature, instead of being the backdrop against which the affairs of humans are played out, is recognized as playing an active role in historical processes' (2010: 2). This thought-figure of the backdrop or background is a frequently repeated leitmotif. Instead, environment is that which is done, instigated, composed and ecologized – which leads us to the question of embedded embodied practices: of slowing down, of listening, of practices of caring and even of different argumentative and storytelling strategies.

We never really stopped talking about environments, and practising amidst them, even if we rarely act in unison, or talk about the same thing. The voices are exhausted, and yet they continue to speak, despite or through their exhaustion. While there is no summary of the environment that can be offered, and it would appear that even the emergence of the environment as a concept is obscured where it is not contested, what I want to insist is that as concept and material surroundings it is less a matter of saying what it is in general or universal terms than getting at what it does in situ, localized *and* muddled with global effects from amidst the trial and error of one's practices.

What we can surely agree upon is that when we address environments today, these are environments in crisis, environments threatened with all manner of material and conceptual exhaustions. Still, crisis is ascribed based on point of view and what carries significance for a form of life. While bleached coral reefs dwindle in one part of the world, jellyfish populations take over in another, and while 'we gain plastic gyres and parking lots, we lose rainforests and coral reefs' (Tsing et al. 2017: G4), which is to say, curious compositions and decompositions take place unevenly. How might we best grapple with our cares and concerns from the midst of such situations?

Environmentalities

Environmentalities, in which can be heard environ-*mentalities*, is a concept that places ecologies of mind in the midst of material admixtures of environmental milieux. This concept becomes especially relevant in today's attention-based economies, where even silicon-valley designers come to regret features they have developed to facilitate the use of ubiquitous screen interfaces, such as the swipe-down-to-refresh function (Lewis 2017). Interacting with online environments and their infrastructures has an impact on the politics and sociality of communities, including the corporeal and psychological behaviours of users. The environment, as I have argued earlier, is a material and virtual admixture as well as a contested conceptual conundrum. As a concept, environmentalities operate as a prompt to acknowledge how far collective thinking at the scale of populations, local and global, has an impact on acts of environing. Mentalities draw attention to tendencies of thinking together, and in thinking acting, and in acting thinking further. These iterative cycles procure certain specialized as well as everyday practices.

So what happens when the fictions/facts, what Stengers and Latour call the 'factishes', we construct and circulate – via our daily practices; via idle chit-chat and gossip; via conventional and Web 2.0 media interfaces; via the brandscapes we daily inhabit, for instance, the brandscapes that inform us which building products and practices are 'green'; and also via the theory we consume, taking in messages obliquely – begin to produce the cognitive architectures of everyday life? What we arrive at, I propose, is something that can be called 'environmentalities'. Environmentalities alert us to how collective intelligence is manifested through complex matrices of data and information flows into which we humans are plugged as fleshy collaborators working amidst multifarious environment-worlds.

The conjunction that can be construed between 'environ' and 'mentalities' compounds the ecological registers of subjectivities, socialities and environmentalities, a triple ecological register that I will discuss later with a close reading of Félix Guattari's essay *The Three Ecologies* (2000). Mentalities should not be mistaken for the mind, explains Brian Massumi, where mind is conventionally understood as attached to a phenomenological self-same subject (Massumi 2015: 179). Mentalities pertain to modes of activity in process, not in opposition to, but through the dynamics of networked systems, something that Gregory Bateson has repeatedly stressed (2000, 2002).

Environmentality is a concept developed in Michel Foucault's lectures presented at the College of France (1975–76, 1978–79), and collected in *Society Must be Defended* (2003) and *The Birth of Biopolitics* (2008). For Foucault, this concept designates how modes of neo-liberal governance direct the performance of populations, making them live and letting them die via 'new techniques of environmental technology' (Foucault 2008: 259). The human subject is collectivized amidst a population that takes shape reciprocally with its environment. It is a specific subject that Foucault has in mind, *homo oeconomicus*, entrepreneur of the self, a collective subject prone to economic incentive whose perceptions, activities and desires are organized by an economic grid.

This discussion of the human subject rendered at the scale of populations is peculiar to the formation that is the city, a material phenomenon that emerges in a recognizable silhouette with the rise of industrialization and takes on new formations and relations through advances in global telecommunications that connect human settlements of various kinds. I will not attempt to offer any back-history to the emergence of the city as a form of human settlement that arcs back to the ancient Greek *polis*, and before, because that would require distinguishing between too many versions of what a city can be, or rather, what a city can do (Frichot, Gabrielsson and Metzger 2016). The city or 'urban problem' is an environmentality par excellence, a constructed milieu that interplays not only with the collective practices of a population, but with how it thinks together, that is to say, its 'noopolitics' (Hauptman and Neidich 2010). Our situation becomes even more challenging today because amidst the contemporary neo-liberal urban contexts of advanced capitalism processes of subjectification are targeted en masse as marketable data are produced at ever greater speeds. While increasingly mediatized environments may well appear to be targeting the individual in all her particularity, Foucault counters that subjectivities are procured at the scale of populations through 'modifications in the variables of the environment' (2008: 269–270). Peter Sloterdijk's account of gas warfare becomes a haunting historical and conceptual comparison here, in the discovery that the specific human subject need no longer be the target, as the broader information environment she inhabits will suffice (Sloterdijk 2007a).

While the neologism that is 'environmentalities' is not to be found in its full form in Foucault, its presence is indubitable. It is a concept that has been further shaped by thinkers such as Arun Agrawal, who claims ownership of it where he explains that he has composed 'environmentality' out of Foucault's better-known concept 'governmentality', as well as Timothy W. Luke and Richard Fletcher (see Fletcher 2017). Governmentality is Foucault's study of the art of governance, with an emphasis on analysing concrete practices, and an insistence on the plural specificity of governmental institutions, which is to say that it is a term that does not presume universality (2007; 2008). Agrawal's focus is on the drift of contemporary societies towards environmental concerns. He explains 'environmental subjects come to think and act in new ways in relation to the environment' (Agrawal 2005: xiv). These are what Verena Andermatt Conley has previously called eco-subjects, directed to behave in certain ways in response to their perceived environmental concerns (1993). There could be counted as many kinds of eco-subjects as there are specified environmentalities, whether characterized by discipline, economic incentive, socialist thought or even a feminist and queer orientation, as well as combinations of all these types, and others. Fletcher argues that combinations of these different environmentalities are what manifest as a politics (Fletcher 2017). The thing is, both environment and subject come to be rethought through their relations, less as singular individual units, not even as the modernist concept of a homogeneous population, but at the complex interchange between thinking together (even if unwittingly) and how concrete material milieux come to be transformed through thinking as such. Environmentalities is a concept that draws attention to how things and thinkables are not lodged in separate domains that divide what is sensible from what is intelligible, but impact on each other amidst environment-worlds.

Worlds and worlding

World as conceptual complex and, more specifically, a shift of focus from world as some stabilized object to processes of *worlding* need to be briefly addressed before I offer an account of what I mean by environment-worlds.

Peter Osborne sets out a distinction between globalization and *worlding*, or between 'globe' and 'world' (Osborne 2014). He defines 'globalization' as the effect of the relative global deregulation of capital markets, including the denationalization of the regulation of markets in finance capital, the implication of which is the evacuation of a social component, resulting in a conceptual space that *has no social occupant*. He is cautious to warn that there are many rich accounts of globalization, but he wants to complicate the aforementioned definition and its evacuation of the social with the Heideggerian existential-ontological notion of 'worlding', and then complement this with philosopher Jean-Luc Nancy's preferred formulation of globalization, that is, '*mondialisation*'. Globalization obscures a world, processes of worlding and associated practices. What this facilitates is a complication between the globe, on one hand, as that geometrically spherical expansion that extends exhaustively all the way to infinity, associated as it is with notions of infinite perfection, and on the other hand, the world, or existential engagements of multiple, located *worldings*, which pertain to finitude and material exhaustion. As Nigel Thrift points out: 'There is no world that is somehow more complete, in other words, but rather a series of incompletes' (2011: 6). By incomplete, I take it that the world is not a project in search of completion (some *telos*), but is open-ended and contingent. The world is only as such because it worlds, it is in process, as any minimal investigation of a world carved out by architecture must surely demonstrate. Home, as one intimate example, is an endless maintenance project (Gabrielsson 2017).

What does Jean-Luc Nancy, whom Osborne brings up, do with *mondialisation*? Among other things he associates it with the mundane, and with the mundane he draws attention to dirt, specifically that which is unclean, *l'immonde*. He draws attention to the dirty material of the real, which, whether he knows it or not, makes him a 'litter mate' with the radical feminist philosopher of science Haraway who repeatedly tells us that we should get back into the mud. Nancy further associates his *le monde* (world) – *l'immonde* (unclean) word play not just with the unclean, but with nonsense, and a world heavy with suffering, disarray and revolt (Nancy 1997: 9; see also Janssens 2012: 54–55). These are the kinds of troubles with which, Haraway argues, we need to stay; we need to stay with the trouble and not clean our hands of it (2016). In his series of interviews and essays called *Cosmograms*, Jean-Christophe Royoux remarks that the 'world can no longer be conceived as a unique and stabilized "nature" upon which our conceptions and representations might base their worth' (2005: 12). This, he concludes, demands an 'aesthetic of cohabitation whereby everyone becomes responsible for the environment that he or she creates' (13).

To *mondialisation*, Haraway appends the 'other', producing *autre-mondialisation*, a concept that she borrows from Paul Preciado (2016: 20). Rather than construct a relation between polis and the police, Haraway extends the possibility of thinking other (*autre*) kinds of relations in the polis such that polis might be related to politeness (Haraway 2016: 92). The place that is called a city supports many worlds and relations that are more-than-human. It is a question of response and respect amidst the encounter, of paying attention to others, Haraway explains, when she forwards her cross-species project (2007: 19). A project subsequently expanded when she writes her more recent book *Staying with the Trouble* (2016). Worlding is entanglement and generative interruption (Haraway 2007: 20), where I am startled out of my self-centred subject position by responding to some other. My mobile position, and this cannot be stressed enough, is not circumscribed and stable.

Nevertheless, there are those who insist that the concept of world is threadbare, if not exhausted.

It is important here to make a pass through the big concept called world, because there are strong voices claiming that this concept has been exhausted and we need to dispense with it altogether. The world is an exhausted concept, Timothy Morton insists, and we need to replace this concept with another.

'World,' Morton explains, 'is more or less a container in which objectified things float or stand. World as the background of the events is merely the objectification of a "hyperobject", ' he argues (Morton 2013). Hyperobject is Morton's preferred term. And to help him define his preferred term, which shows us something that world, environment and nature cannot, he presents a series of large-scale phenomena that fall under this newly coined concept: biosphere, climate, evolution and capitalism. To respond to current social, political and climatic ills, his answer is to 'drop the concepts *Nature* and *world*, to cease identifying with them' (2013: 97). Why? Because they are leading us to out-and-out catastrophe, towards a completely nihilistic 'Noah's Arc'–type adventure, leading us away from a 'coexistence with nonhumans without a world', which is an implicit reference to Martin Heidegger's reflections on animals being 'poor in world'.

A concept like world, Morton continues, is what gives us underground oil and gas pipes, it is an exhausted concept and we must work to transcend it. In any case, the world simply does not exist, he insists. It is not just animals, stones and things that are without a world, we are all bereft of a world. 'What is left if we aren't the world?' he asks. 'Intimacy,' he answers himself. 'We have lost the world but gained a soul' (Morton 2013: 97). This new-found intimacy with non-humans, this promised new awareness 'ends the idea that we are living in an environment' (99). There is simply no such 'container' to be observed out there: 'When we look for the environment, what we find are discrete life forms, non-life, and their relationships,' Morton insists. Yet, surely all of these relationships have been rendered sensible by recourse to discussions and studies of diverse environments, developed through the collective work of the environmental sciences and humanities, I cannot help but interject.

With his conceptual invention of the 'hyperobject', which is supposed to alert us to the 'mesh' that inheres between objects – subjects are also subsumed under his concept of 'objects' – Morton proposes that he is opening a point of view on 'things' that has otherwise been occluded by our fixation on terms such as 'world', 'nature' and 'environment'. His mesh holds things apart, so that relations remain non-relations, for each object must be taken in its unique withdrawnness. Morton will not support relations; this is not 'process relationism', he insists, which he promptly dismisses as a kind of modernist hangover. Relationism is what he calls 'sludge'. Yet what do we give up when we give up these concepts? Is Morton's concept of the hyperobject a sufficient replacement to help us think differently with and through our messy situations?

Unlike Morton, I am not ready to give up the 'world' so easily. More pointedly, I am not ready to give up practices of worlding. I remain unconvinced by his stand-in concept, the hyperobject, which is something we have no access to, which is withdrawn, which we can build no relationship with, and which dispenses, in any case, with all material relations including, it seems, those pertaining to our practices. I will return to this newly coined concept of the hyperobject when I venture an account of things in Part Two of this book.

For now, I prefer to situate my thinking elsewhere and otherwise. Rather than a fixed entity, I cannot help but apprehend and experience a world in process. A world, as it were, continues to world, as vertiginous and overwhelming as that may be. Neither can there be a sense of the world, Jean-Luc Nancy points out, because the world is sense (1997: 8). There is no holding firm to it as it continues to transform everything. That worlds are in process, that worlds are multiple and that worlds emerge through processes of worlding, do not make them 'sludge', and if they do, then this might stand as a reminder that we are all closer to the dirt, mud and sludge, than we realized. And sludge or dirt or mud, bacterial disarticulation, as Haraway is so eager to point out, is the messy stuff out of which we are made and to which we will all inevitably return (Haraway 2007).

While world forming is what is taken to characterize 'man' and his activities, and may well be a concept that has given rise to gas pipelines, underground oil, fracking and other such destructive modes of extraction as well as overheated infrastructural development, that is not to say there are no other approaches to working with worlds and worlding, ones that are less exploitative.

A world continues to world, while creative practitioners continue their worlding labours. Haraway insists: 'It matters what worlds world worlds' (2016: 35). Nevertheless, her take on Heidegger's formulation of the 'world worlds' (Heidegger 2001: 43) allows much more into the world in question. Citing the ethnographer Marilyn Strathern, whom she calls the practitioner of thinking practices, Haraway stresses, 'it matters what ideas we use to think other ideas' (2016: 34). It matters, and we must take response-ability, meaning that we must be responsible, as well as *responsive to* our milieu and to our 'mess-mates' with whom we practise and think amidst our ecology of practices. 'It matters what thoughts think thoughts; it matters what stories tell stories' (34). Haraway is instructional, suggesting that the world becomes a place of storytelling where worlding is the process by which stories are told that construct worlds, at the same time as worlds are constructed by us, the human creature. The world does not have to be rendered as an inaccessible blue marble, a Christmas bauble, nor maintain global homogeneity. It does not even have to posit a big question. Haraway constructs a combinatorial and composes a refrain: 'It matters what thoughts think thoughts. It matters what knowledges know knowledges.

It matters what relations relate relations. It matters what worlds world worlds. It matters what stories tell stories' (35). It matters that in each of these instances, the stress on matter, the messy stuff of material relations, is doggedly repeated. All of this is cultivated through response-ability, our responsiveness to situations, to a local world, which takes shape by way of an ecology of practices (2016: 34). Here Haraway cites Stengers, whose formulation of an ecology of practices, crucial to this book, will be introduced in more detail in the following.

Architecture rolls out environment-worlds and moulds the often-unwitting subject. To rework a phrase from feminist thinker Zoë Sofia (Sofoulis): Aside from their local environment-world, the subject is not (2000: 183). Or, to cite Donna Haraway, a source close to Sofia, 'nothing comes without its world' (1997: 137; see also Puig de la Bellacasa 2012). A similar position is present in Judith Butler's recent argument that, 'We cannot talk about a body without knowing what supports that body and what its relationship is to that support, or lack of support' (2015: 65). Butler positions such a formulation as fundamental to feminism's resistance to a phallocentric understanding that posits the subject as sovereign and independent, and as capable of acting without being acted upon. Rejecting this ontology, she theorizes the human body as 'a certain kind of dependency on infrastructure, understood complexly as environment, social relations, networks of support and sustenance' (Butler 2014). The infrastructures that form an intimate and co-constitutive part of the subject are fragile: They can not only recede or fall apart, but can be designed in such a way as to let us fall, let us die. Butler's position, like that of a long line of feminist thinkers, emphasizes a dependent and interdependent, embodied subjectivity.

Practitioner-theorists such as the Belgian architect Nel Janssens have found it useful to explore this agrammatical construction, worlding, as a way of deepening her creative practice and thinking. She explains that worlding is a way of renewing creative energy to remake possible worlds, specifically towards rejuvenating subjective and community relations. It is a concept that assists in the breaking down of sharp divisions between objects and subjects in an environment-world (2012: 86). The challenge is to acknowledge differences of worlds, and different forms of perception, not to discover some ideal or abstract agreement. Claire Colebrook argues:

> There would not be 'a' world that might be suspended in order to think in a manner that was purely formal or procedural. There would be multiple worlds, each opened from the force of a single becoming. It would be the challenge of perception and thinking to encounter the difference of those worlds, not find some abstract point or field of conciliation. (Colebrook 2014b: 165)

There is no one-world solution.

The questions of world, environment and nature are all worthy for architectural thinkers and creative practitioners. Yet, each time one of these terms is deployed, its parameters must be interrogated again: No assumptions should be made concerning fast and easy definitions. The creative practitioner needs to define her terms lest the terms begin to define her, and seek an approach that is about cautiously opening up her environment-world: 'Opening up to speculative, and so possible material, affective, practical reworlding in the concrete and detailed situation of a here, in this tradition of research, not everywhere all the time' (Haraway 2007: 93). Worlding becomes about acknowledging one's situation and then opening up to new versions of what might be possible today, and in the future.

Environment-worlds

I have pre-emptively made reference to environment-worlds, and now I must offer an account of what might be meant by this conceptual conjunction, which brings the organic and the inorganic, the corporeal and the incorporeal together, and which certainly calls on a mixed material-semiotics. This construction, environment-worlds, is a disjunctive synthesis in that it conjoins two terms while maintaining their distinction, much the same as the conjunction of nature and culture as natures-cultures or how environmentalities can be heard to be composed in two parts, environ-mentalities. The hyphen operates as a connection at the same time as designating a distinction. Importantly, it is not a binary mark, or punctual opposition. The hyphen is more than a defunct postmodern gesture that remembers the delicacy of the texture of text. It is formed by compounding terms and creating combinatorials that mix sign systems with material systems. Rather than regarding these constructions as merely so much word play or metaphor, they can be taken as material semiotic nodes. They mix sense and sensation, what makes sense (semiotics) and how this is achieved via material admixtures (material), relations and encounters in human and non-human environment-worlds. As with all concepts, the concept of environment-worlds comes from somewhere, it is not invented out of nothing. Concepts tend to be patched together from recycled scraps, which incidentally draws attention to the question of the sustainability of concepts.

This brings me to a working definition of environment-world, where I place two of Timothy Morton's least favourite words alongside each other: environment and world, which is to say, I recycle concepts that may seem rather threadbare. I have borrowed this concept from the curious work of a biologist called Jacob von Uexküll, who posits 'signs' as carriers of significance in the construction of a creature's world. Retrospectively, Uexküll has been recognized as laying the groundwork for biosemiotics, and is often identified as an early progenitor of cybernetics in that he was concerned not just with the biological or mechanical accounts of living creatures, but how they construct meaning in their worlds based on environmental signs significant for their survival. This evinces a curiosity about how information circulates in environments, a curiosity that cybernetics would in time instrumentalize through technologies of information. In addition, Uexküll has influenced the field of ethology, or studies in animal behaviour (Else 2010; Wambacq and Tuinen 2017). In the 1930s, Uexküll writes his illustrated book *A Foray into the Worlds of Animals and Humans*. What he illustrates, as Elizabeth Else explains, is a shift in the scientific point of view from thinking about the world solely in terms of its physical and chemical properties to reading the world as composed of 'biological signs and "meanings"' (Else 2010: 28), composed in the contrapuntal relationship between creature and world. In this way, creature and world are witnessed to reciprocally alter each other. This constitutes an alternative to the taxonomical approach, whereby animals are arranged according to *what* they are and not according to *how* they interact with a world. Where the *what* places an emphasis on the discrete object/subject, the *how* pays heed to the importance of relations. The *Umwelt* unfolds a 'subjective perceptual universe' (Else 2010: 29), which Uexküll asks that we attempt to imagine by inhabiting the points of view of different creatures in order to understand what matters for them. Take a walk in the woods, or across a meadow, he recommends, and attempt so far as you can to inhabit the perspective of the other. What emerges in each instance is an extreme perspectivism.

Today, given the non-human turn, and all the work dedicated to studies of the post-human and the more-than-human, Uexküll's storybook might well be called *A Foray into the Worlds of Animals and Humans*. Uexküll is referred to by thinkers such as Gilles Deleuze and Félix Guattari (1987), Giorgio Agamben (2004), Peter Sloterdijk, Elizabeth Grosz (2008) and before them the phenomenological philosopher Martin Heidegger. In his 2013 Gifford Lectures, Bruno Latour remarks 'to define humans is to define the envelopes, the life support systems, the Umwelt that makes it possible for them to breathe' (Latour cited in Walker 2015: 273). Timothy Ingold engages Uexküll, as well as a later thinker James Gibson, to discuss Umwelt in direct relation to architecture, drawing a distinction between human and non-human constructions (2000: 154). This is the contemporary company in which I discover Uexküll's writings. It is also worth noting that the new translation of Uexküll's work appears in a series edited by Cary Wolfe that is dedicated to posthumanities, in which it sits alongside books by Stengers, Michel Serres and Donna Haraway, Timothy Morton, Maria Puig de la Bellacasa, among others, all of whom lay out the dynamics of post-human, or else more than human, landscapes.[5]

There is evidence, furthermore, that the posthumanities paradigm has entered architectural discourse and musings on design practice, for instance, in Ariane Lourie Harrison's introduction to *Architectural Theories of the Environment: Posthuman Territory*, where she makes reference to thinkers such as N. Katherine Hayles, Serres, Haraway and Deleuze and Guattari (2013: 3–33). Harrison presents a post-human continuum between architecture and the environment in the Anthropocene period. Post-human territories, she argues, reorient 'the long-standing conception of the building as an object autonomous from its environment and governed by disciplinary interiority' (2013: 3). This is a reorientation that creative practitioners must continue to struggle with lest they entirely lose themselves within the interior silos of their disciplines, I would add.

Environment-world is my own translation of the German term *Umwelt*, which would usually be translated as, quite simply, 'environment'. I read the German word literally, or at face value: The word Umwelt shelters two parts – *um* and *Welt* – the first meaning 'surroundings', or that which surrounds, and the second meaning 'world'. As Elizabeth Grosz explains, citing Uexküll: 'Each organism in every species is surrounded by its Umwelt, an "island of the senses"' (Grosz 2008: 41). So what I propose is to mimic this two-part structure, organism and environment, which I argue creates this disjunctive synthesis of world and environment. It is a disjunctive structure because world and environment hold together yet do not quite synchronize, because a creature is always out of step with itself, always finding and losing itself. Uexküll explains that 'an enclosing world is present out of which each animal cuts its dwelling world' (2010: 139), hence the notion of carving out an inhabitable shelter and making meaning there. Some action is required, the act of carving out a world or ecological niche from environmental conditions (Grosz 2008: 46), which reciprocally alters those conditions. What results is what Grosz calls 'bubble-worlds', in homage to Uexküll's 'extreme perspectivism' (41–42). What carries significance for each critter (including the human creature) pertains to those environmental challenges associated with its survival. In many instances, the survival of one species will mean the diminution if not wholesale destruction of another, including the environment they inhabit. I will return to this question of perspectivism later because it is what contributes to the formation of subjects amidst their environment-worlds, through processes of subjectification across transforming post-human landscapes.

Uexküll asks the reader to join him on a stroll and, importantly, to take the time to pay attention. Each creature exists as though in a bubble that circumscribes all that is of importance to it – the same pertains to the tick and its three affects (Uexküll 2010: 44–45) as for the housefly, the dog, the grasshopper and finally the human actor with whom Uexküll concludes his foray. All creatures pluck from their environment the perception signs that are relevant to their survival and livelihood, signs that are of 'special biological significance' (53). In responding to perception signs, the creature produces effect signs by means of which it answers to the environmental milieu in which it finds itself. Relations of meaning, signs of significance and the affects they arouse in the recipient together with the effects the creature reciprocally produces create a guide to the reading of environments. A creature distinguishes in its environment as many objects as are of use to it, and while Uexküll describes this as an impoverishment for some creatures whose carriers of significance are few, and Heidegger likewise speaks of creatures that are 'poor in world' (Heidegger 1995: 196), this matters less than the intensity of the relations that each creature secures, by way of its senses, in order to make sense of a local milieu, securing it as a local environment-world. These worlds become as multifarious as the creatures that carve them out of their milieux, or surrounding environments.

Through a series of what look like storybook illustrations (see Sellbach and Loo 2015, 2016) Uexküll describes how different beings hold to different carriers of significance, or different affects, that is to say, what moves them, how they move others in their worlds. While affect (at least for humans) is often defined as the auto-biographical designation of feelings – I feel sad, I feel happy – and the recognition of socially shared emotions, sadness and happiness, affect is harder to grasp and define (Shouse 2005). It is what stirs up the capacity to feel, and in feeling something the onward capacity to share one's emotions with others, even if this is simply to distinguish oneself amidst one's own sorrows and joys. Affect in the way I am using it means capacity, and the reciprocal, though usually uneven, ratio between being affected and affecting others. Affect, feelings and emotions move us and move others. This is where emotions and feelings demand some form of action or some development of a practice, even if this manifests merely as everyday habitual practices.

To affect, and to be affected, is what increases or diminishes one's expressions of life (Deleuze 1988b: 99), and this increase and diminution are necessarily located somewhere, sometime, in relation to something. What is so perplexing about affect is that it does not leave us, the human creature, in a state of equilibrium, but renders us moody. That is to say, affect is dynamic, aroused through chance and planned encounters, and the quality of the relations formed through these encounters. At the same time, the inflations and deflations of affect are delimited, remaining relative to the capacities of a specific creature in relation to their territorial occupations. All of which is to say, the respective capacities and powers of creatures are expressed as clinched with their environments, producing different material dynamics and effects. To chart or else map these creature-worlds goes well beyond the mere description of a territory and becomes projective, allowing us to partake in otherwise unseen, unfelt forces and relations: How might the creature affect and be affected next?

> Every territory, every habitat, joins up not only its spatiotemporal but its qualitative planes or sections: a posture and a song for example, a song and a color, percepts and affects. And every territory encompasses or cuts across the territories of other species, or intercepts the trajectories of animals without territories, forming interspecies junction points. It is in this sense that, to start with, Uexküll develops a melodic, polyphonic, and contrapuntal conception of Nature. (Deleuze and Guattari 1994: 185)

The logic of these relations can quite simply be called 'ecology' – a term that can be variously defined, but which Grosz describes as the 'counterpoint' between organism and environment (Grosz 2008). And while the bubble-worlds that Uexküll invites us to enter are near incommensurate because creatures often remain superficially blind to each other, they overlap forming remarkable patterns, allowing for the push and pull of relationality and process, describing a 'melodic, polyphonic, and contrapuntal conception of Nature'.

Extreme perspectivism, the blindness of creature to creature, operates concurrently with their entangled capacities amidst their respective environment-worlds, to reciprocally affect and be affected by these worlds and each other. What these creatures should not be described as is withdrawn from each other, or inaccessible to each other. The bubble-worlds Uexküll blows with delight out of his soap-bubble pipe illustrate a superficial blindness that is rather a remarkable orchestral entanglement composed of what Uexküll calls different tones. Tones such as the use tones of the forester, the protection tones of the owl and the fear tones of the child who believes she sees a monstrous face in the tree roots are perceived and acted upon depending on how each creature constructs sense in its respective world of sensation, even when these different creatures are clustered around the one oak tree (Ingold 2000: 176–177; Uexküll 2010: 126–131). The spider may not see the fly she catches in her web, and the eyes of the fly may be structured in such a way as to not see the web, thus flying blindly into it, and yet each in its own world has powers of existence which it expresses, and each can be seen to at least minimally overlap with each other, one increasing in power, one decreasing in power as the fly, for instance, is overwhelmed by the web and captured by the spider (Uexküll 2010: 63).

This is why Uexküll invites his reader to take a stroll with him, one fine day, through a blossoming meadow, to witness these relations from proliferating points of view that are more-than-human. Today the simple pleasures of the meadow scene are far too bucolic; the kinds of scenes more likely to be traversed by a reader of Uexküll are composed of ghosts and monsters (Tsing et al. 2017). The stroll we take is less likely undertaken as an amateur biologist than as a creature mired in scenes of anthropogenic disequilibrium. Bucolic scenes become post-human landscapes.

The final illustration of Uexküll's foray into the worlds of humans and non-humans presents the figure of an astronomer perched high above the ground in an improbable tower that extends precariously out from the planet Earth, appearing to puncture the gaseous environment that is the atmosphere (2010: 133–134). The astronomer casts her gaze beyond her world of significance into other possible worlds, searching for signs and carriers of significance there. Yet projected into this celestial field the astronomer, all the same, lays out her *Umwelt*, which is to say, her practice concerns, her field of scientific interest, all that is of significance to her work. She forges a sidereal home, reassured of her partially secure safe haven in her tower infrastructure, accompanied by her instruments and by her disciplinary precedents, obligations and requirements. What is of specific interest in the track I am attempting to travel towards ecologies of creative practice is that *Umwelten*, environment-worlds, are those domains in which creative approaches to practice can be explored. This is where practice takes place, often as a matter of necessity in response to the problems that directly confront the researcher in their immediate milieu.

More needs to be said about this notion of extreme perspectivism as a means of venturing post-human landscapes. What's more, it must be stressed that perspectivism does not assume a ready-made, bounded and stable human or non-human subject. Uexküll illustrates the points of view of a variety of creatures in order to set out their local worlds as complex feedback loops of significance, whereby creature and world are reciprocally affected. The extreme perspectivism of which Grosz speaks is multiplied, performed and enacted in the midst of sense-making ventures so that landscape and subject are both moved and transformed. As W. J. T. Mitchell points out: 'Whatever the power of landscape might be, and of its unfoldings into space and place, it is surely the medium in which we live, and move, and have our being, and where we are destined, ultimately, to return' (Mitchell 2002: xii). Tsing and her co-editors call the overlaid arrangements of human and non-human living spaces 'landscapes' and dedicate their book *Arts of Living on a Damaged Planet* to how human researchers might better pay attention to these landscapes (2017). They are concerned that we are either apt to forget our contemporary environmental crises, remaining blind to the circumstances in which we find ourselves, or else that in the face of crises we boldly move forward and make things bigger and better, consume more, produce more, accelerate capitalism and pack the landscape with stuff: How can we chart another, slower approach through our practices? A significant reorientation is required.

Like Stengers, Tsing and her co-editors insist on the importance of acknowledging the varied knowledge practices that distinguish the different approaches of different disciplines. What they call Anthropogenic landscapes, those affected by human activity, are haunted by pasts and futures. By way of example they explain that when animals become extinct, the seeds they once unwittingly carried on their bodies are no longer disseminated, and then the plant species that depended upon them dwindles or dies out. Species extinctions haunt the present and project their ghosts into a future in terms of the concatenating effects that are produced amidst environments. That is to say, past and future are entangled in the passing destructions of a present. Tsing and her co-editors offer tips on how to read landscapes from the thick midst of this passing-away. They demand that observation be undertaken on the ground, in situ, much as Uexküll insists, as well as framed by a situated point of view that is not exclusively human. From the midst of your circumscribed environment-world, how do you make the effort to widen or even multiply your points of view across post-human landscapes?

What should not be overlooked is how power relations are shaped through the constructed conceit of the perspectival cone of vision. Every landscape presumes a point of view, but who or what is it that is captured by this point of view? What or who is located at the narrow end of the cone of vision? It should be remembered that there are two ends to a cone of vision and neither end can be assumed to be stationary. We might assume that the visual coordinates of point of view secure control over a landscape, over a scene, as in the emergence of landscape painting, an art that paradoxically preceded landscape design. First, carefully curated 'picturesque' landscapes were imaginatively portrayed on canvas, and then, landscape designers took to realizing these visions. The so-called Ha Ha Wall, deployed by the aptly named landscape designer Capability Brown, was a ditch dug between an estate garden and a field to keep the livestock out while maintaining a sweeping, near continuous view. One outcome of this ingenious device was to allow a pastoralist to capture lands well beyond his own simply through visual access. If it is no longer the pastoralist gazing over his Ha Ha Wall visually capturing territories that extend beyond the boundaries of his own landed property, as he projects his gaze towards the chiaroscuro blue of the horizon, who then is looking at whom, or what? What happens if the cone of vision is reversed and the pastoralist discovers that the landscape instead sees him? This question is one that pertains to the Anthropocene thesis: In some distant future what or who will bear witness to the destruction that has been wreaked following what we (human creatures) have bequeathed to a future? The landscape speaks back, but we cannot guess to whom or to what. In his introduction to Deleuze's *Spinoza: Practical Philosophy*, Robert Hurley extends the implications of such sensing by asking a set of deceptively simple questions: 'Which of these actions are we capable of experiencing? What is a walk in the forest (where the tick is waiting to experience *us*)? And what new individual do we compose when we "think like a mountain?"' (Hurley 1988: ii).

In *What Is Philosophy?* Deleuze and Guattari make a remarkable statement with respect to landscape perception. They ask simply: Who or what does the landscape see? If we can work according to the seemingly paradoxical logic that the 'landscape *sees*' (Deleuze and Guattari 1994: 169), what does it bear witness to? Deleuze and Guattari argue that, 'percept is the landscape before man, in the absence of man'. Yet, they also hesitate in order to ask: 'But why do we say this since in all these cases the landscape is not independent of the supposed perceptions of the characters and, through them, of the author's perceptions and memories?' (169). Confounding anthropocentric thinking, Deleuze and Guattari detach percepts from perceiving subjects, allowing percepts to instead circulate in the midst of situated things passing, and passing away. For Deleuze and Guattari, where affects are liberated from affected subjects, and concepts are invented, but never ex nihilo, percepts pertain to encounters with landscapes, which we should not presume to be 'naturally' available. Neither does the percept assume a stable point of view captured by a bounded stable subject. The expression of subjectivity – it cannot be stressed enough – must be radically reframed. Selfhood is not understood here as a 'specific, substantive, personological or universal instance, situated behind the subject, or as an immutable nucleus, but as a relational potentiality, a zone of constitution of subjectivity' (Pelbart 2015: 250). This larval subject, this process of subjectification, leads towards the 'gestures, manners, modes, variations, resistances, as minuscule and unapparent as they may seem' (Pelbart 2015: 250) of subjects in process embedded in their local environment-worlds.

All of the aforementioned assume a logic whereby the subject does not arrive pre-formed at a constructed point of view, but is rather a subject who is formed in relation to a point of view (Deleuze 1993: 19). The 'point' of point of view is where lines perpendicular to tangents meet, but meet with continuous variation; they do not stop meeting and they do not stabilize. Percept is effectively mobilized. Deleuze explains: 'It is not exactly a point but a place, a position, a site, a "linear focus", a line emanating from lines' (1993: 19). This is what he calls inflection, the variation of lines subtending, which is how he explains what we call 'point of view'.

> Such is the basis of perspectivism, which does not mean a dependence in respect to a pregiven or defined subject; to the contrary, a subject will be what comes to a point of view, or rather what remains in the point of view. This is why a transformation of the object refers to a correlative

transformation of the subject: the subject is not a sub-ject, but, as Whitehead says, the subject becomes a superject. Just as the object becomes objectile, the subject becomes superject. (Deleuze 1993: 19–20)

Every point of view is a point of view on variation, even while standing perfectly still. While perspectivism implies relativism, or a relation between mobile subject and changing world, this should not be mistaken for out-and-out relativity. Perspectivism instead draws attention to a plurality of positions where 'variation is enveloped in point of view' (Deleuze 1993: 21). In a celebrated essay from the early 1990s, Beatriz Colomina relates this issue of the formation of the subject and point of view to architecture: 'Architecture is not simply a platform that accommodates the viewing subject. It is a viewing mechanism that produces the subject. It precedes and frames its occupants' (Colomina 1992: 84). Architectural environments participate in the formation of human subjects, contributing to their expressions of subjectivity. Architecture frames, enframes and creates the enclosures from which human (and non-human) subjects in process burst forth.

Deleuze explains that point of view is the 'secret of things' (1993: 22). Rather than focus on visibility as the prime sense motivated through point of view, he emphasizes acts of envelopment, enfolding and wrapping. We would be mistaken to believe that the non-human or the more-than-human is our new 'other', situated in contradistinction to the presumed exceptionalism of the human. There are historically, and to this day, certain points of view and practices that have been obscured or undervalued. As such,

Becoming-woman might possess some privilege or legitimacy, not just because it was not the perception of man, and not because it would be perception from another point of view, but because it would shift the problem of point of view. Becoming-woman would not be perceiving as a woman, but perceiving in such a way that perception would be a form of becoming. (Colebrook 2014b: 154)

The mobilization of percepts amidst post-human landscapes of affect describe transformative becomings, a situation in which to speak of subjects and objects as givens becomes something of an abstraction or a dangerous desire to transcend the world, hold it still and grasp it in one fell swoop.

Different creatures or 'critters' through their creative and destructive acts of environing nature produce their local worlds of sense, capturing them as much as they are captivated by them. They chart out territories via performances of territorialization. Territory, as Deleuze defines it, is the 'coadaptation of the living being and its terrestrial milieu' (cited in Sauvagnargues 2016: 74). For

Deleuze and Guattari, Colebrook explains, 'in the beginning is the territory, in which human bodies assemble according to various rhythms, durations and sympathies with the earth' (2014b: 160). In the beginning is the territory, some specific, place-based site out of which something emerges. These sympathies are also rendered in sonic terms by what Anne Sauvagnargues beautifully describes as the viscosity of the song (2016: 131), or the melody that Grosz has called the counterpoint between organism and environment. A method of sympathy can be drawn forth, one of selection, extraction and the choices made given the available materials, and how these materials are followed. All of this contributes to a suite of practices engaged in relation to a creature's environment-world. Some creatures though overreach what is materially available, as is disastrously evident with the human creature's acts of territorialization.

Included in Uexküll's bestiary is a child on a village street, whose point of view on the local world is compared with his mother's (2010: 65–67). Where for the mother her experienced grasp of depth and space allows her to read the scale of a cathedral they pass by, for the child the cathedral is spatially flattened and he imagines that his mother can pluck the workers off its façade as though it were a doll's house. One primal scene of quasi-architectural settlement is the line drawn around the child as she sings a song to herself. A child in the dark gripped by fear comforts herself by singing under her breath. Lost, she takes shelter in her song, as she attempts to orient herself. The song creates the sensation of a calm refuge in the midst of perceived chaos and darkness.[6] But it is less the child than the song that enables the creation of this portable shelter, Sauvagnargues points out (2016: 131). Extracting a territory from a surrounding milieu as she walks her way home in the dark, singing a song to the emergence of her subjectivity as a performance aimed at self-reassurance. Sometimes, though, the darkness of the provisionally stalked territory moves in and engulfs the child and her song. The demarcated territory abruptly dissipates, or runs to wrack and ruin. The disjunctive synthesis of environment-world collapses as sense and sensation are scattered.

The *Umwelten*, the environment-worlds in all their diversity that we confront today, have come to be denominated at a global geological scale as the 'Anthropocene', denominating massive environmental change registered in geological strata at a planetary level. The exhaustion of environment-worlds, the loss of shelter, floods in. At the same time, this global vision is misleading, specifically leading us away from opportunities to act amidst local worlds of sense and sensation. So look again to your immediate local world in all its worldly mundanity and consider the modes of practice you undertake there and the stories you might tell.

Practice scene: tacit, taciturn, Tacita

This first practice scene will constitute something of an itinerary of encounters with a series of works, each opening onto a specific environment-world where architecture can be located as something of an epiphenomenon, little more than a background or support, a stage upon which some event comes to pass before fading from memory. Rather than formally looming into the foreground, architecture plays a subsidiary role. Critics, such as Anna Gibbs (1997), Irit Rogoff (2003), Gavin Butt (2005) and Jane Rendell (2010) among others have remarked, rarely stand at a distance from such scenes, but are caught up, immersed and affected by the works they encounter. This is the case in what follows. I am deeply interested in the scene of creative practice I discuss here, and the security of some critical distance cannot be assured, but is more likely to collapse. Something takes place in the midst of an encounter, which can result in a reorientation of both thinking and practising. At the same time, a great tactfulness, a certain delicacy is required so as not to overwrite a body of work, to not fix it in place or prescribe it with a determined meaning. This constitutes the first of eight 'practice-scenes' that are included in this book, and rather than commencing with an account of a feted architectural project, architecture as a mode of creative practice will be approached obliquely, by way of art practice.

In 2004, I paid several visits to the Musée d'Art Moderne de la Ville de Paris to view a 16mm film by Tacita Dean called *Boots* (2003), which premiered in London at the Royal Institute of British Architects (RIBA), effectively securing the location of this art project in the proximity of architectural concerns. The exhibition at the Musée d'Art Moderne was accompanied by a catalogue essay written by the French philosopher Jean-Luc Nancy, who spent some time in mischievous word play toying with the artist's first name, Tacita, drawing associations between her name and the words tacit, taciturn and tactful. 'Tacita, the tacit and the one who silences ... Tacita makes use of implicitness, of what must be understood without having really been articulated' (Nancy cited in Eakin 2011). If I picked up the catalogue at the time, I have meanwhile lost it and must work mostly from memory.

My first encounter with Tacita Dean's work took place in 2001, soon after I had relocated to Melbourne, Australia, when I witnessed her 16mm film of women languorously bathing in a bathhouse in Budapest. *Gellért* (1998) was screened as part of a show called *Humid* at Australian Centre for Contemporary Art (ACCA), where Tacita Dean's work would be shown on future occasions too. This was before ACCA was relocated from its old nineteenth-century gardener's cottage in the Melbourne Botanic Gardens to a building custom-designed by the Melbourne architectural firm Wood Marsh, which now looms large like a great rusted hull of corten steel, stranded on a plain of pale gravel to the west of St Kilda Road in what is called the Southbank Arts Precinct.

It must have been in the new ACCA venue, some time in 2008, that I viewed Tacita Dean's hour-long film about five nuns living in a convent in Cork, Ireland, depicting their daily rituals and prayers, their domestic labours and joys (*Presentation Sisters* 2005). This intimate filmic document intimated a future to come, where one by one the nuns would pass away and then the convent would be redeveloped, transformed, fit for other functions, for instance, as a €10 million redevelopment accommodating an educational and heritage precinct (Leland 2014).

I have seen her film about the aged poet and translator Michael Hamburger, moving through the dusty rooms of his house shortly before his death, as the ancient sunlight filters in, and then wandering in his old apple orchard introducing his apple varieties to the artist. He had an apple tree grown from a seed that the poet Ted Hughes had given him. Michael Hamburger was the translator of W. G. Sebald's *After Nature* (2002) and there is a scene from Sebald's novel-cum-travelogue *The Rings of Saturn* where the protagonist, a writer, pays a visit to Michael Hamburger at his 'house in the meadows on the outskirts of Middleton' (Sebald 1998: 181), Suffolk. On his way to Hamburger's house – he travels by foot – the narrator's voice seamlessly comes to occupy the voice of the poet Hamburger, recounting part memories, part dreams or hallucinations, an elegy bound up with the loss of Hamburger's Berlin childhood. Confirming this intimate occupation of one unfolding subjectivity by another, the narrator reflects: 'Across what distances in time do the elective affinities and correspondence connect? How is it that one perceives oneself in another human being, or, if not oneself, then one's own precursor?' (182). Sebald's books, especially his last novel, *Austerlitz*, are much loved by architects on account of the way the dust motes of architectural atmospherics come to be entangled with the emotional lives and unreliable memories of inhabitants, often as a means of obliquely addressing difficult political histories, suggesting an affective approach to history writing (Stead 2015: 41–48). Sebald died an untimely death in a car accident in 2001.

Tacita Dean has captured the dancer and choreographer Merce Cunningham in his studio a short while before he passed away. Offering homage to his life partner John Cage, Cunningham performs Cage's composition *4'33'*, which Tacita describes across a spatial assemblage of six films depicting six performances in which Cunningham's minor readjustments of his seated position are near imperceptible. She seems to have a knack for moments of impending extinction, or what I prefer to call exhaustion. Her tacit sense for and tactful treatment of the passing away of people and things have often been remarked upon. I have seen Tacita Dean's slow filmic lament for the last rolls of 16mm film manufactured by Kodak, a material extinction in its own right. I have seen her footage of the Alex Fernsehturm in Berlin, observing a slow line of elderly patrons arriving and seating themselves in the revolving restaurant at the top of the famous television tower (*Fernsehturm*, 2001). Tacita Dean explains that following the fall of the Berlin Wall, the revolving floor of the famous Alex tower was made to turn at double the speed, achieving a full revolution in just half an hour (Dean and Royoux 2005: 253). All the while our consumption of a life becomes ever more voracious.

There was a film describing her fascination with an amateur sailor lost at sea, Donald Crowhurst, whose body was never discovered (*Disappearance at Sea*, 1996), but who, Dean argues, had developed time sickness. There are her attempts to document the green ray (*Green Ray*, 2001), a legendary flash of light that is said to appear at the horizon as the sun goes down. Does the green ray exist, or is it but a sailor's forlorn hallucination? Tacita Dean explains that 'looking for the green ray became about the act of looking itself, about faith and belief in what you see'.[7] She is not only an artist, but a writer known for her 'asides'. The one mentioned here is taken from a voiceover that accompanied *Green Ray*. Something appears, only to disappear again with such celerity we wonder whether it ever existed.

I visited the emptied, defunct Finance Office at Documenta 13 in Kassel in 2012, climbing up and down its elegant, ornamented central staircase between its mezzanine level and ground floor. On both levels, entirely occupying the walls, Tacita Dean had drafted more of her famous blackboards, an exhausting exercise, one no doubt prone to repetitive strain injury in the hand that drafts. This time she depicted a storm coming in across a landscape, the rain arousing a thunderous flood of water that raged down the valleys and gullies of the mountains outside Kabul, Afghanistan. This project had been based on something of a failure, or an experiment that did not quite work out as she expected, in that she had hoped to collaborate with a young Afghani who had been tasked with capturing film footage in Kabul. The footage turned out to be unusable, and instead the drama of the storm moving in across the sky and the great torrent of flood waters were depicted in white chalk, smudged in with fingers here and there for atmospheric effect. A storm that smells of chalk and blackboard paint.

I followed and took pleasure in her work in a more profound way than I had followed any architect, and began to wonder what was happening in this lack of faithfulness to my own first discipline. Still, architecture is that which sets up the frame and the possibility for some of Tacita Dean's environment-worlds, as well as setting the scene for many of her non-narrative stories. As the poet Susan Stewart points out, Tacita Dean wanders through the thick medium of time and 'discovers evidence of the ruin and the disappearance of all made things' (Stewart 2001). This, at least, reassures me of further connections between her art and questions close to architecture, as well as Tacita's own concession that she is interested in 'failed architectures' (Obrist and Dean 2013: 30).

Boots was neither the first nor the last work that I would witness, nor necessarily the one that haunted me the most. While a great many of her works use architecture as a motif, support or specifically framed background (the Alexanderplatz television tower, the bathhouse in Budapest, a poet's house, the 'Bubble House', the convent where the Presentation sisters lived), there was something particular about the confounding scenes of *Boots*, which challenged the validity of history, suggesting in its place the kaleidoscopic play of fragments of memory and the importance of a story to be told. No doubt great caution needs to be taken here, because when the reliability of history is under threat, then there is the risk that the most powerful voice will take on the storytelling function, leading collective memory into frightening identity formations.

Boots was shot in an empty Art Deco Villa in Porto, Portugal, called Casa de Serralves, and followed the difficult progress of an old man leading someone on a tour, remembering and misremembering events that might have taken place there. The murmuring of an old guide's unreliable narrative, his orthopaedic boot and his two walking sticks echo through the quiet spaces of the vacated house, the sound often proceeding him and remaining after he has departed a scene. The emptiness of the house suggests its abandonment, and what's more, unless you have access to supporting source material, or an intimate knowledge of the regional variations of the Art Deco style, it is not possible to locate the house in its context. Much like an unreliable memory, or dreamscape, its geographical specificity remains uncertain. Dean wrote instructions for herself in preparation for the film: 'I am going to film on three different days, at three different sunsets, once in English, once in German, once in French. Each film will be a version, not a copy: a different fiction, a different version of events' (Trodd 2008: 386).

Three narrative strands, none of which is quite aligned, three possible worlds, are all cast simultaneously onto three different screens in three different languages. The trilingual man, comfortably at home in none of these languages, who plays the role of Boots, was an old friend of the Dean family, and he too passed away shortly after the film was shot. He did not particularly like the villa in which he was asked to perform his part three times. Again, Tacita Dean captures a flickering image in celluloid before exhaustion sounds its final toll as the sun sets three times over. The same can be said of her shift to a large-scale format when commissioned to produce work for the Unilever series in the Turbine Hall at the Tate Modern in 2011, where she projected a

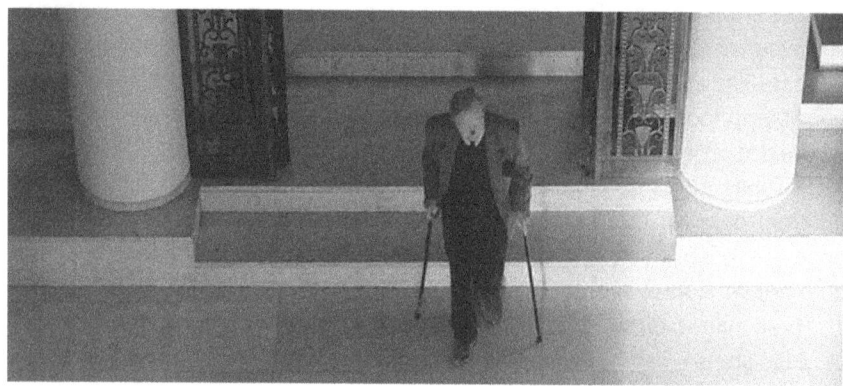

FIGURE 1.2 *Tacita Dean – still images from the 16mm colour film* Boots, *2003. Three films (English, French and German versions). Each film: 16 mm colour anamorphic, optical sound, 20 minutes. Courtesy the artist, Frith Street Gallery, London, and Marian Goodman Gallery, New York.*

35mm film on a loop to lament, critique and creatively resist the passing of the age of celluloid, its impending extinction, in *Film* (2011).

Years after I had seen *Boots* in Paris, over twelve years later in fact while I was living in Nuremberg, I took a day trip to Munich, just an hour away. There, in the upper levels of the Museum Brandhorst is to be found an atmospheric depiction of a battle at sea. A sea battle, Daniel Barber once explained to me, is the location for at least one origin story of the word or concept 'environment'. The sea battle in question was rendered atmospheric by Cy Twombly, one of Tacita Dean's influences (Obrist and Dean 2013: 23) and yet another subject she has captured on 16mm film (Dean 2011). Twombly's *The Lepanto Cycle* of 2001, first prepared for the Venice Biennale, occupies twelve large canvases now displayed in a custom-designed upper room at the Museum Brandhorst. Dripping yellow, red and hot pink dashes; semicircles and spears demarcate boats aflame, sinking, the annihilations of a battle at sea. The event in question took place in the Gulf of Paltras in 1571, and resulted in the destruction of the Turkish fleet by the Holy League. It stands as a depiction of a battle between competing religious belief systems that continues in varying permutations to this day, as we witness in contemporary timelines of terror. Yet the immersive atmospheric affect, otherwise lost in a distant past, rather than the narrative is what is supposed to take precedence here.

Tacita Dean's project *Boots* is quieter in setting out its interior atmospherics, with its suggestion of past spectres, half-forgotten stories, love affairs and the coexistence of conflicting points of view collapsed into the figure of a 'dilapidated' old man played by a man who is in fact an architect. An architect with a foot that stopped growing after he was 12 years old following a skiing accident. An architect without much of a reputation, whose nickname really was 'Boots', who had a remarkable life story, parts of which Tacita relays to Hans Ulrich Obrist. *Boots* is interesting because, as I recently discovered when reading an interview between Tacita Dean and the ubiquitous conversationalist Obrist, soon after completing this project Tacita Dean, with her self-confessed fascination in 'a swollen foot, a crippled foot, a withered foot' and her early blackboard pieces dedicated to 'big swollen feet' (Obrist and Dean 2013: 11–13) herself succumbed to a foot problem, commenting that her fascination turned out to be an 'uncanny physical presentiment' (12). Eakin, who interviewed Tacita Dean in 2011 at her studio then located at the Hamburger Bahnhof in Berlin, explains that Dean suffers from rheumatoid arthritis, has had a surgery on one hand and can no longer straighten her right arm, has had a knee replacement and walks with a pronounced limp. Exhaustive series dedicated to loss and the passing of time with an emphasis on the compelling remnants of technological obsolescence are matched with the corporeal exhaustion of an artist.

Throughout all these encounters what is announced is a lament, a loss, but a certain material pleasure taken in this passing away, as though we can feel it slipping through our fingers like a ribbon of film. In an early written work that is supplemented with images, Tacita Dean in collaboration with Jeremy Millar composes a short piece entitled 'Magic World' (1999). It is what I would call a ficto-critical narrative addressed to a dying world in overlaid scenes depicting various temporalities that extend a critique on the passing of time, a humble peregrination with the subtitle: 'A Report on a Future Visit to Shepperton.' It could be called a site-writing walk, recomposing and distributing temporalities of occupation across the landscape of Shepperton, in the county of Surrey in England. The ancient time of the earth, its material histories and flows are juxtaposed with the incremental settlements of ancient peoples; the gradual cultivation of the land; series of historic events, 'Things are happening more quickly now' (Dean and Millar 1999: 118); and the construction of bridges, roads, film studios and airport terminals, all of which are gathered into an afternoon walk that vertiginously collapses these different registrations of geological, prehistoric and recent historical times. Its mood very much reflects the quiet though haunted ruminations of Sebald's narrator in *The Rings of Saturn*: 'From the earliest times, human civilization has been no more than a luminescence growing more intense by the hour, of which no one can say when it will begin to wane and when it will fade away' (1998: 117). The present casts its consideration towards the past, at the same time as tripping into a future, extending inexorably in two directions that do not admit to being easily disentangled. 'The stream passes below them, through them, over them. They do not move, we can follow them no more' (Dean and Millar 1999: 119). The entire piece is set out as something like notes in anticipation of a short film treatment. In the end, the question of whose point of view, onto what kind of vista, revisiting what kinds of past events, projecting into what kind of unknown future, lingers.[8]

Notes

1 I use these terms specifically, as they make reference to thought-images that have been developed by companion thinkers Donna Haraway and Karen Barad.

2 See http://environmentalhumanities.org and *The Routledge Companion to the Environmental Humanities* (2017).

3 See https://www.kth.se/en/abe/inst/philhist/historia/ehl/ehl-events/stories-of-the-anthr/stories-of-the-anthropocene-festival-1.664943 (accessed 29 June 2018).

4   See http://nelson.wisc.edu/che/anthroslam/ (accessed 26 September 2017).
5   Haraway takes issue with the 'posthuman' arguing instead that we have 'never been human' (Haraway 2007).
6   Here I adapt a passage from Deleuze and Guattari's chapter 'Of the Refrain' from *A Thousand Plateaus*. The child they describe is a boy, I displace him with a girl, to produce another effect altogether (1987: 311).
7   See https://vimeo.com/38026163 (accessed 6 October 2017).
8   As final work was being undertaken on the manuscript of this book, Tacita Dean's three-part exhibition dedicated to Still Life, Portrait and Landscape at the National Gallery, National Portrait Gallery and Royal Academy of Arts, respectively, were all opening in London between March and August 2018, raising yet further questions that cannot be addressed here (see Dean 2018).

2

Ecologies

A term more easily recognized and less idiosyncratic than my hyphenated environment-worlds is ecology. Much like Uexküll's idiosyncratic illustrations of creaturely *Umwelten*, ecology emerges from something like a picture book approach, composed of a startling array of creaturely and botanical worlds, highly detailed and colourful, singled out or else plunging back into environmental milieux. Ernst Haeckel, the German biologist who coined the word ecology was in the habit of colouring his discoveries as vivid and finely drafted illustrations, some of which are to be found on the cover of Didier Debaise's recent book *Nature as Event* (2017). Alexander von Humboldt, the 'inventor of nature', likewise finely illustrated the environments he explored (Wulf 2016). Peg Rawes explains that Haeckel defined ecology as the 'household of nature', thereby drawing into proximity what we understand by habitat, natural milieux, places and shelters (Rawes 2013: 1). The word 'eco', as is often pointed out, comes from the ancient Greek term *oikos*, which means house or home, designating the basic unit of ancient Greek society (Bennett 2010: 365). To organize and be responsible for a household, including its economy meant that one could count oneself as a legitimate citizen in the ancient Greek *polis*. Ecology might designate the household of nature and its economic organization, but it is also a domain of knowledge dedicated to the study of this household, the relationship of the organism, individually and collectively, with itself and within its environment. Ecology draws attention, first and foremost, to complex interconnections: 'ecology explains that all organisms are connected in a network which makes what is called an ecosystem. Interconnection is a touchstone of ecology' (Armiero and Sedrez 2014: 1; Reisinger 2018). Furthermore, as Bateson argues: 'We are not outside the ecology for which we plan – we are always and inevitably part of it' (2000: 512). Guattari has critically cast this relational interconnected embeddedness across three ecological registers in his influential essay *The Three Ecologies*, where we find that the 'natural' cannot be so easily isolated from the 'cultural' and socio-political. More recently, the editors of *General Ecology: The New Ecological Paradigm* draw attention to how ecology today, which extends across all manner of technological systems and infrastructures, has 'started to designate the collaboration of a multiplicity of human and nonhuman agents' (Hörl 2017: 3).[1] This is a process to which Guattari contributed early on.

Guattari's essay appears in many of the places where a relational approach to rethinking ecologies in architecture and elsewhere is discussed: in Verena Andermatt Conley's edited book *Rethinking Technologies* (1993); in Rawes's edited collection (2013: 48–49), where it is cited by Rosi Braidotti and Conley in their contributions; and again in the same volume where Anita Berlin discusses healthcare spaces and complains that Guattari is virtually silent on the question of gender (2013: 210–211). It is cited by Brook Muller, where he focuses on how the asignifying rupture of the three ecologies makes us think differently about our architectural practices (Muller 2014: 152), and it is cited by Renata Tyszczuk and Stephen Walker in their editorial introduction to an edition of the journal *Field*, dedicated to the theme of ecology (2017: 1). They too open with Guattari's epigraph dedicated to Bateson. Notably, it is an important essay for Nicolas Bourriaud in his highly influential book *Relational Aesthetics* (2002: 90–92), where *The Three Ecologies* is placed in connection with artistic practice and an ethico-aesthetic paradigm sketched out by Guattari. Peter Pàl Pelbart explains that Guattari's ecosophic conception complicates environmental, social and mental registers (2015: 91) and Stengers reads Guattari's *The Three Ecologies* as an urgent cry of warning: 'we must think and feel with a triple devastation: psychic, social, environmental' (Stengers 2013: 176). That is to say, we should be alert to the intertwinement of the three ecologies that Guattari presents.

Guattari opens his fiery essay *The Three Ecologies* with a quote from Gregory Bateson's *Steps to an Ecology of Mind*, a quote that I propose can be used as a mantra: 'There is an ecology of bad ideas, just as there is an ecology of weeds' (Bateson 2000: 492; Guattari 2000). It is a quote that I carry around in my head as a refrain, and I know that I am not alone in this. It is a small song that influences what is to follow where I come to discuss 'things' and 'thinkables'. It is a mantra that could be supplemented as follows: *Mind Fracking*, the high-pressure extraction of ideas, leaving behind desolate mental landscapes. That is to say, it also speaks to the problem of environmentalities, how we think together in relation to our local environment-worlds. Another kernel of ecological thinking from Bateson reads, 'the basic unit of survival is organism plus environment' (Bateson 2000: 491), after which he goes on to explain that creatures who choose to destroy their immediate, or even their proximal, environment will soon enough discover that they have destroyed themselves and their well-being as well as their fellow creatures, 'and everything gets into a rather peculiar mess' (492), including the environment that is composed of our shared and circulating concepts.

Having opened his essay with a warning where he speculates on the limit condition of planetary exhaustion, Guattari continues. He writes with urgency as he goes on to decry, as others do before and after him – the exhaustion of human relations; the ossification of marital life via patterns of standardized behaviour; the poisoning of family life through mass media consumption; and neighbourhood relations diminished and mean. Strife intersects and runs its course in the construction of subjectivity in relation to its environment-world (Guattari 2000: 19). What is needed, Guattari argues, is an ethico-political articulation, what he calls ecosophy, which allows for transversal relations between the three ecological registers of environment, social relations and human subjectivity. He places ways of living and modes of life in question, drawing attention to practices and their relation to the good and bad habits that are formed from the midst of a creature's habitat. Guattari goes through each 'ecosophical' register in turn: social, mental and environmental:

1. Social ecosophy, he explains, must develop 'practices' to modify and reinvent the way we live together, specifically challenging the nuclear family unit as unsustainable, and thus challenging, I would add, the capsularization of society (Cauter 2004; Sloterdijk 2007b). Guattari argues that we have to reconstruct group being, what it means to exist and work together. We must experiment, and use subjectivity as the motor to rebuild 'human relations' at every level of the socius (Guattari 2000: 33). This is not a matter of achieving a stupefying consensus, but a *dissensus*, pre-empting the importance of disagreement for thinkers such as Jacques Rancière and Chantal Mouffe (2000: 33).

2. Mental ecosophy (2000: 24), Guattari explains, is where the relationship between the subject and the body must be reinvented, and the answer is not ever more demanding exercise regimes that transform the body into a 'flesh corset'.[2] Mental ecosophy must be able to cope with mass media and social media bombardments, and resist conforming patterns of fashion and advertising. Like artists of the mundane and every day, Guattari recommends looking again at the mental ecologies of everyday life: 'individual, domestic, material, neighbourly, creative or one's personal ethics' (33). Labour practices, to which I would add reproductive labour, need to be recalibrated according to a logic not determined by profit and yield (38). New

approaches to how we imagine, and even daydream, must be experimented with.

3   Environmental ecosophy, as has been suggested earlier, needs to get out of the funk of bucolic visions of an ideal nature. Even serious environmental concerns, Guattari argues, have not begun to 'prefigure the generalised ecology' (2000: 35), a figuration he attempts to sketch out with his ecosophy. Environmental ecosophy must be associated with more than small nature-loving minorities and specialists.
The specialists are those whom Stengers names the guardians of knowledge, who sequester knowledge and in the process suggest that those without the training and expertise have nothing to offer (2015). Instead, environmental ecologies, natural, constructed and mixed, are a concern for all.

Ecologies are expressed via habits, habitat, habituation and inhabitation, all of which can be bundled together in terms of the conceptual and material lessons they offer. Inhabitation concerns habituation, and how well maintained you keep your habitat, based on what kinds of daily habits and existential refrains you entertain. This then draws us into the disciplinary domain of practices. Depending on what you do amidst your ecology and what your ecology does to you, you might contract a good or a bad habit, make a mess of things or else ameliorate your environment-world. Demos stresses that, as creative practitioners, 'we confront a politico-ecological imperative to mobilise creativity itself as a desperately needed resource in the reconstruction of the conditions of life's ongoingness' (2017: 21), which will also place us, from time to time, in situations of exhaustion.

An ecology of practices

The key thinker upon whom I draw inspiration, the one with whom I dare to think, is the philosopher of science Isabelle Stengers. She speaks in complex and eloquent terms for scientists and their practices. From this location the emphasis on practices can, I argue, be extended to other modes of practice, specifically those belonging to architecture, design and art. Speaking to an audience that extends beyond the sciences, Stengers launches forth what she calls her cosmopolitical project concerning an ecology of practices, which is based on her long career studying the practices of scientists. She expresses her respect for these practices, but issues warnings about science where it is sung out with a capital 'S', where it becomes a monolith and claims expertise in such a way that other voices are silenced or suppressed (Stengers

2012). Much the same complaint could be issued about architecture when imposed with a capital A. Stengers charts a delicate path between respect and critical regard for the sciences, and she undertakes this work across the seven scientific landscapes of her double-volume project dedicated to a cosmopolitics (2010, 2011a).

When she offers her introductory notes to an ecology of practices to a cultural studies audience (Stengers 2005a), Stengers responds to a formulation from Brian Massumi, who writes, 'a political ecology would be a social technology of belonging, assuming coexistence and co-becoming as the habitat of practices' (Massumi cited in Stengers 2005a: 183). Here Stengers states a direct correspondence between practice and habitat, by which she effectively defines what ecology means for her, in the process setting out something of a manifesto. While I have enumerated her terms previously (Frichot 2015, 2016), I return again to what contributes to her call. It is indeed a call she issues as a speculative gesture thrown out towards future practice formations. In the following, I offer a summary of her ecology of practices, which supplements Guattari's three ecological registers in useful ways.

Stengers's first step towards an ecology of practices is a simple sign of respect: no practice should be defined as just like any other 'just as no living species is like any other' (2005a: 184). She argues that practices deploy non-neutral tools for thinking through what is happening, tools which can be passed from hand to hand, thereby transforming both the situation, the tool *and* the one who handles the tool. She emphasizes that practices are obliged to frame what is happening in a minor key and in direct response to our local habitat or from the midst of those issues that confront us. A reorientation is at stake in this understanding of the specificity of practices and what they can achieve in relation to what they claim are pertinent problems. It is about listening to the kinds of questions practitioners ask without too quickly judging them. At the same time, there is an acknowledgement that fields of practice, like habitats, can be destroyed. But this should not be an excuse to make the claim that something more important or worthy will take its place, because it may very well not. For Stengers, because ecologies are always and necessarily open to transformation, it is less about recording a current ecology of practices than creating connections and relations so that new practical possibilities might emerge. Finally, she stresses that we should never believe we have arrived at an answer once and for all, but must maintain an affirmative and not a negative, not even a *deconstructive*, demeanour in relation to our circumscribed problems. The question of practice and its relation to thinking is one that is shared by architecture and the creative disciplines more generally. Practice (research, teaching and the development of research in the professional sphere) focuses on local and particular problems, which immanently define a practice's relations amidst its environment-world (Stengers 2011a: 389). An ecology of practices operates in action, on the go, testing, venturing and feeling out possible sites of investigation (Frichot 2016).

Practices, such as physics, and here we can also think of architecture, require a habitat, upon which they rely for their survival and ongoing dissemination. Stengers herself locates her first 'step' in the proposition that a practice should not be defined as just like any other, that is to say, it cannot be generalized and rolled out but should be understood in all its particularity (2005a: 184). This also means, she explains, to feel out its borders, which may well expand and contract and even disappear over time, dissolving into other fields. These borders resemble the way in which Uexküll describes the delimited environment-worlds of creatures based on the extensive array of what matters to them. Environment-worlds of practice are necessarily delimited lest the chaos of excess noise obscures everything (Uexküll 2010: 135). Step two pertains to how an ecology of practices takes up tools, and that tools are used to think through and with a situation – to think through what is happening. The tool becomes enormously important, and I will return to it when I address concepts in Part Three. The tool, Stengers explains, is passed from hand to hand, and the 'gesture' of passing the tool on to another, as well as the 'gesture' of taking the tool in hand, points to a specific, even intimate relationship between a tool, the tool's user, and the environment or situation in which it is being applied. Where we take up our tools for thinking, there habit must be resisted (Stengers 2005a: 185).

Taking up Stengers's ecology of practices in *Five Ways to Make Architecture Political*, where she dedicates a chapter to 'How to Study Ecology of Practice', Albena Yaneva argues that an ecology of practices for architectural design requires the redefinition of complicated relations between all beings and things, including habits, skills, buildings, sites, city regulations, the designer's tactics and strategies, clients, institutions, models, images, urban visions and landscapes (2017: 33). Ecology, Yaneva asserts, 'dissolves boundaries and redistributes agency' (33), and alerts us to how artefacts, whether these come in the form of bridges or prisons or public squares, are composed from a range of interested human and non-human actors, all of whom can show us yet another point of view on things. The dissolving of boundaries pertains to how a bridge infrastructure, for instance, cannot be extracted from the politics of its construction, occupation and even its failure. Politics for Yaneva involves shaping, fabricating, inventing and assembling, and it happens in process. This is a shift away from a primary emphasis on the point of view of the architect as a master designer, for instance, to a diversity of points of view framed through encounters with designed things. Yaneva stresses that ecology is not a naturalizing metaphor, but an opportunity to think with practices, which requires a slowing down. To engage in practices requires that one immerse oneself in one's respective milieux.

An ecology of practices must 'think by the milieu', an orientation that Stengers takes from Deleuze and Guattari (Stengers 2012). In an essay on animism, she directs her attention to creative practices by making reference to the 'milieu of art' and speaking of the importance of writing as an indeterminate art that resists dismembering experience (2012). It is an imperative of sorts, though Stengers would, perhaps, avoid the imperative in favour of the pedagogical benefit, alerting us to where we are, that we must surely start, as J. K. Gibson-Graham stress, from where we are (Gibson-Graham 2011: 2).[3] Stengers explains that this does not mean addressing an ideal situation, affixed ground or foundation, because: 'We do not know what a practice is able to become; what we know instead is that the very way we define, or address, a practice is part of the surroundings which produces its ethos' (Stengers 2005a: 195). A provisional collective of practitioners comes together around a problem, and it is not that we can refer to a 'we', as in 'we architects' or 'we creative practitioners', in advance of our practice. Instead, it is *through the practice*, and I would add, by *following the material*, that this 'we' emerges. The milieu and its associated problem are entangled, and the problem should not be extracted from its milieu without the risk of obscuring its condition of emergent possibility.

Ecologies of creative practices

A long excursus has been taken from environments to environmentalities through worlds and *worldings* towards a definition of environment-worlds, then by way of ecology towards an ecology of practices to arrive finally at ecologies of creative practice. Where is the creative practitioner amidst these concerns and world-weary cares? Why the modifier 'creative'? The creative practitioner stays with her troubles amidst her ecology of practices, where practices are theorized and theories practiced. The 'creative' of ecologies of creative practice draws predominantly on Deleuze and Guattari's creative philosophy, where the creation of concepts, affects and percepts is identified as the driving force that is shared across disciplines. Those acts deemed 'creative' are those that remain at the greatest risk of becoming recuperated, derailed, captured and turned to economic ends. Much like the ambivalence sheltering amidst ecologies, creative practices can produce both positive and negative outcomes.

An environment of sorts has emerged across architecture and cognate fields, where the benefits of ecological design, design ecologies and urban ecologies are discussed by way of case studies and illustrated samples

(Mostafavi and Doherty 2010; Orff 2016; Tilder and Blostein 2012). To call a practice ecological seems to suggest positive relations in a world, as though 'ecology' could be characterized as a general good. To 'ecologize' can even be identified as the new catch-call that replaces to 'modernize', but this is where we must maintain a tireless vigilance, and test again each time what we mean by ecologies. To assume that ecology demarcates a basic good is to overlook Bateson's reminder that there is an ecology of weeds, much as there is an ecology of bad ideas; ecologies flourish and ecologies produce the scent and scenes of death. Error can be propagated despite the best of our intentions.

There are edited collections that address architectural environments, such as Ariane Lourie Harrison's *Architectural Theories of the Environment* (2013), Brook Muller's *Ecology and the Architectural Imagination* (2014) and David Gissen's *Subnature*, which considers architecture's 'other environments' (2009), again, all of which highlight exemplary projects, designers and artists. All the while, an architectural status quo is maintained by signature architectural projects and well-known architects and practices. It is not these kinds of recognizable practices that I am after. Instead, the practice scenes that will punctuate this book, both in dedicated chapters and embedded in the general discussion, are non-normative forays into the more peripheral works of creative practitioners.

Perusing the literature that highlights an ecological turn in architectural practice and discourse, Peg Rawes, in her introduction to *Relational Architectural Ecologies*, finds with each reference she cites something that is missing, something that draws her into the terrain of her own project demands, framed as a tripartite dedication to: feminist work on relational ecologies; expanding understandings of ecological architectures and challenging what we might mean by ecology in the first place (2013). Concerned with a similar ethos, the practices I discuss move slowly, contravene the expectations of what an architectural project should be or should do and are often rather messy and uncomfortable, even indisciplined. They are less likely to be represented in mainstream architectural media.

Edited collections such as Doina Petrescu's *Altering Practices: Feminist Politics and Poetics of Space* (2007) as well as Lori Brown's *Feminist Practices: Interdisciplinary Approaches to Women in Architecture* (2011) come closer to the kinds of practices I foreground in that they make space for minor practitioners and explorative practices that mix thinking with practising, including experimental approaches to writing. Returning again to Rawes' work, I am encouraged by the explorative approaches that have been collected in her co-edited volume *Poetic Biopolitics* (Rawes, Loo and Matthews 2016), where the editors argue that spatial, material and textual poetics and practices can form 'affirmative ethical relations between people, and places' (2016: 1), to which I would add 'things'. Aesthetic practices can at the same time be ethical practices, and this is what the editors demonstrate in these volumes. It is a cause I likewise share. It was by engaging in this ethos that with Catharina Gabrielsson and Helen Runting I recently edited *Architecture and Feminisms: Ecologies, Economies, Technologies* (2018), where it was important to situate practice scenes broadly defined alongside theoretical discourse.

To engage in ecologies of creative practice is to argue for an understanding of how practices, like ecologies, are situated and jostle alongside each other, some practices taking precedence over others, resulting in diminutions and destructions, as well as surprising flourishings. Such shifts in status will often depend on how much institutional support is achieved for a practice and to what extent research funding bodies are influenced by the stipulated 'national interests' of a geopolitical context.

Ecologies, it should not be forgotten, pertain to many kinds of organizational matrices interlacing the natural and the technological. How do you situate yourself in the scene that is the Anthropocene as a creative practitioner? How do you achieve this? What works, and how do you make yourself worthy of what happens to you in terms of the encounters you suffer and enjoy? Part of what I argue is that how you conceptualize what you are doing makes a significant difference, likewise how you share your stories of practice. Creative ecologies, Demos has recently argued, call for connectivity and relationality, aimed towards generative rather than destructive ends, recognizing, at the same time, that ecology is not value free, nor, I would add, is it free of power relations. Creative ecologies suggest a counter-project, requiring a process of decolonizing nature, which, Demos hastily adds, also means decolonizing culture (2017).

The situated difficulties of living together, alongside each other, jostling amidst ecologies composed of mixed human and more-than-human actors is what practising a cosmopolitical approach to design allows us to deal with (Yaneva 2016: 5). As Stengers argues: 'Some people love to divide and classify, while others are bridge-makers – weaving relations that turn a divide into a living contrast, one whose power is to affect, to produce thinking and feeling. But bridge-making is a situated practice' (Stengers 2012). What *processes of subjectification* are facilitated or quashed according to environmental conditions, and what environments are likewise diminished or ameliorated? What I want to map is the relationship between human subjectivities engaged in creative practice, striving, yearning, succeeding, failing amidst the environments within which they find themselves both enabled and constrained. How they exhaust their environment-worlds at the same time as exhausting themselves becomes a further matter of concern. How exhaustion, as improbable as it sounds, might be formulated as a methodology will be ventured in the final section of this first part of the book dedicated to environment-worlds.

For now, in what follows, I will introduce a second practice scene.

Practice scene: Katla Maríudóttir's volcano

From 14 to 20 April 2010, ash from the volcanic eruptions of Eyjafjallajökull in southern Iceland spread across much of Europe, disrupting air traffic for a week. Even as far away as Australia this environmental event had sociocultural implications. The Australian Institute of Architects' annual international conference was thrown into disarray when several eminent European guests were unable to attend after their flights were cancelled. A diagram of the ash cloud emanating from the volcanic eruptions shows a ghostly smudge across a large swathe of northern Europe as small fragments of rock, minerals and volcanic glass were dragged through the atmosphere like pigment dropped into a bowl of agitated water. When Eyjafjallajökull blows, then Katla, its larger neighbour, usually follows suit. Katla is a subglacial volcano and when it erupts it causes massive flooding of the glacier Mýrdalsjökull in which it is located. Aerial images of the landscape show a blossom of white ice around Katla. Leading southwards down from the volcano towards the sea, a furrowed carpet of green is visible, and towards the south-east, a dark stain of soil, the lava fields through which Iceland's ring road (*hringvegur*) perilously passes. When you dig into the field, deep brown and black bands are revealed, the black tephra bands geologically indicating when the resident volcanoes last erupted. The coastal ring road constructed in the early 1970s is an infrastructure that offers no guarantee of safe passage through the lava fields. After a heavy rain, bridges and roads are washed away and inhabitants must be airlifted to safety. Recent rescue efforts were made in the settlements of the southern coast of Iceland as I write these words.

When imagining volcanoes the temptation is to picture inverted cones, but Katla, even though she rises to nearly 5,000 metres above sea level, does not reveal herself as such. Katla is lodged in a glacier and her shape shifts depending on where you are standing in the landscape; it depends on your point of view and how far you have been caught up in landscape events. Even though she has not erupted since 1918, Katla is considered active and she continues to be carefully monitored. She is editorialized as 'notorious', as the 'mother of all volcanoes', and the Icelanders have been waiting anxiously because every recorded eruption of Eyjafjallajökull has been shortly followed by Katla blowing her top.

Katla is also the name of an architect who completed her degree in architecture at KTH (Royal Institute of Technology) Stockholm in 2012, two years after Eyjafjallajökull erupted, and who now teaches in Reykjavik at the Iceland Academy of the Arts at the same time as caring for her infant.

Challenged with the demand to produce a final project for her five-year degree in architecture, Katla Maríudóttir returned to the environment-world she knows best, coastal Iceland where she grew up in the vicinity of her namesake. She describes the house she lived in as an adolescent, located on a small grassy hillock protruding from the dark lava fields, a white box on a green hill. Both of her parents were pastors in local churches, of which there are many as locals usually walk across the landscape in order to join their community in prayer. There is no place name on Google Maps given for the scattered settlement of houses in the vicinity of which Katla spent her adolescence. The nearest settlement is towards the north east at Kirkjubaejarklaustur, a town of around 120 people.

What we are presented with here is a landscape heaving upwards messily as the fiery underworld pushes through the earth's crust, erupting here and there, procuring what Katla, the creative practitioner, calls 'landscape events'. Landscape events impact on architectural events, which together produce narrative events. This schema is what organizes Katla's creative survey, and so as to orient herself she produces a compass. It is important that the compass is not determined in advance of her material-semiotic engagement with the landscape, rather it comes from within its messy midst. Like her namesake, Katla is embroiled in her situation, but in seeking to undertake a survey she must open up other points of view too. Her compass operates somewhat like Maria Reiche's ladder in that it augments her sensory apprehension of a local post-human landscape that is an environment-world she has occupied during a formative period of her life. Yet this is neither simply a personal story nor the transcription of childhood memories. Katla tentatively situates herself as a spokesperson for the landscape. She explains of her local environment-world: 'It is a place where every small little thing is alive and has a story to tell' (Maríudóttir 2014).

Katla visits her adopted blind grandfather who tells her ghost stories. He can see spirits and local sprites and entertains conversations with them. He lives near an old turf-house, a vernacular architecture in various states of repair and disrepair. Katla spends time in a small local library discovering letters from the wives of shipwrecked sailors. She takes numerous photographs of rudimentary and pre-fabricated fishermen's huts. She happens upon strange tales of churches that have uprooted and wandered across the Icelandic landscape in the vicinity of the volcano Katla. A church was destroyed and then rebuilt, destroyed and rebuilt, and with each reconstruction shifting its

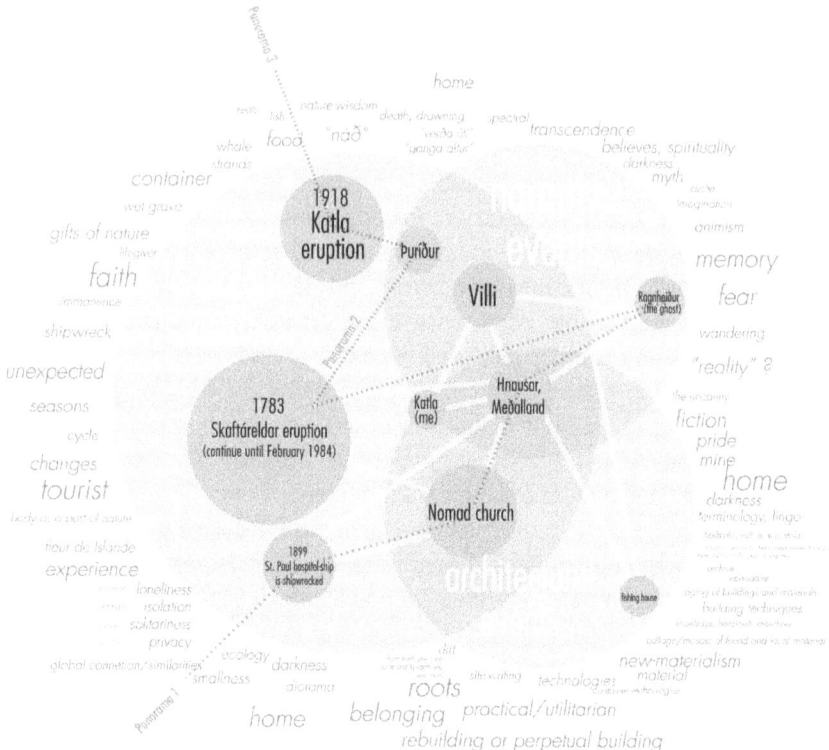

FIGURE 2.1 Katla Maríudóttir, *Compass*, Jarðnæði: Tranquil Terra. *Drawing by Katla Maríudóttir (2014).*

location, re-establishing its ground and reconvening a local community, an assembly.

Katla follows the material of this lively diverse archive, and by thinking with her landscape encounters she comes up with her compass, which is composed of these three kinds of events: landscape events, narrative events and architectural events. The events are provisionally distinguished only to see more clearly how their minor stories are deeply entangled. She explains that the events overlap, forming a four-dimensional web through time and space. They include a flood, a wandering church, a turf-house, a shipwreck, a ghost, a migrant mother, a volcanic eruption and so on. Characters and places and materials come to be intermixed, but the compass she constructs helps Katla to orientate herself. Each spatio-temporal event is demarcated using the indefinite article – *a* turf-house, *a* ghost – which draws our attention to their singular and immanent expression. In dialogue, Gilles Deleuze and Claire Parnet speak of the power of the indefinite article, which refers to nothing but itself in its impersonal specificity (2007: 79). The indefinite article rests on neither subjects nor objects, but draws attention to processes taking place in their own specific immediacy, and to glimmers of a landscape event, a wandering church, a migrant woman and a fleeting encounter in which something happens. Each event draws together an assembly of those who are concerned, and these may be more than human participants, ghosts, for instance. As Latour has pointed out, the Icelandic word *Althing* was that around which 'thingmen' would gather, manifesting as the issue that brings people together because it divides them (2005a). Each thing about which we care is framed by specifically located interests in various situations of alignment and misalignment so that a multiplicity of points of view are made manifest in an encounter with things.

Importantly, for Katla's attempts to survey her environment-world, landscape, narrative and architectural events can be said to raise 'very complex questions about composition and decomposition, about speed and slowness, about latitude and longitude, about power and affect' (Deleuze 1991: 95). Between Katla, the events she witnesses and the material life of these Icelandic coastal plains, something is made to circulate, which beckons to another way of seeing things, to other visions and sonorities and other forms of assembly.

Katla's own composition, as modest witness to these events, expresses no ambition to propose a built project for this mutable plane of relations, this fragile ecology. The built project as the inevitable outcome of an architectural investigation is exactly what Katla resists, as she aims to reclaim other ways of doing architecture. Instead, with great rigour and exactitude, she documents a turf-house in a state of decay, she maps a history of shipwrecks along the shore, she follows the migratory passage of a woman whose home has been flooded in the aftermath of a volcanic eruption in 1918 and she sketches the metamorphic transpositions of a church that travels across the landscape.

FIGURE 2.2 Katla Maríudóttir, *Architectural Events*, Jarðnæði: Tranquil Terra. *Image by Katla Maríudóttir (2014).*

This willingness to let things be by drawing them out through means of architectural documentation sets fire to the core assumptions of the discipline of architecture where it is most rigid and dogmatic. No, the answer posed by architecture does not have to take the form of the built edifice, the form of a cultural centre, a museum, a housing block, nor does it even have to comprise a series of delightful follies that can punctuate a path across a curated landscape. What does Katla propose instead?

Katla argues that it is sufficient to deploy her architectural skills towards the challenge of surveying a local environment-world, to convey its affects and percepts to a people who are not witness to the things and events she has apprehended. To survey an environment-world means bringing sufficient sensitivity and humility to the event itself, to a place as it unfurls; it is not to presume that such a place is in need of your authorial gestures and additions – yet more stuff, more program, more combinatorials of things and their associated 'solutions' – but to map invisible forces. To experience joy in providing a conduit through which a landscape with a life of its own persists requires the development of ethico-aesthetic skills with respect to following the materials, for which an adequate lexicon of concept-tools is also required.[4]

When Katla presented her final work in the form of a small installation at the KTH School of Architecture, Stockholm, in June 2014, the architectural critics assembled there to judge her work were slowly drawn into her story. Her installation was composed of mixed media, including her compass diagram; material samples from the lava fields; a patch of turf; drawings of turf-houses in various states of decay; panels telling of the stories she had gathered populated by such aesthetic figures as a migrant mother, ghosts and a blind psychic hermit; and composite landscape images inspired by the artist Tacita Dean. These composite images collapsed the temporalities of her site into one mise en scène as though the landscape, architectural and narrative events were depicted in a slow exposure that lasted over a century. Volcanic eruptions took place at the same time as shipwrecks at the same time as flooding glaciers at the same time that the landscape bore witness to the wandering itinerary of a church and the displacement of peoples. The project was entitled 'Jarðnæði: Tranquil Terra' and Katla called her task that of an architect-cartographer. Much like Maria Reiche, her challenge was a documentary one, a means of rendering sensible rather than insisting on the imposition of new forms. The Icelandic word Jarðnæði brings together estate and land management, but also means an earth of peace and quiet, hence, Tranquil Terra. Though the tranquillity is belied by the upheavals of the landscape Katla engages in, the longue durée of the earth's persistence speaks of other moods and speeds, and all manner of cohabitations of human and non-human participants and their material relations. At the conclusion of her presentation, there was silence. It was hard to know what the silence held in store. Everyone waited, holding a collective breath. Who would speak first?

Exhaustion: of environment-worlds

To broach the theme of exhaustion, which traces a weary passage through this book, I commence simply with a list as a means of explaining this thematic orientation:

1. Exhaustion is both corporeal and conceptual; it is about the breakdown of things (human things, non-human things, infrastructural and architectural things, other kinds of things both corporeal and incorporeal) and it is about the falling apart of concepts. It is material and it is semiotic, both/and.
2. Exhaustion pertains to the exhaustion of habitats, territories and environments. It is the exhaustion of the assemblage of living creatures (human and more-than-human) and their local environment-world.
3. Exhaustion can be described as a methodology, offering a way of practising from the midst of the spaces and temporal paces of exhaustion.
4. Exhaustion is distinct from out-and-out extinction, as extinction is what threatens the ends of exhaustion – beyond exhaustion, extinction.
5. Exhaustion is not about being tired, instead exhaustion can be partnered with creativity, specifically with ecologies of creative practice – beyond exhaustion, creation.

This first round through exhaustion, which closes the first part of this book, concerns itself with the exhaustion of environment-worlds and by association the exhaustion of the potentialities of space. It is a simple yet complex formula I test: At one end of a spectrum of exhaustion there is extinction and at the other end the possibility of creation. Deleuze's essay 'The Exhausted' ('*L'Épuisé*') is one of the primary sources from which I draw my discussion of exhaustion, which will be a recurring motif installed to conclude each section of this book. Here we commence with the exhaustion of environment-worlds. At the culmination of Part Two I offer a reflection on the exhaustion of things, and then, at the close of Part Three, the exhaustion of thinkables. This leaves one final step in the methodology of exhaustion, which pertains to the exhaustion of the creative practice scenes that punctuate the more theoretical essays, but now I am leaping too far ahead.

Returning to my point of departure, the place where I discover exhaustion as a concept is in Deleuze's essay 'The Exhausted', first published in 1992 in Samuel Beckett's *Quad et autres pièces pour la télévision*, and subsequently collected in the English edition of *Essays Critical and Clinical* (1998a). Samuel Beckett's script *Quad*, composed for television, is exemplary of exhausted environment-worlds. *Quad* takes place in an architectural space stripped bare of all but its minimal coordinates. Despite the movement of recognizably human figures, its scale is indeterminate, and the architecture could in fact be imagined as a vast, empty, post-human landscape. A square is marked out in Beckett's instructional script, A, B, C, D; a square crossed twice by diagonals through a centre marked E. With the use of a detailed diagram and associated instructions, four trajectories are mapped out for four figures who enter *a* quadrilateral, *a* square, from the four outer corners, A, B, C, and D. Each figure is draped in a differently coloured cowl to distinguish them, and their different entry points further signify that they hearken from different places. They arrive from nowhere and leave again. No origin is allocated, nor any end point, and their trajectories through this near-empty space could continue indefinitely, but at a certain moment, just as the figures have entered the space marked out by a square, so they depart again. Gilles Deleuze explains that Beckett's script for *Quad* is clear, 'it is a question of exhausting space' (Deleuze 1998a: 163), and for my purposes, this pertains to the exhaustion of those spaces I have called environment-worlds. Exhaustion as a concept grapples with the exhaustion of territories, habitats and milieus, that is to say, of environment-worlds. What is at stake is the mutual exhaustion of the living creature (human and non-human) and its local environment-world.

It is from Deleuze's dense essay that something of a methodology of exhaustion can be extracted, composed of four steps. In this chapter I venture a discussion of what I have identified as the third step in a methodology of exhaustion, that is, the extenuation of space and the conceptual emergence of an 'any-space-whatever' occupied by 'any-characters-whatever' (Deleuze 1998a: 162), aptly illustrated by the cursory description of Beckett's *Quad*. Space becomes depotentialized, and subjectivities rendered near imperceptible, like shadows or hollowed-out figures wandering about seemingly homeless, seeking refuge, seeking some encounter. Impossible as it may seem, at the extreme moment of environmental exhaustion something may yet emerge, and that is the direction towards which I aim to lead each of the concluding essays that address the threshold of exhaustion. I aim towards the speculative gesture of ecologies of creative practice that may yet emerge out of exhaustion. As Peter Pàl Pelbart affirms, 'Exhaustion may be the term that acutely defines, albeit enigmatically, the hesitant and unnecessary passage from catastrophe to creation' (Pelbart 2015: 122). To culminate this journey it will be necessary to cross the three parts of the book to arrive finally at the scene of exhaustion that pertains to ecologies of creative practice.

The potentialities that emerge at the outer limit of the spectrum of exhaustion, before something like extinction wipes out everything, is what concerns me here. On the other end of the spectrum of exhaustion there is vitalism, a particular attitude to life as that which courses through and with all things, animating environment-worlds. Art critic Jan Verwoert describes the ends of the affective spectrum of exhaustion as exhaustion and exuberance (2007). In her book, *Exhaustion: A History*, Anna K. Schaffner offers an etymological explanation: Exhaustion is derived from *Exhaurire*: Ex – out; haurire – to draw out (2016: 7). Something is drawn out, which either means it is extenuated, stretched to its limits, or perhaps drawn out so as to map a new possibility. The opposite of exhaustion, Schaffner points out, as do many others, is vitality, that is to say a life force, or vitalism (2016: 8). For me, the other end of the spectrum can be called joy, what the philosopher Baruch Spinoza designates as a most adequate idea. Exhaustion is that which is drawn out, resolving itself in dissolution, or else in the glimmer of some new possibility.

Exhaustion, it must immediately be stressed, is not simply about tiredness. When one is exhausted the dominant desire expressed by the one who is tired is: If only I were simply tired and could finally rest. Exhaustion is more profound than mere tiredness; its structure of feeling is rather about an anxious restlessness. Exhaustion is about wakefulness and the distance of sleep. It is insomnia. Exhausted, awake, not tired, a constant wondering plagues you, as you ask yourself: Have I exhausted all that is possible? Have I done everything I can to ameliorate my local environment-world? It is an exhausting challenge.

It is exactly the space and pace, the local and global extent of exhaustion that I wish to explore. I have previously (2012, 2013, 2014) extracted a methodology of exhaustion from Deleuze's brief and dense essay 'The Exhausted' so removing and abstracting it, without some attendant risks, from the specific application he has tested in his reading of Beckett's novels, plays and television plays (Deleuze 1998a). Taking some liberties with Deleuze's essay, I enumerate four ways of exhausting the possible, accepting that this list should not be taken as exhaustive. I wilfully extract these four approaches from what Deleuze identifies as three 'Languages': Language I, II and III, respectively. It is important to note, as I will continue to stress, that the results of the methodology of exhaustion can proceed towards a more powerful composition of materials and forces, as well as towards a decomposition of our relations and encounters amidst our local environment-worlds. That is to say, the methodology produces what could be judged as both 'failures' and 'successes', but this very much depends on point of view and situation and what you do about the things that matter to you.

Where in Deleuze's argument he progresses from exhaustive series or 'combinatorials' of things (and things include images and concepts, not just things we can conveniently grasp hold of), through the exhaustion of voices, followed by the extenuation of space and finally towards the dissipation of the power of an 'Image of Thought', it is useful to see what happens when the methodology is followed in both directions, back and forth between combinatorials of things and the Image of Thought, which overdetermines how we are apt to think about things. The four approaches to a methodology of exhaustion include:

1. Language I: The composition of combinatorials arranged through the formation of exhaustive series of things (including concepts and images understood as things, including any such thing that can be named). A combinatorial can also be composed of a series of moves, such as those choreographed moves taken by Beckett's four pacing figures in *Quad*. Exhaustive combinatorials of things will be addressed most closely in Part Two dedicated to things.

2. Language II: The drying up or exhausting of the flow of weak and strong voices. Notably, in Beckett's *Quad*, the four figures shuffle 'without words, without voice', their voices seemingly exhausted, dried up (Deleuze 1998a: 162), their heads are bent over facing the worn-down ground. What is suggested is the exhausting work of discourse wherein some voices are heard, while others remain under-represented. This particular mode of exhaustion becomes acutely relevant in terms of the feminist ethos I weave into this book, and my repeated attempts to bring to the fore otherwise overlooked minor practitioners across the creative disciplines.

3. Language IIIa: The extenuation of the potentialities of space by way of the 'any-space-whatever', which can include the exhaustive dissemination of images of designed living spaces, found in the architectural and design media and in proliferating feeds, such as ArchDaily.[5] This is of particular relevance when it comes to the exhaustion of environment-worlds, but it also touches upon the exhaustion of things and thinkables.

4. Language IIIb: The dissipation of the power of the Image of Thought, which can be an iconoclastic confrontation that leads either to a new, more positive Image of Thought or else towards a more dogmatic one. It depends on what kind of problem you are currently grappling with and how far you are constrained by or at liberty to critically engage

with your milieu. I will return to the construction and destruction of an Image of Thought in Part Three.

I take the liberty of revising Deleuze's taxonomy, as he himself explains that the last two ways of exhausting the possible are 'united in Language III, the language of images and spaces' (1998a: 162). Further to the extenuation of environment-worlds, it is worth mentioning that there is a mathematical and geometrical definition of a method of exhaustion that allows the area beneath a curve to be calculated by approaching the problem of exactly measuring curvature without, strictly speaking, arriving at anything more than a sufficient answer, creating what might be called a working method. To be exhaustive, in the sense of a search party, is to survey an area as completely as possible, but there is always the suspicion that some thing still remains to be unearthed, or that we missed some crucial detail. And so the search may well be taken up at a later date. Crucially, the methodology of exhaustion, as well as confronting the dissipation of sense, leads to the breakdown of the organic or inorganic body, defined in the broadest way to include, for instance, a human body, a body politic, a built environment-body, an ecological body, an environment-world body and so forth: 'A body can be anything; it can be an animal, a body of sounds, a mind or an idea; it can be a linguistic corpus, a social body, a collectivity' (Deleuze 1988b: 127). It is important that a body can be considered as so many things, separate and apart, and further, what happens between bodies takes place because of their encounters, which can proceed in two directions when it comes to the spectrum of exhaustion, towards exuberant joys, or complete exhaustion and then decomposition.

Where Deleuze reads the seventeenth-century Dutch Jewish philosopher Baruch Spinoza, he argues: 'When a body "encounters" another body, or an idea another idea, it happens that the two relations sometimes combine to form a more powerful whole, and sometimes one decomposes the other, destroying the cohesion of its parts' (Deleuze 1988b: 19). He explains that following such encounters 'we experience joy when a body encounters ours and enters into composition with it, and sadness when, on the contrary, a body or an idea threaten our own coherence' (Deleuze 1988b: 19). Remember that this 'we', as I have already pointed out, can be composed of many kinds of bodies.

In this first foray into exhaustion I focus upon the extenuation of the potentialities of space, which pertains to what Deleuze calls Language III, or what I have specified as Language IIIa. Following on from exhaustive combinatorials of things and exhausted voices, Language IIIa is that part of the methodology of exhaustion where language is no longer used to denominate innumerable things, or to transmit voices, but is entirely dissipated in a confrontation with the immanent limits of space. With Language II, the relationship with language is effectively stretched to its limits. Then, to arrive at an Image of Thought via Language IIIa, one proceeds through what Deleuze has named an any-space-whatever, which is the extenuation of space (1998a: 160). Space, conventionally defined through extensive measurements, enables the demarcation and determination of localized places and their respective assemblages of singularities, 'a sample of the floor, a sample of the wall, a door without a knob, an opaque window, a pallet' (Deleuze 1998a: 165), so supporting the taking place of some event. Yet, 'To exhaust space is to extenuate its potentiality by making any encounter impossible' (163), as witnessed in Beckett's *Quad*, where the four figures repetitively approach each other on the square, but always turn away at the last moment before actually meeting. In *Cinema 1*, Deleuze describes the any-space-whatever in relation to post-war towns, apprehended as disconnected and empty spaces (1992b: 129). Across a selected series of cinematic images he describes in detail how the any-space-whatever is composed or rather 'extracted' from a given state of things, through means of light, shadow, white and colouration (1992b: 111–122; see also Frichot 2009a). It is of relevance here that one step of the methodology of exhaustion pertains to spatial exhaustion, which speaks to the exhaustion of environment-worlds composed of subjectivities and the shelters they attempt to carve out of their surroundings.

In addition to spatial exhaustion or attenuation, Deleuze's Language III includes the labour of image making, where Deleuze suggests that making an image is a very difficult thing to do. Images in this sense must be distinguished in two directions: They are distinct from those found or received images, which alongside things, and concepts, might be enumerated and named or even 'branded' within combinatorials under Language I; but they are also distinct from the 'Image of Thought', which organizes how we think unreflectively, by way of habit, opinion and cliché. The any-space-whatever and the images treated in Language IIIa finally lead to an encounter with the Image of Thought, Language IIIb, which is not some representation of an object or a subject, but a movement in the mind suggestive of all manner of noopolitical effects, of which more will be discussed in Part Three. Suffice to say, noopolitics, which is based on noology (understood as a logic of mind or minds), takes advantage of our collectively networked, unreflective habits of thought and comes to be expressed through the imposition of preconceived ideas.

Why might exhaustion be a conceptual theme of interest, and why in the form of a methodology? As Deleuze puts it: 'The problem is: In relation to what is exhaustion (which must not be confused with tiredness) going to be defined?' (1998a: 163). For the purposes of this exegesis the methodology of exhaustion alerts us to the many crises of our local environment-worlds. These environment-worlds operate at many scales, and no doubt some kind of more graspable architectural experiment is required to explain the exhaustion of designed habitats.

Alex Schweder, an architect whose day job was at one point checking the compliance of buildings with local fire regulations, is an architect-artist. He troubles such disciplinary distinctions with his series of performative works undertaken by his studio Performance Architecture. The work in question, of which he has tested previous permutations, is called *Your Turn*. It is a helpful example to supplement the bleak humour of Beckett's exhausting combinatorial experiment, as well as helpfully illustrating aspects of Uexküll's logic of *Umwelten*.

Your Turn speculates on minimum habitable living conditions, and in this way contributes to a discontinuous genealogy of techno-architectural experiments dedicated to the cell and the capsule, from Archigram's living cells, through a range of questionable speculative experiments dedicated to minimal approaches to sheltering migrants and the homeless, all the way to the living cells designed by Pier Vittorio Aureli's studio Dogma, presented as their contribution to the British Venice Biennale of Architecture in 2016 (see Runting and Frichot 2018a and 2018b). This is a discontinuous genealogy in that each time the minimal unit of the cell is explored, it is directed at answering a different question and is obliged to respond to its specific socio-cultural, economic and historical Image of Thought. *Your Turn* expresses neither

FIGURE 2.3 *Alex Schweder,* Your Turn, *Aldrich Contemporary Art Museum, Ridgefield, CT, 2017. Photography by George Brenner.*

techno-euphoria nor the presumed joys of co-living in maintenance-free cells. Schweder's work is different. He pushes the minimum to an extreme limit, and whether intentionally or not, gently mocks *ad absurdum* the desires of the architect to test the minimum by exploring design scenarios.

Uexküll's model describes scenarios in which different creatures coexist for the most part unseen to each other, and yet impacting on each other's worlds, affecting and being affected, like the spider and the fly. It is as though Schweder has taken this diagram as his brief in designing a minimal habitable wall to be occupied by two tenants, each taking up residence on either side of the wall and sharing a cell wall in effective co-isolation (Sloterdijk 2007b), as well as – and here is the crux of the experiment – dependent on the sharing of minimal resources. *Your Turn* requires that two occupants cohabit in co-isolation the two sides of a habitable wall. Each occupant is invisible to the other, but must share all the available resources generally assumed to compose minimal living conditions. As the email invitation to the ten-day performative event, commencing on 1 October 2017 in Ridgefield Connecticut, explains:

> The artists [Alex Schweder with his colleague Ward Shelley] will occupy either side of a twenty three foot square wall until October 8th, during which time they will share six domestic functions (bed, bathroom, desk, dining table, kitchen, and comfortable chair) by sliding them back and forth through the wall. Only one person can use the amenity at a time, thereby creating the need to share a limited resource.[6]

When I first met Alex he was undertaking another architectural performance experiment in Berlin at the Magnus Müller gallery, which at that time was located across the road from the Volksbühne theatre on Rosa Luxemburg-Platz. For this exhibition, he made himself available for free architectural consultation. It was a work he called 'Free Architectural Advice', advertised as such with a glowing sign in the gallery window. Either people would make appointments or walk in off Weydingerstrasse, and he would sit down with each one of them to discuss their architectural problems. He would then prepare, in duplicate, a prescriptive specification detailing how the 'client' could resolve their architectural problem. He called these instructions, and clients would be invited to take one copy home to interpret and enact while the other would be kept as a record, pinned for the time being to the gallery wall behind Alex's consultation desk. Sometimes the problem would be as simple as a plant that was slowly dying on a shared apartment stairwell and how to best negotiate its care, or else small territorial workplace problems concerning the sharing of open-plan offices (which happened to be my problem). What Alex demonstrates about architecture is that it can be performed through the smallest gestures and the most minor shifts in one's environment-world. He writes: 'Herein lies the opportunity for an occupant to claim authorship and thereby shape his own subjectivity' (2011: 144).

Alex's experiments with the artist Ward Shelley form a series he calls Architect Performed Buildings. He points out that even the simple gesture of writing 'living room' on a house plan designates a set of particular actions, or performances, which are open to interpretation (2011: 131). Performing can get exhausting after a while. Before *Your Turn*, Schweder and Ward had performed *Counter Weight Room Mate* (2011) and *Stability* (2009), the former coordinating the movements of two occupants tethered to either end of a climbing rope, and the latter experimenting with how two occupants might cohabit a miniature see-saw house. In *Stability*, the occupants lived and worked at either end of the see-saw house and had to counterbalance each other's performances in order to carry out basic daily tasks. They exhaustively practised this occupation for a week. It was an exercise in synchronizing rhythms, even though the occupants had no visual access to each other. The aim was to carve out one's own environmental niche as well as one's subjectivity to the point of making this distinction near indiscernible. This was undertaken by experimenting with one's performance of occupation within considerable constraints: 'Through the overlap of performance and architecture subjects are constructed that create, occupy, are impacted by, and modify their environments in a continuing process' (Schweder 2011: 133). It could be a prescription for environment-worlds. In 2016, they took this experiment a half-step out of the laboratory that is the art gallery and created *ReActor*, a house balanced on a single column responsive to the live load of the wind and the movement of its orange-overall-clad inhabitants. While out of the gallery, the site nonetheless is a controlled one in that it forms part of the 'architecture field' of Art Omi International Art Centre in Ghent, New York.

The methodology of exhaustion always conjoins the 'exhaustive *and* the exhausted' (Deleuze 1998a: 154), and how these work together, organizing the proliferation of events of sense *and* material mixtures of bodies as independent yet co-constitutive series. An exhaustive approach is applied to an exhausted body, simple or complex. Exhaustivity *and* exhaustion together present us with urgent ecosophical questions such as the overconsumption of our environment-worlds described via a long litany of contemporary plights. Exhaustivity, as Deleuze explains, demands that one combine the variables of a situation, but by renouncing any preference (1998a: 153). A logical process of exhaustivity and its production of relations of sense (or sense-making procedures) suggests a compositional method that resists hierarchization and even judgement: Any choice is as good as any other, though *we need to make ourselves worthy* of the choices we make, as Deleuze emphasizes in a stoic manner (1990: 149). In *Cinema 1: The Movement Image*, he argues: 'If I am conscious of choice, there are therefore already choices I cannot make, and modes of existence I cannot follow – all those I followed on the condition of persuading myself that "there was no choice"' (1986: 114). Choice is established over and again with every choice that is made, in such a way that what is at stake is situated anew each time. This question of choice draws attention to an ethics, or more specifically, an ethico-aesthetics of the encounter, which returns us to the question of what we do once we have run through all the things it is possible to name (or else, brand, colonize or claim dominion over), when our discursive voices are exhausted (and thus no longer capable of critique), and once we have extenuated the possibilities of space towards a limit point of de-potentialization (of, for instance, all worldly resources, all human and non-human relations).

Now we can return to these four figures, silent shuffling sentinels, ceaselessly traversing the space of a square, moving across what might be an emptied-out post-human landscape. We can do anything we like with them, interpret them with humour or pathos. Observing different low-resolution versions on YouTube can be a mesmerising exercise. From the comfort of your laptop screen it is like witnessing the exhaustion at the end of the world, at the end of ends. The figures might be the first or the very last humanoids. Yet, as Pelbart intimates: 'Something must be exhausted, as Deleuze sensed in *The Exhausted*, so that a different game may be conceivable' (Pelbart 2015: 53). What kind of spatial environmental game do we set up or discover ourselves within next? And how will we make the best of it?

Notes

1. I want to thank Vasily Sitnikov for drawing my attention to this book, and the series within which it sits, dedicated to Theory.
2. This is an expression and critique I have gleaned from my colleague Daniel Koch.
3. For those who have not yet encountered the work of J. K. Gibson-Graham, this pen name denominates the collaborative work of two feminist economic geographers, Katherine Gibson and the late Julie Graham.
4. A brief, earlier version of this account of Katla Maríudóttir's work can be found in Hélène Frichot, *How to Make Yourself a Feminist Design Power Tool* (Baunach, Germany: AADR Spurbuchverlag, 2016).
5. See http://www.archdaily.com
6. Alex Schweder and Ward Shelley, *Your Turn*, October 1 to 22 April 2018, Ridgefield, CT: The Aldrich Contemporary Art Museum. https://mailchi.mp/0e6932cba352/schweder-shelley-at-the-aldrich-museum?e=e86371e3f0 (accessed 24 September 2017).

PART TWO

Things

3

Object oriented

From environment-worlds to things, this second part of the book addresses the cacophonous discourse on objects and things. An awful lot of noise has been made recently about things, or objects, depending on your preferred terminology. It is as though we had not been discussing them already; handling them; measuring them; inventing, discovering and managing them; and being deeply affected by them, as well as affecting them. For some it would appear that we have finally apprehended the object, only for it to withdraw from us, as it becomes inaccessible, as we share no relation with it except by way of our limited human senses. The sensory object has been held up to us, or at least its shadow has been cast yet again on a screen or a cave wall, and we are told that all we can do is describe it through a poetic phenomenological rambling, applying a delimited and paltry aesthetics, grasping at it blindly as it continues to elude us. How, instead, can we address objects, or rather things, with care?

Story two: Agnès Varda – gleaning

Women mostly. In groups and alone. Casting across what appear to be fields that are now empty following the harvest. What are they looking for? Their heads are heavy, their necks are bent and their eyes are lowered to the ground. Their skirts are pulled up as fabric baskets in which they can collect remainders. What has the harvest left behind? They are scavenging for scraps; they are attempting to supplement their meagre livelihood with leftovers. They are attempting to make do.

Such scenes as these are depicted in Agnès Varda's *The Gleaners and I* (2000) (*Les Glaneurs et la Glaneuse*) and in her follow-up documentary film, *The

Gleaners and I: Two Years Later, where she returns to many of the characters she has encountered, and pays visit to some new characters who have written to her in the interim. She follows the material of environment-worlds.

The gleaner's labour exhausts fields that are already exhausted. Still, doggedly, she goes in search of remainders. She fossicks in the dirt following the material to see where it will take her. As Shelby Doyle and Leslie Forehand point out: 'According to Wajcman, women have always been designers and manipulators of technology, as their role as laborers – harvesters, weavers, potters, and caretakers of the domestic economy – placed them into an early and intimate relationship with technology' (2017). A view supported by Zoë Sofia's discussion of container technologies, and her emphasis on the undervalued technologies of containment and supply discovered in bowls, jars and vats, and where architecture is understood as a facilitating environment (Sofia 2000). Gleaning is perhaps the most humble technological redeployment of resources of all, relying on calloused hands, empty stomachs, urgent need and skirts reshaped as simple container technologies.

Varda demonstrates that gleaning, formerly reserved for bucolic rural scenes, enters the urban context where marginal figures eke out an existence. She tells the story of sitting in a cafe across from a street market. Anyone who has spent time in Paris and who enjoys fresh produce will be aware of the remarkable celerity with which a street market is mounted and dismantled on the boulevards and squares. Street market architectures are based on the simplest of infrastructures of uprights, and canvas, and trestles, and the most inconspicuous of holes scored into the bitumen where the uprights are lodged for the duration in order to hold up this rudimentary shelter. Varda is looking across at the market as the trading day closes around 2 pm, and happens to observe, between the moment of closure and before the street sweepers come along to clean away the refuse, a number of figures descending quietly on the scene, like flies, she says. What are they doing? she asks herself, and then she realizes they are scavenging for leftovers, they are urban gleaners, and this sends her on a trajectory that takes her into the countryside, then back into the city, towards the sea and even into museums, as she wanders across France entering into dialogue with people who tell her why and how they glean.

What do we do when we glean? We select, extract, gather, pull out of context, recombine and often we have to be prepared to pick up the leftovers because, no doubt, someone has been there before us. This pertains to well-worn concepts too. We compose exhaustive combinatorials of things and string them together in search of some meaning, of some thread to follow, however artificially strung out. We listen, as Varda has listened, to the weak and the strong voices before they fade away, lifting them briefly out of obscurity.

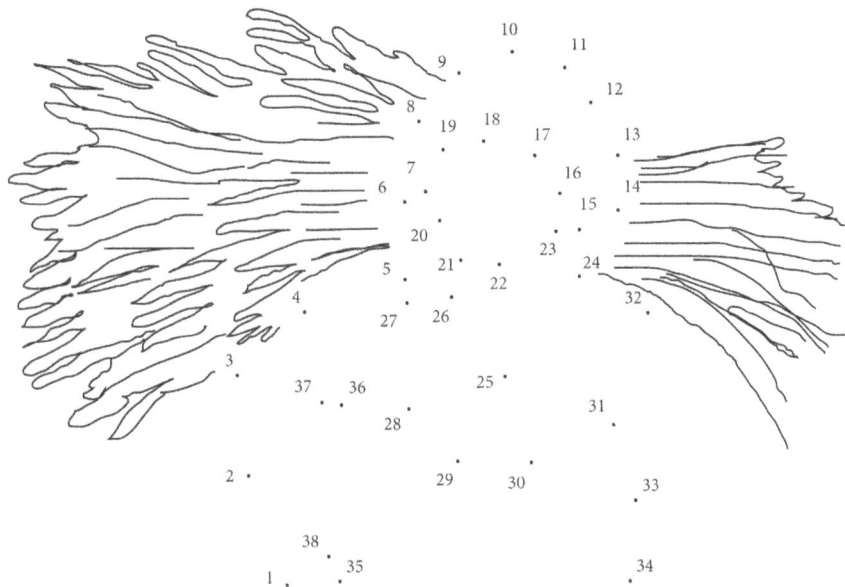

FIGURE 3.1 Agnès Varda dot-to-dot. *Drawing by Hélène Frichot, 2017.*

We attend to the places where spaces are threatened with exhaustion, and we challenge the status quo, the dominant Image of Thought that tells us how to collectively think.

Gleaning is an art of stooping down to pore over what has been forgotten, to pick at the earth, to pluck at the pavement in the dishevelled aftermath of an event. It is an art of survival. It is an art of creative resistance in response to a fast-paced consumptive lifestyle. Too often it is not a choice, but a necessity, Agnès Varda humorously, generously, demonstrates as she enters into dialogue with a cast of marginal characters.

This stooping over is an important embodied gesture to linger with, a stooping over again and again, a non-upright position, which is also a retort to the configuration of the human form as an upright figure, lifted up off the ground and able to face the horizon with his hands dirt-free, ready to manage weapons and tools. By contrast, the *glaneuse* is not afraid to get her hands dirty. Varda's (2000) voice-over tells us: 'It's always the same humble gesture.'

Varda calls her documentary film-making technique *cinécriture*, and she is frequently identified as a feminist film-maker. She points out early on that *glaneurs* or rather the *glaneuse* are historically women, and usually depicted working collectively in clusters. Gleaning was women's labour, and it can be understood as a labour of caring and maintenance, as well as a means of sustenance. Today, Varda laments, gleaners are usually discovered working alone, furtively, quickly exiting and entering a scene.

As part of her documentary film making, which is a creative practice, Varda allows her subjectivity to become collapsed into the scenes of gleaning, into the filmic story, the *cinécriture* she is composing. She explains that her approach to her art is to glean filmic fragments, conversations and visions. Witnessing urban gleaners at work, she describes the image of a forgotten orange scavenged by an ancient hand that passes slowly up the black expanse of an old woman's coat. Film for Varda is not utilized as an illustration, but a way to arouse feelings, what can also be called affects, a capacity to affect and to be affected. This requires paying attention to and respecting the encounters we enter into. Varda includes what might seem to be extraneous scenes in *The Gleaners and I*, where she reflects on her own mortality, observing her greying hair and the backs of her wrinkled aging hands. In interviews she confesses to distracted moments when she has forgotten to turn the camera off, and ends up filming happenstance textures, her trousers and the grey inside of the car. The camera goes for a walk as she concludes an interview, and then she realizes she can glean this apparent filmic refuse too. Waste not, want not.

She recycles things and images in future films. Her heart-shape potatoes reappear in a project she does for Hans Ulrich Obrist at the Venice Biennale in 2003, 'three large screens showing the lives of old sprouting potatoes', which she calls *Patate Utopia*.[1] The buttons from *The Glaneurs and I: 2 Years Later* reappear in a short film about an adolescent girl's coming of age. Cats frequently appear across her early and later films and documentaries as though in acknowledgement of non-human encounters. This is important, because with her cats and potatoes and buttons she also demonstrates her engagement in the life of more than human things. She operates according to a free association of ideas, which is distinct from random association. She describes it like this: 'It's about these transitions from one impression to another ... you glide from one impression to another one.'[2]

What she calls her 'recycling idea' comes from her failed films. She has reels and reels of filmic stock left over from failed projects, or unused footage. *Les Créatures* with Catherine Deneuve and Michel Piccoli is a flop (shot on Noirmoutier Island in 1966), so she thinks to herself, I'll do something with this material, I'll make a house out of the film. Filmic refuse is gleaned and becomes *Ma Cabane de l'Échec* (2006) exhibited at Fondation Cartier.[3] At first she calls it the cabin of failure, but it gives her such pleasure that she calls it the cabin of cinema. She is interested in the on and off screen, the life that surrounds the image that she captures. Her aim is to 'try to find ways in reality that lead to dreams and to other landscapes of the soul'.[4] She follows the material so as to discover movements in the world of the mind that express more than mere platitudes.

@helenejuliaf Tweet, 18 September at 9.08pm: Better to be a glaneuse than a flaneuse any day ... sustainable critique vs consumptive critique.

A *glaneuse* is better than a *flâneuse*, I have claimed, and even though characters such as Cléo from Varda's early film *Cléo from 5 to 7* (1962) have been described as coming into their own by claiming the art of flanerie, becoming flâneuse, it is the glaneuse who sustains the life in things, who does more than merely consume what she discovers in her local environment-worlds. The flâneur or flâneuse only cares for images of himself cast back from the reflective surface of the shop window, whereby he can superimpose his worn-down suit with the latest season's fashions displayed behind the glass. The flâneur never quite makes ends meet and is on the verge of becoming a sandwich man or even a ragpicker, Susan Buck-Morss explains, descending through the aesthetic psychosocial types (1989). Rebecca Solnit points out that the main problem with the flâneur is that he did not exist. Try to name one actual flâneur, she demands of her reader. He is not an individual, but a type. Walter Benjamin speaks of the flâneur taking a turtle for a walk through the Paris arcades as a gesture of slowing down, of requiring the progress that he haptically and visually enjoys to nonetheless reduce its fast pace; yet, as Solnit suggests: 'No one has named an individual who took a tortoise for a walk' (2000: 200). Instead, whenever this wonderfully improbable scene is conjured, the source is invariably given as Benjamin. There is the suggestion that he may well have dreamed up this sequence. The flâneur, as Solnit points out, is both seduced by and resistant to the emerging commercial culture he apprehends as he strolls through his favourite arcades. The glaneuse, on the other hand, is gendered originally in the feminine, and we can find her on the streets, as Agnès Varda has done. The glaneuse is not merely a type, or not only a type, but really does have to make do with minimal means; she can descend no lower.

Lauren Elkin writes of Varda's ecological conscience, and her vision of collectivity, that we are all in it together. As Elkin points out, Varda is happy to include the work of artists under her definition of gleaning, discussing the work of Louis Pons, who assembles trash and collects things, or Bodan Litniaski, a Ukranian brickmason who builds a house from scraps. The urban gleaner, as Elkin explains, is also called a *chiffonier*, a rag picker, which is one of Walter Benjamin's types. Elkin is also the author of *Flâneuse: Women Walk the City*, one of those thinkers who want to suggest that women can be flâneurs too, yet the gleaner is a far more modest, if meagre, and perhaps less well-dressed mode of life. As we all know so well, and as Elkin stresses, the 'threat to the environment posed by waste is incredibly pressing; the need to recycle is a question of ethics' (2017). Yet, will sporadic gestures in *recyclage* and minor shifts in consumptive habits have been enough? Isabelle Stengers thinks not, lamenting that riding bicycles and using the right kind of energy-saving light bulbs will not save us. There is a risk that these gestures will not suffice, even though they express a growing consciousness of our worldly exhaustions and how fast we run through the things we consume daily, barely cognizant of their inbuilt obsolescence.

Things

> All those things, that is to say, those things which occur to me, occur to me not from the root up but rather only from somewhere about their middle. Let someone then attempt to seize them, let someone attempt to seize the blade of grass and hold fast to it when it begins to grow only from the middle.
>
> Franz Kafka, *The Diaries of Franz Kafka* (1992)

All these things being said about things, and objects too, arrive from a diversity of situations and disciplinary points of view. Distinctions between things and objects are ventured or overlooked. A life of things is called upon, or else an orientation towards objects is recommended (Graham Harman). A thing becomes an arche-fossil, existing before as well as after the passing of human creatures, even situated as a cure to human finitude (Quentin Meillassoux). The thing in itself remains inaccessible, and things continue to bother us. An *être-en-soi* (being in-itself) is self-contained, a realized object that simply is, and in its thisness it contrasts with a properly human being's *être-pour-soi* (being for-itself); a human being for-itself that is, in turn, ever in tension with *l'être-pour-autrui* (being for others) (Jean-Paul Sartre). There are things-in-themselves (*noumena*) and things for us (*phenomena*) (Immanuel Kant). More recently, with the theoretical stirrings of new materialism, things turn out to have a power all of their own, a thing-power (Jane Bennett). Things rendered as hyperobjects have been inflated into objects of such massive environmental scale, with murky outlines, that they are located beyond our (human) ken, except for the symptoms and signs we meagrely glean (Timothy Morton). A social life of things is commented upon and questioned, which situates the thing inextricably amidst social relations (Arjun Appadurai).

There are things that can be abstract and concrete that are called boundary objects, which constitute the information embedded in things (artefacts, specimens, field notes, maps) that mark out thresholds between one situation and the next depending on their application. Such things turn out to be both plastic and differentiated, but able to maintain some minimal identity across sites and situations of use and meaning (Susan Starr). Things are slippery and become something rather like quasi-objects, changing guard with quasi-subjects, because subject and object are flung together and intermixed into temporal flows and upheavals and complex relations (Michel Serres). There is something that can be called a thing-feeling of outgoing, generous and jovial things, where things are decidedly not withdrawn (Lars Spuybroek). We momentarily gather around a thing to argue about our matters of concern, whether they are political, scientific or aesthetic (Bruno Latour). Young girls are offered as examples of sweet young things (Martin Heidegger). Live human subjects are, with historical regularity, reduced to bare life and rendered as exceptional things removed from the human rights of citizenry (Giorgio Agamben). Things, it probably goes without saying, have a long conceptual history (Elizabeth Grosz) – a long and illustrious genealogy that divides and endlessly subdivides into so many tributaries of thought, not to mention material instantiations. Given all these variations on the theme of things, it should be no surprise that such a thing as thing theory has emerged (Bill Brown).

Any one thinker or reflective doer who turns to address a thing, or an object, and behaves as though this is a novel practice of *epoché*, of bracketing out the world in order to get at the kernel of things, forgets the exhaustive forays that have already been undertaken before them. This leaves the thinker (and the creative practitioner too) in the awkward situation of wondering what exactly to add to this exhaustive array of contemplations and interactions with things. Things and/or objects (terms used both as synonyms *and* carefully distinguished, depending on who you are reading) appear like so many items that have been set out on a shop shelf, ready to be taken down and purchased, and cherished, and then forgotten, as they eventually collect dust, and discover themselves forsaken on someone's front verge or in a yard sale. The things that are left behind. The effects of the deceased. Things bereft of relations. The things that pile up as landfill upon which skyscrapers, in some parts of the world, then come to be hastily constructed, or else wheat fields sown as an aesthetic gesture of critical feminist defiance (Rawes 2013). The pile that famously rises higher and higher before Walter Benjamin's iconic Angel of History, who, with his back turned and horror-filled, is flung at full speed blindly towards a future while bearing witness to the mounting debris of a past (Benjamin 1992: 249). It will not be possible to be exhaustive, and like others, I will have to rag-pick my way through the trash. It will be a process of 'gleaning'.

Rock, grotto, inscrutable thing

In architectural discourse, the object as a rarefied kind of thing has appeared on the covers of journals, in essays and dialogues between architects and philosophers who would appear to be speaking of different things altogether, in different languages. I offer an example.

What is that thing, seemingly without an identifiable scale adorning the cover of a 2016 special English-language edition of *Arch+ Journal of Architecture and Urbanism*? It could be a meteorite, it could be a stone dug up from the ground or it could be one of Maria Reiche's stones writ large. It even resembles a piece of chewed-up and spat-out gum. But it is not. While it looks like a naturally found object, it is in fact manufactured, reproduced by means of sophisticated digital scanning and three-dimensional (3D) printing techniques. The final thing has been arrived at following iterative model-making tests that pass through many sets of invisible hands as well as through technological instruments and processes. This rock, grotto, inscrutable thing composed the central installation featured in the Swiss Pavilion of the Venice Biennale of Architecture in 2016. This thing is called *Incidental Space*, and it is signed by the 'Swiss-based' architect Christian Kerez.

Anh-Linh Ngo, the editor of the special issue of *Arch+*, where *Incidental Space* and the work of Kerez are copiously treated, describes the grotto-rock as 'alien, exalted, inscrutable' (Ngo 2016: 3). It is worth noting that grotto can be etymologically related to the grotesque, which arouses a mixture of wonder and horror. Ngo fiercely defends Kerez, who has apparently been critiqued for his lack of responsivity to curator-architect Alejandro Aravena's brief, which was directed at social architectures for the occasion of the 2016 Biennale. It would seem that the rock, grotto, inscrutable thing has nothing to say about social matters of concern, though it should not be overlooked that elsewhere in the main Arsenale buildings, Kerez and his students' speculative explorations of iterative favela forms are on display. Here too, through exercises in form-finding inspired by the favela, the theme is the wonder to be experienced in those incidentally produced spaces that emerge incrementally as though by happenstance. Some might call this a 'taste for the slums' (Dovey and King 2012; Gabrielsson 2018: 83).

Mario Carpo, a theorist of digital architectures writes an essay on Kerez's thing, part lump, part grotto (2016: 70–72). Carpo sees something remarkable in the idea that this thing has been digitally scaled up from an undisclosed object that was the size of a shoebox to fill a considerable part of the main exhibition room at the Swiss Pavilion. He expresses an architectural delight in inhabiting a 'model' for real; we can get right into the 'matter of concern' that this 'thing' presents. From a small model built of sugar and dust (Mairs 2016), from a source unknown, which Mario Carpo claims the architect is unwilling to divulge, the origin of the thing is meant to remain obscure. In obscuring its origins, or multiplying the possible stories of its formation, such a thing is all the more likely to arouse wonder, a favoured architectural affect. Still, what exactly is this thing doing inside the Swiss Pavilion?

FIGURE 3.2 ARCH+ Journal for Architecture and Urbanism: Release Architecture, *May 2016. Cover design: Meiré und Meiré. ISBN 978-3-931435-35-6. Cover photo: Top view of the geometry of Incidental Space – rendered 3D scan, 2016. Rendering by Melina Mezari © Christian Kerez.*

Writing in the popular online design magazine *Dezeen*, Jessica Mairs calls *Incidental Space* an inhabitable cloud-like structure, explaining that Kerez wants to raise 'controversial questions' about how architecture is produced and experienced. She quotes Kerez who explains his ambitions as follows: 'What we were looking for here is an openness in terms of meaning; it's not a symbolic space, it is not a referential space, it allows you to initiate a pure encounter with architecture' (Kerez cited by Mairs 2016). It is a pure and autonomous form, standing for itself. Do with it what you will.

Sandra Oehy, the curator of the Swiss Pavilion where Kerez's inscrutable thing stands, describes Kerez's installation as an architectonic project, which is important to stress lest it be mistaken as some kind of *objet d'art*. She explains that:

> This space is an event that takes place at a specific location and justifies itself there. This space is meant to stand only for itself, as a claim or a thesis; not to serve as an illustration of some other space beyond itself, or gesture toward some particular tendency in architecture. It is not a reproduction or portrayal; instead, it is a process and an ephemeral manifestation. This space is an experiment: a fundamental research project investigating how architectural spaces might be conceived and might be built, both in the imagination and in technical terms. (Oehy 2016)

That is to say, Oehy argues for Kerez's thing as a thing very much separated out from a political gathering; it stands there to arouse aesthetic and technical pleasures alone. In a way it refutes the kinds of 'things' that are usually 'carriers of significance' for architects, including drawings, and scale models, but also sites, the work of other architects and precursor architects. Likewise this thing that Kerez has manufactured as a factish of sorts stands there to express its technical and aesthetic wonders. Beyond being astonishing, and even arousing affective wonder, what kind of thing is remarkable? What kind of thing helps us think about and engage in our discipline in a different way?

Why should a thing call for a social gathering in any case? Isn't a thing simply that which we (humans) apprehend, get our hands on, or not, purchase, own and finally discard as trash? Isn't a thing merely that which we 'phenomenologically' enjoy, as privileged, self-same and secure human subjects? Or else, as architects, designers, creative practitioners, isn't a thing that which we mould between our hands, or through the use of simple and advanced technologies? Again, why should a thing have anything to do with a social gathering?

Let me explain by way of a further definition of the 'thing', offered by Bruno Latour.

FIGURE 3.3 *Christian Kerez*, Incidental Space, *Swiss Pavilion, Venice Biennale of Architecture, 2016. Photography by Hélène Frichot.*

In his essay 'Why Has Critique Run Out of Steam? From Matters of Fact to Matters of Concern' (2004), Latour offers what might seem an idiosyncratic definition of the thing by playing on the German word for thing, *das Ding*. Rather than being some thing for which we have no better name than to point at it and say 'that thing there', Latour draws attention to the German philosopher Martin Heidegger's meditation on things, a meditation with which Latour does not entirely agree:

> Martin Heidegger, as every philosopher knows, has meditated many times on the ancient etymology of the word thing. We are now all aware that in all the European languages, including Russian, there is a strong connection between the words for thing and a quasi-judiciary assembly. Icelanders boast of having the oldest Parliament, which they call Althing, and you can still visit in many Scandinavian countries assembly places that are designated by the word Ding or Thing. (2004: 233)[5]

What Latour draws out from Heidegger, the thinker of things, is that the thing is not merely something mute, which we designate as such because we cannot otherwise identify it, or give it a name. Instead, the thing is something that has stirred up attention and given rise to a political gathering. As an aside, it is also interesting to note that Latour's essay has been cited by the architectural theorist Reinhold Martin as a means of arguing against the loss of criticality in architecture that seemed to be threatened with the turn towards projective or post-critical practice in the early 2000s (Martin 2005).

Now, despite Kerez's thing appearing to have no truck with social or political considerations, it is towards this definition of the thing that the editor of the *Arch+* issue, Ngo, goes, creating some mixed messages about how we are to get a hold of Kerez's *Incidental Space*. Ngo, who also deploys Timothy Morton's concept of the hyperobject (more of which below) draws attention to Latour's discussion of things, specifically from Latour's introduction to a large volume of essays and project accounts called *Making Things Public: Atmospheres of Democracy*, which was edited with Peter Weibel as an accompaniment to an exhibition at ZKM Centre for Art and Media Karlsruhe, Germany, in 2005. Again, Latour associates an apprehension of the thing (*das Ding*) with the event of a political gathering, a place around which all those who are concerned (human and non-human) assemble. A thing, importantly, is bound up with something we care about, something that has aroused our concerns, and not just as an individual (or a singular sovereign subject apprehending a circumscribed object), but as a social collective, a gathering of concerned humans and non-humans struggling to find some common sense in our situation.

Latour is interested in the complexity and promise of 'things that cannot be thrown at you like objects' (2004: 237). To get the reader to descend into the everyday melee of things, he opens a newspaper, peruses a collection of articles and announces that from what he has gleaned therein he could 'unfold the number of former objects that have become things again' (Latour 2004: 236). What does he mean by that? In the introduction to *Making Things Public*, he suggests a simple thought experiment. He asks his readers to reflect on any contemporary issue that has struck them recently, whether it is the Islamic veil in France, genetically modified organisms in Brazil, the melting of Greenland's glaciers, the repairs to be made to your apartment or the closure of the factory where your sister works. Today we could add recent news that over the past twenty-five years insect populations monitored in the German context have diminished by 75 per cent (Carrington 2017), or that Australia's Great Barrier Reef, possibly the largest complex organism on the planet, is suffering from coral bleaching and is nearly exhausted (Haraway 2016). That is to say, Latour asks us to reflect on things closer and further away from home. Following such reflection, he argues, we are likely to find that the objects of our concern, our 'issues', are each composed of 'a different pattern of emotions and disruptions, agreements and disagreements' (2005a: 14–15). While these objects of concern may be various and differentiated and we may passionately disagree about them, nevertheless each object gathers around itself a different assembly of relevant parties that effectively binds us to a public space that differs from that which is usually called political. What emerges, Latour argues, is a hidden geography, and it is this that he invites his readers to survey and map, for it lays out a 'whole new ecology loaded with things' (2005a: 17). This is what Latour calls a *dingpolitik* (2005a: 22), a politics of things (*Dinge*) that are of concern to us, pointing out that an archaic definition of *das Ding* designates an assembly.

The *thing* becomes interesting when a gathering forms in its vicinity, something arouses the attention of those gathered, there is some controversy at hand or there is some shared work to be done. The 'thing' for Maria Reiche is her *seemingly* barren landscape of stones, which from another point of view reveals complex patterns and shapes that she spends the better part of her life surveying. The 'thing' for Agnès Varda composes an assemblage that brings gleaners together with assorted situated debris. The question of how this secret geography can then be presented becomes the next challenge.

Around this wondrous, craggy, grotto 'thing', no social gathering takes place, except for that highly specialized gathering of architects, students and exhibition attendees, concerned with the aesthetics of digitally manufactured (anti)forms. All the while, behind the scenes of enjoyment and pleasure around this grotesque, rock-like thing, remaining for the most part unseen, it is worth reflecting on that gathering of students whose unpaid labour enabled the production of iterative tests towards the final prototype for *Incidental Space*. In exchange for their labours one can only hope they achieved pertinent pedagogical discoveries.

While there is a very specific technological material problem at work in Kerez's thing, we might want to question whether it really matters. Or whether it is rather an exceptional expression of rarefied hubris that arouses architectural affects without really challenging the architectural status quo.

Before leaving this curious thing behind, it is relevant to note that in the same edition of *Arch+*, there is an edited excerpt from Timothy Morton's book *Hyperobjects* (2013). By association, and even though we have been warned against interpretation, *Incidental Space* stands in as a hyperobject. Certainly, this is one of the conceptual associations Kerez appears to want to make as a means of thinking the project that is *Incidental Space*.

Hyperobjects

The work that the hyperobject concept has to undertake is immense and unruly. For instance, it must displace more familiar, even if threadbare terms such as 'world', 'nature', 'environment' and even 'ecology'. The urgency that drives Timothy Morton who coins this concept is an ecological question, which means it is a socio-political question too, and the capitalist tendency to stockpile objects is included in his argument (2013: 113). The hyperobject is situated as a novel ecological concept that denotes the vague outlines of biosphere, climate, evolution and capitalism. That is to say, it is indiscriminate when it comes to natural and cultural phenomena, and as such can be aligned with the project of challenging the Great Divide between nature and culture. To respond to current social, political and climatic ills, Morton's answer is to promptly 'drop the concepts *Nature* and *world*, to cease identifying with them' (2016b: 97). He remarks in one of his earlier books that 'the very idea of "nature" which so many hold dear will have to wither away in an "ecological" state of human society' (2007: 1). Why? Because these old concepts are leading us to out-and-out catastrophe, towards a completely nihilistic 'Noah's Arc' type of venture, which is to say, our nostalgia for such concepts as world and environment is leading us away from an ability to look beyond an anthropocentric worldview. Nature has infected our imagination, and we need other ways to redirect our thinking about things. Nature, world and environment, we are to understand, are all concepts constructed with a specifically human subject, or a specifically privileged *Anthropos* in mind. It could be true that these over-familiar, nearly exhausted concepts are not helping us think and practice amidst the concatenating local and global emergencies we suffer, or witness at a distance on the news and across our social media pages. Yet cautions must be issued, because it cannot be as simple as replacing one concept with another, unless such a displacement can make a difference that succeeds in reorienting our practices.

The question that needs to be addressed to the concept of hyperobject is whether it is a concept that helps us think what we once called the world in useful ways, specifically in terms of the crises that cluster, mesh and combine amidst the Anthropocene. In conversation with the architect Christian Kerez, Armen Avanessian explains that Morton's hyperobjects, which are directed at naming large-scale phenomena of naturescultures in disarray, 'are objects which no longer have the consistency of objects' (Avanessian and Kerez 2016: 78). They are, furthermore, a means of thinking the world beyond the human, an inhuman world, a more-than-human world. Why would we need to do this? Our new-found intimacy with non-humans, denominated by feminist thinkers as the more-than-human, is a new awareness that 'ends the idea that we are living in an environment', asserts Morton (2016b: 99). There is simply no such 'container' to be observed out there, he continues. Instead, 'When we look for the environment, what we find are discrete life forms, non-life, and their relationships' (2013: 128–129).

Just when it would appear that a concept like the hyperobject enables a better grasp of things that are otherwise beyond our human ken, Morton explains that: 'An object is profoundly "withdrawn" – we can never see the whole of it, and nothing else can either' (Morton 2011: 165). For Morton: 'Objects are unique. Objects can't be reduced to smaller objects or dissolved upwards into larger ones. Objects are withdrawn from one another and from themselves' (2013: 116). Everything, it would appear, even subjects, are some kind of 'object', isolated, unique, irreducible and withdrawn. We cannot gain a purchase on any other world, not even our own, according to Morton.

The ecological era we have entered is the time of hyperobjects; this is Morton's way of thinking the Anthropocene and the after-effects of the Great Acceleration, which follows in the wake of the Industrial Revolution and then the nuclear age. He credits Graham Harman with the 'discovery' that things do not depend on human perception for their reality. Object Oriented Ontology (OOO), which I will introduce in the following, allows us to 'think deep down things', Morton explains (2011: 185). Deep down, entities exist in a flat ontology where there is 'hardly any difference between a person and a pin cushion' (Morton 2013: 14). Furthermore, relations between things are merely vicarious and as such aesthetic, that is to say, merely a matter of one's sensibility, a sensitivity that supports an ability to sense and describe the remarkable phenomena of a world, or rather, the confounding, concatenating phenomena of hyperobjects. Hyperobjects, though allowing some kind of limited sensory and thus aesthetic access, are really 'real entities whose primordial reality is withdrawn from humans' (2013: 15), except that the human sensory apparatus picks up some signals, here and there. The problem is that these meagre messages do not get us to the real thing, and may even lead us astray. This, for instance, is what happens with climate change deniers; they cannot gain access to the real thing, so they claim there is no such thing as climate change.

While there are no relations, and notions of flow, process and becoming are taken to be misleading; there is, nevertheless, a strange interconnectedness of things, Morton explains. Something must allow things – or rather 'objects', which, again, is Morton's preferred handle – to hang together. An explanatory model is needed. Morton's solution is to propose that things cohere on account of the 'mesh', which floats on top and in front of them (Morton 2013: 28). This mesh appears to have uterine qualities, as Morton describes a 'sticky mesh of viscosity' and the 'interuterine' solidarity between things that makes us all slimy (Morton 2013: 30). *The Matrix* (1999) is the filmic reference he delivers to help the reader feel this stickiness, with the important distinction that there is no transcendence, no way out of the sticky mesh. For Graham Harman, whose philosophy Morton closely aligns his own project with, it is not mesh but a curious stuff, also with qualities of viscosity, called 'plasma' that allows things, or rather objects, to hang together, while remaining withdrawn and inaccessible. When Morton subsequently wrote his *Dark Ecology*, which followed *Hyperobjects* (2013) and *Ecology without Nature* (2007), these inaccessible, withdrawn objects became weird objects, a little bit disgusting (2016a: 124) and decidedly loopy. In *Dark Ecology*, he warns, ecology is that which makes things weird and loopy, as well as sticky.

What I do hear Morton stridently arguing is that somehow our old concepts have got us into this mess, and this is something worth reflecting upon. Morton's cry is clear, and needs to be heard. It is a primary motivation behind his desire to coin a new concept, in order to find a way out, a line of escape. Even if the hyperobject risks being the bad answer to an ill-formed question, and the weird object something that architects risk taking as a prescription for the design of new projects, as I will explain further here.

Object-oriented things

Between 2009 and early 2011, at a women-only show called *Elles* at the Centre Pompidou in Paris, a small section of the exhibition was dedicated to female architects. In a glass vitrine clustered amidst the other exhibits, a model of ambiguous scale represented a sample of computationally generated architectures from file to fabrication. It was composed of delicate, allusively biological curlicues set against a luminescent tangerine-coloured ground. When apprehended at this scale, enclosed in a vitrine, the model is maintained as something of a *nature mort*, a still life or life stilled. It is impossible to know how large it should be, or whether it should simply be apprehended as an aesthetic wonder in its own right, referring to nothing outside itself, much like Kerez's thing. It is itself and nothing else, beyond a registration of the potentiality of the 'chain' from file to fabrication, albeit a fabrication restricted to the role of the architectural model. A computational wonder.

The project in question is Alisa Andrasek's *Probiotics' Agentware*, and the name of her studio is fortuitous given the title of this second part of the book: It is called Biothing.

The conjunction 'Bio-thing' is that thing which acknowledges the strange biological liveliness of things, challenging the presumed threshold between the living and the non-living. If a thing is supposed to be inanimate, mere stuff, then a 'biothing' radically contravenes this limit, and we had best acknowledge its 'thing-power' (Bennett 2010). In addition, there is the emergence of what Andrasek calls 'computational ecologies' populated by multi-agent systems creating complex webs of relationality, and a computational capacity 'to descend into the cellular grain of matter, flow of light, heat, vapor, and friction' (2012: 52). Architects, she asserts, can now 'go beyond geometry to directly design the structure of matter itself' (2012: 53). All of this is achieved

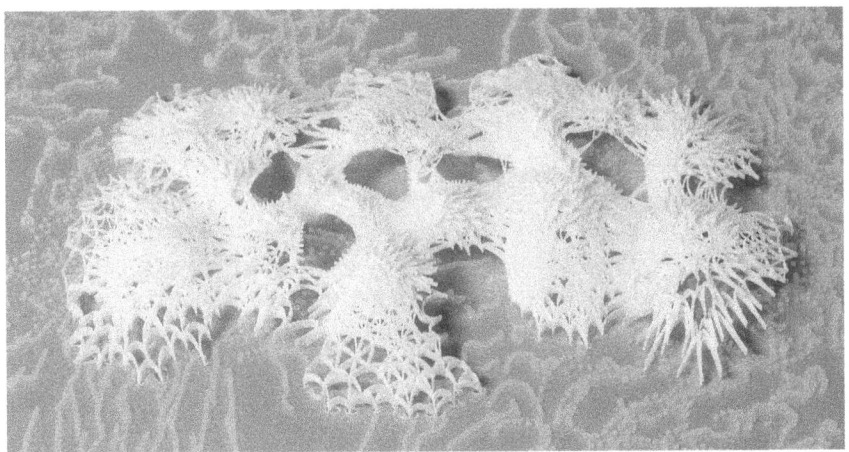

FIGURE 3.4 *Alisa Andrasek*, PROBOTICS AGENTWARE RESEARCH *2008–9, directed by Alisa Andrasek DRL/Architectural Association London 2008–9. Students: Knut Brunier, Diego Rossel, Jose Sanchez and Anica Taneja. Part of the permanent collection at the Centre Pompidou Paris.*

by 'algorithmic, process centred, data rich and iterative' means, enabled by technological advances that are 'eroding the difference between the artificial and the natural, tempting designers to embrace a mode of operation which is suggestively similar to that of biology and of the natural world' (Andrasek and Andreen 2016: 106). Andrasek contributes to a post-digital revisitation of natural form, now expressed less in terms of aesthetic mimicry than at the micro-dynamic level of algorithmic codes appropriated from biology. These are codes that map the unfolding of life processes, which can in turn be transferred into architectural form-finding experiments.

The experiments of Biothing are fascinating, compelling, evanescent in their aesthetics and allusively lively, and they seem to swarm before your eyes like germs in a petri dish. This swarming, seething, shimmering is supported by Andrasek's compelling computer animations, many of which are available for view on her website. Biothing begins with experimental algorithmic poetry, as witnessed in Andrasek's early essay for Neil Leach, David Turnbull and Chris Williams's edited book *Digital Tectonics* (2004), and eventually institutes itself according to scientific research expectations as Andresek co-publishes research in peer-reviewed journals like *Intelligent Buildings International* (Andrasek and Andreen 2016).

What interests me in particular when it comes to a consideration of things is a small note, an aside that Andrasek makes in an essay in *Log Magazine* (2012), a non-peer-reviewed journal, where she discusses the benefits of

Object Oriented Programming (OOP). This is a computational process that allows for the distributed independence of discrete units of data, cellular automata and multi-agent systems, towards the simulation of discrete models as an alternative to procedural programming (Andrasek 2012; see also Andrasek and Andreen 2016). It is worth noting in passing that when Bruno Latour describes what he calls his Object Oriented Democracy in relation to his neologism *dingpolitik*, he too draws on the new phenomenon of 'object-oriented' software (2005a: 14), which he pointedly deploys as a conceptual metaphor. As I will show, such metaphoric transfers can place a thinker-practitioner at risk of saying something she perhaps does not intend.

In the margins, hidden away in Note 6 of the *Log Magazine* article in question, Andrasek suggests a comparison between OOP (Object Oriented Programming) and Graham Harman's OOP (Object Oriented Philosophy), explaining that: 'Object-oriented philosophy, as proposed by Graham Harman, considers the life of things as grounds for a new metaphysics. See Graham Harman, *Tool-Being: Heidegger and the Metaphysics of Things* (Chicago: Open Court, 2002)' (2012: 49).

But what is this Object Oriented Philosophy, or rather, Object Oriented Ontology, as the name of this paradigm has shifted? Like something of a theoretical virus it has spread across annals of architectural discourse. We find it discussed or cited in *Log Magazine* issues 25 and 33 (Andrasek 2012; Gage 2015; Gannon et al. 2015); in the German architectural journal *Arch+*, where its influence informs an explanatory framework for a curious artefact; and in a recent essay in the new Italian journal *Ardeth* (Harman 2017). Graham Harman has taken on the position of Professor of Philosophy within the world-renowned Los Angeles private school of architecture Sci-Arc, and earlier this year took part in a public event at that school presenting his work in moderated dialogue with no less than Slavoj Žižek (Harman and Žižek 2017). These cross-disciplinary infiltrations need to be taken seriously, and their symptoms assessed.

OOPs!

When we turn to a reading of Graham Harman what we find is a so-called realist philosophy of the autonomy of all things, where objects (not actors or agents) are withdrawn and inaccessible. Objects, for Harman, cannot be explained by overarching systems (what he calls overmining), nor can they be reduced to smaller and smaller parts or atoms or processes (what he calls undermining); instead, they stand in a middle ground, thereby seemingly corresponding to a human scale, and yet his philosophy supposedly refuses to privilege the human subject. It is crucial that the human is not privileged, as Harman subscribes to a flat ontology allowing the predominance of no thing in particular. Despite being withdrawn, and inaccessible to us, except perhaps for their sensual effects, Harman nevertheless structures his objects. He asserts that objects are split into two: (1) They are real, but this reality remains inaccessible to us (human creatures), and (2) they are sensual, which is to say objects are allusively and phenomenologically arousing, alluring us by the power of their sensory effects. Objects are further divided into a schema that Harman calls the quadruple object, whereby a real object has real qualities and a sensual object has sensual qualities, which Harman describes in terms of objects like dogs and melons, and by calling on the categories of space and time, and such thinkers as Plato, Aristotle, Husserl and Heidegger (Harman 2011: 95–109). Most crucially, and repeated frequently, Harman's objects are non-relational and anti-materialist, and this is exactly what is said to secure their reality. He is a philosopher who will not get his hands dirty, nor bend his head to the ground to go gleaning for things as a matter of survival. Finally, and most unsettling in this account is that objects are anti-political. The object procures no gathering, it does not hold together an assemblage in relation to a shared matter of concern or care. Harman states that one of his aims is to overthrow epistemology in favour of aesthetics. He has publicly called himself a phenomenologist, which raises the spectre of the apolitical stance of architectural phenomenology. In all, when conjoined with architectural practice thinking, Harman's thesis risks becoming a deeply conservative architectural phenomenological project, influencing a third wave of architectural phenomenology where master narratives and master-pieces are reimposed as architectural goods, as I will argue further.

Why would an architectural practitioner like Andrasek feel compelled to dedicate a footnote to Harman's OOP when discussing the use of Object Oriented Programming in her design work? OOPs! I would venture that the chance sharing of an acronym, OOP, has led the architect astray in response to the rising volume of the discursive chatter surrounding Harman's name and strategically branded philosophical paradigm in architectural publications and at schools of architecture. Harman's name is currently topical, close to the top of the charts in architectural discourse, as have been, each in their time, the names of philosophers such as Foucault, Derrida and Deleuze, each one taken up and then dispensed with as their conceptual wares are exhausted by architectural practitioners eager to source novel concepts, though to place Harman in this company is misleading.

The explanatory logic and metaphysics of OOP or OOO bear no resemblance to the argument that Andrasek makes about the benefits of Object Oriented Programming, with its distinctly manageable if complex dynamic. Her computational agents are certainly not withdrawn and inaccessible objects;

instead they emerge as dynamic trajectories operating in layered fields of data-driven relations, which can and do divide into smaller and smaller parts, at the same time as being organized by an overarching 'universal' system that further purports to be political, or at least social in its potential engagement with a public. Because...

Like a lively virus, dead and alive at the same time, the experiments of Biothing eventually escape from the computational petri dish, leap out of the vitrine, and arrive in the public sphere with the 2012 project *Bloom*, first rolled out for the 2012 Olympic Games in London. Here is an experiment in universal applicability achieved through mass variation, or a method of responding to specific situations by deploying what Andrasek argues is a universal code. Her experiment manifests in a toxic hot pink unit that can be interlocked in various permutations, and which is designed with the scale of the human participant in mind. The architectures of Biothing, as documented in architectural publications, joyously enter into a relation with children, students and researchers, expressing a desire to form human and non-human connections and curious artificial natures. Though it is difficult to discern whether these blooming things create potential democracies, or only cute distractions. It is hard to say from the published images what kinds of relations are formed, and what kinds of relations are sufficiently durable to make a significant difference amidst local environment-worlds.

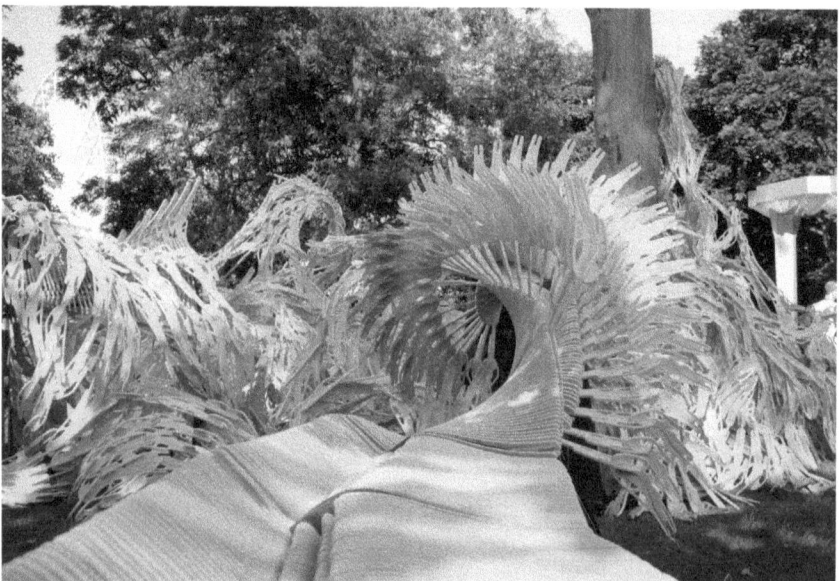

FIGURE 3.5 *Alisa Andrasek and Jose Sanchez,* BLOOM, *Bloom Games, London Olympics 2012.*

OOOh, no!

With great hesitation lest I draw more attention to a paradigm I deem deeply problematic, I admit that more needs to be said about the plague of OOO, or Object Oriented Philosophy, as it was first formulated in Graham Harman's PhD thesis subsequently published as *Tool-Being: Heidegger and the Metaphysics of Objects* (2002). It is important to reflect on the implication of what happens when an architect cites a philosopher, and likewise, when a philosopher makes reference to an architect and architectural projects to forward an argument. I want to insist that there should be no prohibition with respect to citational practices, because open conversations across disciplines and practices are crucial: We need to vent our passionate agreements and disagreements when it comes to our matters of concern and care. No one wants to live inside a disciplinary silo; there is way too much to be learnt from each other. At the same time, citational practices are always political, suggesting implicit or explicit games of power, as feminist theorists and researchers know so well. That is to say, referencing is an ethical act (Rendell 2017: 24), and citation is the means by which one announces one's stance, one's location and one's affiliations. What must be treated with wariness are those weak links in an argument where a source is cited as a gambit to achieve legitimacy, when a reference becomes a prop or a signifier that one is ahead of the discursive game. References are like currency. Who are your references? In architecture today it is crucial to ask: What are the implications of being a woman (researcher, architect, practitioner), for instance, without references? That is to say, a woman or minority researcher whose work could be referenced, but remains overlooked. One of the startling things about the emergence of speculative realism, a theoretical cluster to which Harman has contributed, is the lack of women and minority representatives and the dominance of specifically male-gendered voices. I will touch on this concern as I proceed.

The 'discoverer of objects' Graham Harman comes along and tells us (architects, designers, creative practitioners, cultural theorists, whoever happens to be listening in) that we have been undermining and overmining objects, and even middle-mining them, and thus getting farther and farther away from what is at stake when it comes to objects. To forward his philosophy of objects, Harman makes reference to many philosophers, but primary among them is Martin Heidegger, and in particular what is known as Heidegger's tool analysis. This analysis is where Heidegger distinguishes Dasein's relation with tools as shifting between being ready-to-hand (*zuhanden*; *Zuhandenheit*) through habitual use and present-at-hand at the moment the tool intrudes into the tool-user's reflective considerations (*vorhanden*; *Vorhandenheit*)

(Heidegger 1993a, 1993b, 2001). Usually this intrusion takes place when a tool, object or thing breaks down, or breaks apart. Dasein is a specialist concept, signed by Heidegger to designate the 'being-there' or 'there-being' (*da sein, dasein*) in the world of the human creature, of how each human creature discovers himself or herself as thrown into a situation that precedes them and persists after them. We could call this situation the local environment-world where the human creature finds, invents, designs, improves and manages her tools, material and conceptual.

Harman challenges what he argues is the habitual interpretation of Heidegger's tool analysis, which is often used to distinguish practice from theory, a distinction that Harman describes as a merely 'anthropological' shift 'from practical know-how to hyper-alert knowledge' (2002: 167). Where the 'ready-to-hand' tool paradoxically withdraws from us exactly while it is being put to use, receding from our consciousness as we become accustomed or habituated to handling it, the same tool transforms into something that is present-at-hand when attention is abruptly drawn to it, for instance, and most explicitly when it breaks or falls apart. This is what Harman describes as the difference between the tool and the broken tool. That is, a shift of awareness, sometimes dramatic, from the know-how of the ready-to-hand tool that is taken up and used to the sudden apprehension of the tool as an extraordinary thing and the theoretical reflections thereby aroused in this encounter. Harman complains about Heidegger's analysis, suggesting that it is 'mistaken to say that in the passage from hammer to failed hammer, the previously concealed hammer-being becomes visible in the second case, or even "more" visible than before' (2002: 219). As Harman further explains, Heidegger dismisses certain objects as being too technological, and later in his writings preserves instead the hermeneutically circular 'thingness of things', only to privilege human ontologies too emphatically. In contradistinction Harman argues that 'the true chasm in ontology lies not between humans and the world, but between objects and relations' (2002: 2). Harman's OOO aims to remove both humans and relations from the equation, in order to place primary and singular importance on objects without relations.

Harman's stated aim is to relocate the drama in the heart of objects to the objects themselves, which he lays out across a flat ontological field. No object, as such, should be privileged over any other, and certainly not the object that is the human subject. The distinction between practical knowledge and theoretical knowledge, so useful to architects and creative practitioners, is one that Harman dismantles in order to lay out his serene world of objects. It should be added that, as with Morton, a world is also an object for Harman (2002: 159) – not aphasic, not even solipsistic objects, but objects in solitary confinement, not even present to themselves. What this overlooks is the usefulness for creative practitioners of the modes of learning enabled when they manage their tools and instruments and designed things, now intimately close to the process of their creation, now stepping back in order to analyse their designs at a relative distance, only to move forward again to take up the creative process further. The practice–theory relay between tool and so-called broken tool is one that creative practitioners should be wary of dismissing too quickly. This is not to privilege the human actor as designer amidst a creative problem, because as well as respecting a theory–practice relay, a creative practitioner must question their own authorial stance and not assume that it is stable or immune from the influence of other thinkers, practitioners and their encounters with things.

Another of Harman's key targets is a thinker who contributed to the formation of Harman's reputation, Bruno Latour. Harman's discussion of Heidegger's tool analysis can also be discovered in an essay included in Latour and Weibel's edited collection *Making Things Public: Atmospheres of Democracy* (Harman 2005a: 268), where Latour as an editor can be seen to be supporting Harman's project, or rather making space available for Harman to set out his distinct matters of concern. Latour likewise dedicates his essay *Why Has Critique Run out of Steam?* to Graham Harman (2004: 225), which I take as a sign of great generosity on the part of Latour, who recognizes how important it is to create assembly spaces for vehement disagreements, as well as agreements between thinkers.

First, to distinguish Harman's project from Latour's, the conceptual terminology is what needs to be renovated. Harman goes right ahead and dispenses with Latour's use of the concepts of 'actor' and 'actant', and in their place inserts the object – not the thing, but the object. What does this fix on the object allow him? Latour's actor and actant are dependent on the relations and specific environmental situations from which they emerge and back into which they plunge, and this is what Harman takes issue with. For Harman, objects should be characterized neither in terms of relations nor processes of becoming and fading away. This exhaustion of the object via its relations is an instance of what Harman calls undermining, where objects are assumed to be too shallow. When we undermine objects, we reduce them, for instance, into smaller and smaller parts caught up in fluxes and flows of matter. Objects are then overmined in being explained away through overarching systems such as social and cultural constructivism, or else in terms of a privileging of relations. Harman's key enemies, as such, are materialism and constructivism. He further stipulates that objects should not in any way be associated with political concerns, an argument that is crucial, as we have seen, to Latour's account of a *Dingpolitik* (Harman 2002: 158–159; Latour 2005: 22). Politics and ontology must be separated out, and eventually Harman will suggest that epistemology should be placed to the side in order to privilege aesthetics. Objects come first. One effect of the disagreement between Harman and

Latour's approach to things is that the former will only allow for those particles that he calls objects, while the latter is rather more concerned with what Karen Barad would call the intra-actions (2008) between particles and waves, between actors and their relations. Intra-action is what Barad describes as the mutual constitution of entangled agencies producing different practices with different inclusions and exclusions. As a practitioner and thinker one must be responsible both for the inclusions and the exclusions one enacts, a seemingly daunting task in response to one's local environment-world. Diffraction, another related term from Barad that acknowledges patterns of difference, avoids fixing on the object and/or the subject in advance (2008). Harman offers a direct retort to Barad in his recent book *Immaterialism*, where he restores Barad's conceptually inventive 'intra-actions' between objects and thought to interactions so as to secure again his world of discrete inaccessible objects (2016: 16).

Why not return to the thing and its game of hide-and-seek, appearing now as it becomes present-to-hand, disappearing again when it is ready-to-hand? Why not resist fixing its intra-actions in advance? Harman wants to overcome a Heideggerian philosophy of things, the elusive thingness of things, which he deems to be too romantic, characterized as it is by bucolic scenes populated with peasant shoes and milk jugs, but not allowing any space for technological objects, which must be urgently considered, especially from the point of view of the present. In agreement with Harman, Latour likewise suggests that Heidegger's privileged things do not allow for a discussion of technological artefacts, both where they function and fall apart. Rather than 'object' what the term *thing* enables is a recognition of the relations of difference with which objects with seemingly recognizable outlines are co-constituted, and how objects are apt to fall apart once exhausted, or else be composed of multifarious relations during the process of their formation. Furthermore, there are many things that can only be called things, as they quite simply lack clear and distinct attributes. It is, I argue, a more restricted and rarefied category of things that can be identified as objects, which Latour draws attention to when he makes his own distinction between objects and things (2005a).

Specifically, and pointedly, Harman wants to remove all relations from a consideration of objects; only he gets stuck, because, what holds one object to another? At work here is a refusal of any productive play of differences. How can objects all be irremediably withdrawn, not even allowing relations between each other, not even allowing a relation with themselves? Following Harman's account with its Platonic shades, the only thing we are left with are the effects produced, as of shadows of things cast on an interior wall or screen, things given to us sensuously, and that is all. Socrates' analogy of the cave, recorded by his student Plato, is fitting here, as it would seem that Harman is remaking himself as a twenty-first-century Platonist. That is to say, everything that there is is divided according to two conditions, the intelligible and the sensible, which, as I have explained, Harman further divides so as to situate his quadruple object. While the intelligible is taken to be the eternal and the immutable, up there in some imagined heaven, transcendent and inaccessible to us, the visible, on the other hand, is that which is merely sensuous, mutable, changeable, constituting all that is apt to decay, to exhaust itself, all of that which supposedly expresses itself as poorer copies, or copies of copies (simulacra) of the heavenly ideas, the *eidos*, eternal immutable forms, which we can never gain access to, unless perhaps we are a philosopher king, the only privileged figure Plato allows to depart from the cave in order to apprehend the reality of things.

Steven Shaviro, who at first remarks charitably on the power of Harman's body of work to date, notably offers a firm critique of Harman's eradication of relationality. He uses the difficult work of A. N. Whitehead, the 'process philosopher' whom Stengers reads closely (2011c), and Haraway cites, and who is notably a companion philosopher for Deleuze's thought practices, in order to mount his critique of Harman. Before I rehearse this critique, I want to comment first on the generous tentativeness with which critics have raised concerns about Harman's project. Stengers, for instance, even though she is frequently invited to the speculative realist party by being included in their edited collections (2011b), obliquely suggests that Harman and his associates deserve the problems they have constructed for themselves. Rather than refusing their practices, following her ethics of respect for other practices she simply states that she shares no affinity with their thought (2014: 192). Similarly, when Celia Åsberg, Kathrin Thiele and Iris van der Tuin (2015) call attention to the feminist archive in its relation to what they call ontologies of immanence, an umbrella under which they collect speculative realism, OOO and (feminist) new materialism, they argue that we should resist calling out the bad guys and the good feminist gals, wanting instead to underline relationality and affinity: a generous intellectual offering.

Let us get back to Shaviro's concerns with Harman. Shaviro outlines Whitehead's and Harman's distinct approaches to relationality, and explains that this 'stand-off' that he is presenting is admissible because both thinkers aim to shift a point of view on things so as to challenge the privilege of human perception and understanding, and both thinkers want to frame a 'speculative philosophy', or what Harman with others have come to call 'speculative realism' (Bryant, Srnicek and Harman 2011), which, it should be stressed, is by no means a shared, but rather a loosely related project. Coined by Harman, OOP's early association was with speculative realism, also associated with the French thinker Quentin Meillassoux, a student of Alain Badiou, who mounts his own critique against what he describes as the conceptual habit of 'correlationism'. Correlationism determines that there are no events, objects and beings that are not already correlated to a point of view, or subjective access (Meillassoux 2008), a situation Meillassoux and other speculative realists strongly critique. Likewise, Harman's aim is to extract us from the trap of assuming that the world can only be accessed via a subjective understanding assumed to be specifically human, which thereby removes us from any speculative consideration of the real.

Shaviro quotes the opening of Whitehead's *Process and Reality* to explain what a speculative philosophy might do: 'the endeavour to frame a coherent, logical, necessary system of general ideas in terms of which every element of our experience can be interpreted' (Whitehead 1985: 3; Whitehead cited by Shaviro 2011: 279). As Shaviro explains, where Whitehead is promiscuous, allowing for a diversity of relations among all entities, which he explains by way of his concept of prehension, Harman's account deprivileges all such relations. Instead, all entities are taken to be ontologically equal, not in terms of their relations but because they are all equally withdrawn from each other. As Shaviro points out, Harman posits a 'strange world of autonomous subterranean objects', what Harman himself describes as a 'universe packed full of elusive substances stuffed into mutually exclusive vacuums' (Harman 2005b: 75–76; Shaviro 2011: 282). It is upon such inaccessible substances in vacuums that we are then asked to speculate.

When Graham Harman launches his conceptual brand, OOO, the response of architects, artists and those who deal with all manner of material and malleable stuff is likely to be one of recognition: Oh yes! We deal in objects too – we intimately know and handle objects, as they constitute our crafted artefacts, which we are occupied with designing, imagining, constructing and liberating into a world. The object seems a welcome relief from process, flow and vectors of dematerialization, all of which can be associated with the rise of computation in architecture, as well as the conceptual signature Deleuze. To grab hold of the object means to thwart relationism, because, as Harman remarks, 'relationism has spread like a virus and become horribly stale without anyone realising it' (Gannon et al. 2015: 75). Mark Gage further explains that architects can be terribly anxious about how their projects stand out, protrude and avoid sinking back into the 'shallow background of the everyday', which is something that a stress on relationality risks doing to the architectural object (Gage 2015: 106). Architectural commentators are anxious not to overmine the architectural object by embedding it into the logic and relations of urban ecologies (Gage 2015: 100), and anxious not to undermine the architectural object by breaking it down into smaller and smaller parts.

Unfortunately, and as is often the case, a paradigm such as OOO ends up being taken as prescriptive, for architects are keen to apply their appropriated concepts, for better or worse. A dialogue that takes place between Harman and three architects, Todd Gannon, David Ruy and Tom Wiscombe in *Log Magazine*, is of particular interest here (Gannon, Ruy and Wiscombe 2015). Gannon commences by saying that everyone is tired of process and flow. Everyone has a dog-eared copy of Deleuze and Guattari's *A Thousand Plateaus* (1987) on their studio desks, he explains, but if we are caught up in process and flow – as is presumably recommended in this popular handbook – how can we grasp hold of the architectural object and assess it in its own right? He complains that if 'architecture is robbed of its objects, it is also robbed of all the wonder, mystery, surprise, and power' (74). Power, Harman adds, is 'overrated as an intellectual theme' (75). It is a comment that any architect concerned even minimally with social, cultural, historical and political contexts, not to mention the enduring issues suffered by repressed minorities in the discipline and practice of architecture, should respond to with grave concern. Tom Wiscombe pointedly uses the term 'exhausted' to speak of previous paradigms where architecture has been deconstructed or else set loose amidst material flows and processes. To recover from the vertiginous sensation of flux and indiscernibility, what OOO promises to architects, Wiscombe suggests, is 'a new formal lexicon' composed of 'Chunks, joints, gaps, parts, interstices, contour, near-figure, misalignment, patchiness, low-res, nesting, embedding, interiority, and above all, mystery, [all] terms that resonate for me' (76). David Ruy goes so far as to ask: 'Is it possible to design a withdrawn object?' adding that following the linguistic turn (Derrida) and the virtual turn (Deleuze), we now, thankfully, have the 'object turn' (85, 94). Todd Gannon talks of weariness in the face of too many years engaging in 'serious sensual immersion' (90). In dialogue, the architects all come perilously close to arguing for how a philosophy like OOO offers a new architectural program, though Wiscombe is the most cautious of the three architects and suggests that we should not literally apply this new program, a mistake that has been previously made, to which Harman also cautiously agrees, suggesting that, 'Philosophy absolutely must not try to be an instruction manual for architecture or for anything else' (86). Nevertheless, the shape and form of an Object Oriented Ontology take on distinctly architectural qualities as the dialogue proceeds. It is an architecture that is 'weird' and composed of chunks and patchiness, and it is coloured black and chrome, so as to achieve a kind of withdrawn aesthetics. Exemplary projects can be discussed and illustrated, at least according to the architectural interlocutors. In all, though, the autonomous withdrawn architectural object is witnessed begging fast retreat from social and political concerns, and the central mood meanwhile is one of exhaustion.

Whitehead remarks in *Process and Reality* that, 'while a philosophical system retains any charm of novelty, it enjoys a plenary indulgence for its failures in coherence. But after a system has acquired orthodoxy, and is taught with authority, it receives sharper criticism. Its denials and its incoherences are found intolerable, and a reaction sets in' (1985: 6). The dialogue between architecture and philosophy is operating differently in the reception of OOO. It is less about one system (let us say the Deleuzian one) becoming an orthodoxy and another (let us say OOO) coming to replace it. Rather, it is about the ease with which a non-systematized concept is applied to an aesthetic object in formation to the point of tedium, until a kind of boredom sets in and a renewed search for novel concepts is attempted. Less than being taught with authority, such concepts are more often lifted out of context and directly applied. While it would be easy to complain about how architects misappropriate philosophical concepts, this would be to overlook the happy accidents that do sometimes result from such appropriations. The problem is rather the kinds of claims that come to be made so as to legitimize a form-finding experiment, and the excuses made so that an architect might wash their hands of the implications of installing a design project on the ground in relation to its specific environment-world. A further, no doubt irritable, complaint is, yet again, the lack of representation of women and minorities in these ventures. Speculative Realism emerged as a distinctly male-oriented game from the get go when a group of men convened at Goldsmiths to discuss their overlapping philosophical interests on 27 April 2007 (see also Shaviro 2014: 5). The collection of essays that form *The Speculative Turn* includes only one woman thinker, and that is Isabelle Stengers (Stengers 2011b). Harman's edited book series with Edinburgh University Press, to date numbering eleven books, includes no book authored by a woman.[6] The conversation between the three architects and the philosopher mentioned earlier, as well as all the projects represented in their dialogue, further normalizes these kinds of exclusions, which are embedded in the very language we use to discuss things. Furthermore, the architectural objects they treat risk becoming circumscribed as autonomous aesthetic exercises.

Isabelle Stengers wryly remarks: 'Certainly the meditative question "what is a thing?" or the evocation of the "thingness of things" have an enticing philosophical flavour' (Stengers 2014: 190), identified and mulled over by the likes of Heidegger, Harman, Morton and a prodigious list of others. The problem, which Stengers draws attention to, is that the meditative subject is a very specifically male, and unmarked, subject, a pure locus that transcends 'what matters for us' (Stengers 2014: 191). Stengers takes Latour and his *res* as an example, to remind us that things must be a matter of concern that bring us together (in agreement and disagreement) around a problem. Rather than casting judgement, Stengers, where she discusses OOO in passing, comments that philosophers create the problems that require them (2014: 192). At the same time, she remarks upon how thinking is a drama that transforms thinkers into larvae or prey (189). When thinking makes a thinker its prey, surely this suggests the ways in which a problem can take advantage of a thinker in unexpected ways, constraining how they think and act in a world.

The great risk I want to stress is that, without looking any further than the conceptual brand name OOO, creative practitioners might leap to the conclusion that this paradigm is made for us. I speak less *for* than *with*, or *alongside*, those engaged in the creative disciplines when I raise these concerns. The object begs for a reorientation that recognizes its distinct mode of being (in a world), its 'ontology'. Though this is not what Harman delivers, and while the conceptual brand name is compelling, something else entirely is at work. There pertains the risk of cutting off relations between things (human and other), or rendering things inaccessible and 'withdrawn' (like sulky children), and of begging a retreat into a retrograde and conservative form of phenomenological fascination. Descriptive poetics and list-making frenzies replace more complex accounts of the truly messy relational matrix that entangles things and their transformations. To this I want to cry out in response, OOOh! No!

Practice scene: Chelle Macnaughtan's *Trottoirs*

I try to imagine her making her first discovery, then coming across these pavement markings repeatedly, puzzling out their system, their structure of non-representational sense, attempting a cartography of their 'material-semiotic fields of meaning' (Haraway 1991: 195). There persists the concern that she will exhaust herself in the process, because can she ever be sure that she has covered the full territory of the given city? Has she mapped every mark? The material part of the conjunction 'material-semiotics' is a reminder that significations are not just tied to language and linguistic form, but include all manner of embodiments, material transformations and non-discursive expressions in relation to concrete places. She brought to her work such an extreme intensity, such an exactitude on account of her eye for detail, that I could only stand back in awe.

The work in question is composed of photographs taken of the mundane surface of pavements across four seasons and twenty *arrondissements* in Paris. Chelle Macnaughtan is very specific about this (Macnaughtan 2012: Prelude xix, Essay IV). The pavement markings could be abstracted, that is to say, selected and extracted from all the other material signs available across the Parisian *trottoirs*. One useful definition of abstraction is the process whereby something is taken from one situation and transferred to another for

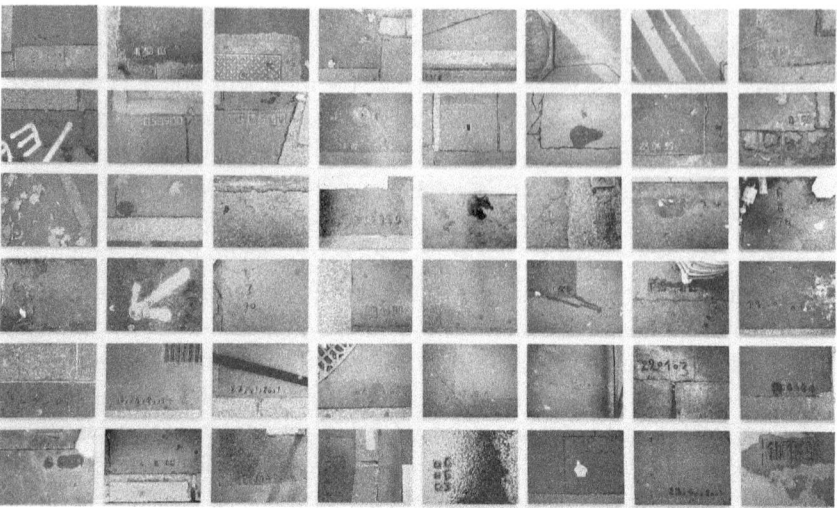

FIGURE 3.6 *Chelle Macnaughtan*, Les Trottoirs de Paris, *Spatial Listening Exhibition, 2011, RMIT Gallery. Installation image by Mark Ashkanasy.*

further experimentation. Here, as Didier Debaise suggests in conversation with Isabelle Doucet and Benedikte Zitouni, to abstract meaning is to extract something from a creature's milieu, which is an act of interpretation of that milieu (Doucet, Debaise and Zitouni 2018), to affect and to be affected by a milieu. Abstraction, according to this definition, comes after, and not before, an experience-based engagement amidst an environment-world. Great care needs to be taken in this process lest everything is lost and nothing is learnt, like a designer who deploys a paltry metaphor for a project that gets him nowhere. It appears there is always much to be lost. Gilles Deleuze and Félix Guattari write that, 'through having seen Life in the living or the Living in the lived, the novelist or painter returns breathless and with bloodshot eyes'. It is as though they have seen 'something in life that is too much for anyone, too much for themselves' (1994: 173), which places the quiet mark of exhaustion on them. This exhaustion, while threatening artists in their intense material-semiotic relations, is nevertheless that which at the same time sustains them according to their capacity to respond to the milieu in which they find themselves.

Chelle Macnaughtan was my second PhD student, and the first of my students to be deeply invested in research *by*, or *through*, design, or by way of 'creative practice' works. Such prepositions locate the creative practitioner with respect to their work in the domain of research: This is not an investigation *about*, *for* or in support of some aesthetic project, but how the process of the creative project itself carries a capacity to enable discovery and experimentation amidst environment-worlds.[7] Because this domain was still so new at the time, and there were so few precedents, I see her as something of a trailblazer. Her work was further complicated on account of its transdisciplinary interests, located as it was between architecture and art. Chelle described her work as 'design research beyond the disciplinary classification of either architecture or music, instead providing support for a consideration of a disciplinary "between-ness" as a further idea of the "open" work' (2012: 13). Jane Rendell was a great influence in Chelle's dedication to carving out a disciplinary space of action between art and architecture, and ended up being one of Chelle's examiners.[8] To further elaborate on the map of her expertise, Chelle came from a background in music, interior design and architecture. Her thesis undertook a series of experiments in the 'transdisciplinary terrain of negotiated exposition', between notational systems in music composition and in architecture, with an in-depth focus on John Cage's methods of indeterminacy. She was dedicated to an investigation of the sounds of architecture and the spaces of sound.

By its conclusion her thesis was composed of a suite of five major and three minor works, all of which were mutually cross-referenced, and in many instances co-dependent – one project exploration begetting a further project, each being considered individually, and, when collected as a suite, intended to remain an open work. To support her cause, Chelle undertook her own specific reading of Umberto Eco's concept of the open work. The thesis and creative works composed an array of concatenating intertextuality that could have unfurled indefinitely – only the PhD, being a finite project aimed towards satisfying the criteria of a degree in research training, obliged Chelle to settle upon a provisional border. When Chelle's examiners first received her thesis, they all discovered (with mixed feelings of both joy and dismay) that it was contained in a specially hand-crafted box, the contents of which included: a prelude; four essays, one of which she identified as an interlude; a postlude; and representations of the project work, many illustrated on transparent acetate sheets in reference to a material used by Cage, and all of which were arranged as loose sheets, like a music composition. And yes, should these pages have become muddled, this would be part of what the one who received the work had to be prepared to play with within each section of the PhD.

It is her third 'major' project to which I wish to return, Project III *Les Trottoirs de Paris*, which depicted Chelle's journey-form through Paris, commencing in October 2003 when she was undertaking fieldwork there. Wandering the streets, gazing with her head bent to the pavements in thought as she was trying to resolve a detail associated with her first major project *AI*, she discovered date markings, both mechanical and handmade that signified subterranean work on utilities. The series of photographs that resulted can

FIGURE 3.7 *Chelle Macnaughtan, Spatial Listening Exhibition, 2011, RMIT Gallery. Installation photography by Mark Ashkanasy.*

be understood as a spatio-temporal map of the city, informing a creative practice of 'indeterminacy', which, she argues, leads from experimentation to liberation (Macnaughtan 2012: Prelude, xix). Liberation from what exactly it is hard to say, except that John Cage was a central precursor for this work, and so liberation in part means a liberation from the overdetermining ego of the author-creator. To remove the overweening authorial gesture, to make the captured, bordered images about a rhythmic reading, a serial encounter: 'There is the operation of opening the arrested spatio-temporal moment of each photograph's audible cartography in relation to each viewer's reading and recollection' (2012: IV, 15). She wants us to listen to the street sounds as we view the images. The smallest signs of life visible in the photographs are supposed to enable an entry point into audible urban landscape environments swelling beyond the borders of the images and manifesting so many layered worlds: 'These impressions simply exist in an interpenetrating non-obstruction that is environmental ambient noise' (2012: IV, 16). Sometimes it is as though she unfolds a landscape without a subject, a post-human landscape.

It occurred to me as I was gathering many practice scenes, of which I could only include a selection, that Chelle's *Trottoirs* illustrate the humble exercise in gleaning with which I have opened the second part of this book. Chelle's neck is bent, she faces the pavement and her wanderings across Paris are somewhat at random. She slowly exhausts herself while exhausting her territory, in a world city whose image is likewise exhausted. In these wanderings, she can be seen to be reclaiming some of the exercises in stalking that the surrealists famously practised, except this time it is a she, and not a he who stalks, and it is not a human but a non-human actor who is pursued. She follows the trail of a non-human actor that speaks of the complex, mostly invisible infrastructures supporting cities, and towns and smaller settlements. Underground works designate an invisible yet fundamental infrastructural system connecting industry, commerce and residential quarters alike. As Jane Bennett argues, when speaking of the electricity grid, 'to the vital materialist, the electrical grid is better understood as a volatile mix of coal, sweat, electromagnetic fields, computer programs, electron streams, profit motives, heat, lifestyles, nuclear fuel, plastic, fantasies of mastery, status, legislation, water, economic theory, wire and wood – to name just some of the actants' (Bennett 2010: 25). Though Chelle's pavement gleaning could by no means take this full assemblage on, instead she extracts other threads, producing other combinatorials of concepts and things.

The forty-eight pavement photographs finally included in Project III *Les Trottoirs de Paris*, Chelle explains, perform an intertextual relationship with: time, space, architecture, listening, ego, signature and authority; and draw attention to: gesture, apparatus, cartography and borders. These are the concerns she extracts, and each is located amidst an intersecting matrix of relations. Time, *différance* and signature, for instance, come from her reading of Jacques Derrida (Macnaughtan 2012: Essay IV, 1). The signs impressed into the bitumen by hand describe the unique signature of the invisible workers who undertook the maintenance of underground utilities, and who thereby become unwitting participants in the project. Even the date markings mechanically impressed suggest some invisible worker, or group of workers, and pinpoint a specific moment in time, whether that be 22 October 2003 or 6 July 1999, or the pavement image that shows two date markings, 15 March 2001 and 25 February 1998, and so forth.

Chelle's photographs of the pavements led her to further projects. Her first two projects had commenced with questions: (1) Project I *AI*: How can sound be spatialized through indeterminate procedures? (2) Project II *74' 56"*: How can the sound of architecture be expressed in two-dimensional etchings? With Project III *Les Trottoirs de Paris*, a chance encounter instead led her to a question, which inspired her to commence the composition of a work. Collected photographs of the 'date' markings constituted an investigation in their own right, which subsequently led to a mapping exercise that informed further projects. She lifted the dates off the pavement, and redeployed them as instructions or notations to assist her to compose her fourth and fifth major projects, *Les Saisons* and *La Voix*. In this way, Chelle identifies *Trottoirs* as a 'fulcrum' in relation to her suite of major and minor projects (2012: Essay IV,

14). She describes the collected photographs of the pavements as instruments or tools to be used for creating something else, operating at the same time as raw information, a map and an apparatus for creative composition. Something happens in this work; her chance encounter with these incidental markings provokes her to ask questions, which remain open, and which propel her forward.

The *Trottoirs* project composes a non-functional map, but this only becomes evident when all forty-eight images are mounted and displayed, and something of a system is rendered legible. With just one image of one circumscribed patch of pavement, a restricted point of view or portal is framed onto the city, and the 'carriers of significance', to borrow from Uexküll, are considerably reduced or rarefied. The pavement images form a map, but one that shows none of the usual landmarks; it is a map that is not just spatial but spatio-temporal, as the images are taken across the seasons *and* across the Parisian *arrondissements*, gathering up spaces and times. The date markings are non-intentional signatures, they shelter no deeper meaning, they merely compose a registration of a completed task. Chelle speaks of how her methods are often deployed to afford her a degree of authorial withdrawal (Macnaughtan 2012: Essay IV, 27). Mierle Ukeles's project of care, 'Touch Sanitation Performance' (1979–1980) shaking the hands of 8,500 municipal workers who would accept her gesture, can be brought to mind. Chelle, operating at the other end of the spectrum of care, shakes so many invisible hands at a distance, and her photographic documents produce what she calls counter-signatures. Sheets of the past, layers of the registration of time, including the time the mark is made, the photograph captured, the multifarious times and points of view of those who view the work all speak to its contingent durability.

Chelle spoke to me of her fascination with what can be revealed in even the meagre details allowed in her close-vision depictions of the pavements. While interpretation is conditional, provisional and inconclusive, we are nevertheless apt to read into things: autumn leaves, scraps of blossoms, the sun slanting across the ground at a certain angle with a certain intensity, the inexorable passing of the seasons, but also the detritus, a cigarette butt that someone has smoked, a metro ticket stub someone has used to travel from one metro station to another, chewing gum, paint, a paperclip, a key. The thing is, we are compelled to read these signs as something like signs of life, even though this attempt to make sense of the material-semiotic field may mislead us into installing specific kinds of pre-determined human agency. We are apt to privilege the human point of view on things; it is what we believe we know best. Jane Bennett offers advice here, which has been reiterated by Rosi Braidotti, and that is, 'a touch of anthropomorphism can catalyze a sensibility that finds a world filled not with ontologically distinct categories of beings (subjects and objects) but with variously composed materialities that form confederations' (Bennett 2010: 99). Even though at every turn we must be wary of making assumptions about how this human is composed, to acknowledge our own shape in its awkward fit with an environment-world is more ethically sensitive than insisting on an anthropocentric point of view. How, without privileging the human, but by acknowledging our human modes of life can we think and practice otherwise?

Claire Colebrook, with her argument for 'extinct theory', a theory that imagines the unthinkable – theory without a (human) point of view, theory post-apocalypse, beyond the human or with only dwindling human witnesses – speculates on a situation in which: 'One can think here of texts as remaining, unread, dead objects without authors or audience' (2014a: 39). To this she adds: 'Imagine a species, after humans, "reading" our planet and its archive: if they encounter human texts (ranging from books, to machines to fossil records) how might new views or theories open up?' (2014a: 39). Where popular media and fiction regularly imagine such post-human landscapes, why does theory lag behind? Embedded in her discussion is a worrying dismissal of what I have called creative practice; instead she asks about '"life" without the human look? Life without praxis, life without meaningful action, life without production or labour: such would be theory *after* theory, or theory that opened itself to the thought of extinction' (2014a: 38). She is sceptical about the emergence of so much earnest activity between practice and theory, work that joyously affirms living, productivity, pure potentiality and futurity, as well as embodied and affective life, including any assumptions about a substrate composed of human life. All this furious activity, she suggests, is in denial of the looming global crises, current and past terrors, 'viral, political, economic, climatic and affective' (41). Instead she asks: What of impotentiality, what of becoming-imperceptible? A thought experiment seemingly without a practical component in which there is no future of open creativity and unbounded possibility. Theory after theory, extinct theory, is instead 'destructive of such an imaginary' (45).

The problem is, theory after theory, extinct theory, renders such practice scenes as are gathered in this book near meaningless remainders. At the same time, there is something to be said for the extreme slowing down that comes with becoming-imperceptible with the earth.

This takes us a long distance from the questions the creative practitioner might want to raise, and away from the humble gestures of the practitioner head bent towards the pavement making do with what she has, perhaps making more sense, that is to say proposing more directions forward than the pavement markings might merit. We are a long way from the practitioner who chooses to tell different stories. For Chelle, it is rather a question of what she will do with her 'discovery', how she will make good her encounter, what future compositions she will experiment with. It is not even that she attributes an excess of meaning to the markings – in fact, she extracts them, abstracts them from their context and following procedures of determined indeterminacy redeploys them.

Thing-power

Whether broken down or in good use, whether present-to-hand or ready-to-hand, things have a power all their own, intra-acting and intermingled as a complex tangle of human and non-human relations. In her book *Vibrant Matter: A Political Ecology of Things*, Jane Bennett introduces what I like to call post-human landscapes manifested as assemblages of so many vibrant, material things, combining human and non-human actors. She tells stories of complex networks of things at various scales, manifesting through precarious material forms. Her examples of vibrant matter support my emphasis on things over an OOO, with which she likewise has an argument (Bennett 2015). She urges her readers to pay attention to the thing-power of things and the way they issue a call concerning their predicament. Even though it is not always clear what they have to say, things nevertheless, I would add, enter into circulations of affecting and affected relations. Her head bent to the pavement, much like Chelle Macnaughtan, Bennett opens her book with an encounter with some trash she has spied on the street, assembling the kinds of things that cannot in any easy way be identified as objects and yet which produce effects and affects that have implications at local and global scales (see also Massey 2005: 182–183). The vibrant thing-power of things arrests her attention and the assemblage in question is the shimmering detritus that has been captured in a stormwater drain, 'glove, pollen, rat, cap, stick' (2010: 5). It is an inauspicious opening image bringing together things that do not normally belong together; like dirt, they express matter in the wrong place. Yet inventories such as these compose our worlds and enter into relations with us precariously positioned human creatures. The broader scenes that Bennett then analyses by way of thing-power and thinking through assemblages include the event of an electricity power grid blackout in North America in 2003; edible matter and the contemporary problem of obesity; the inorganic material that is metal and stem cell research. In each case, something is at stake, some problem is addressed, of the kind we are unlikely to find in OOO.

Bennett draws on the work of Deleuze and Latour, among others, to tell her story of thing-power expressed as vibrant matter. In *We Have Never Been Modern*, Latour argues that such philosophers as Heidegger attempt to purify the messy world according to subjects and objects, things that pertain to nature and things that pertain to culture and society, but things are far more complicated and intertwined than this, as Bennett demonstrates so compellingly with her situated examples. Thrift, who shares aspects of the theoretical framework of Actor Network Theory (ANT) with Latour and Bennett, continues this line of work with his non-representational theory (2008). For his part he defines what it means to be human as part of a 'situated flow within which human bodies are just one set of actors' (2008: 226).

Less than a prohibition against forms of representation understood in an aesthetic sense – the drawings, renderings, models composed by architects – non-representational theory asks us to resituate these disciplinary paraphernalia. For instance, how can a creative practitioner's modes of representation be less about re-presenting what she already believes she knows based on the acceptable norms of her taste community, and more about a cautious sketching and testing in order to draw out a situation in which she finds herself immersed? In many ways, this concerns orientation and paying attention to situation, not to speak *for* or *about* but to think *with*, much as Julieanna Preston thinks with the mud she hauls, a practice-based encounter to be discovered subsequently, or Chelle Macnaughtan bends her head towards the dirt and refuse of the pavement thinking with the marks she discovers there by chance.

If we take full flight from the Heideggerian account of the thingness of things, if we mobilize our relations with a broader spectrum of things and accept our reciprocal and dynamic relationship with things, rather than letting them sit about in a warehouse, or on a shelf, we can place ourselves in contact with what Latour has called the parliament of things. A parliament suggests a setting in which all those assembled come together to discuss pertinent *matters*, and as I will discuss, such an assemblage relies on different modes of representation. Latour and after him Bennett's radical move is to introduce apparently inanimate things into such a gathering. It is a reconsideration of things that Albena Yaneva introduces to architecture with her ANT-inspired studies of architectural assemblages of things, for instance, where they are to be found in Rem Koolhaas's architectural studio (Yaneva 2009, 2017). Likewise, it is the means by which something like the thing that is a public urinal turns out to be a matter of concern at an urban scale, as Isabelle Doucet has demonstrated (Doucet 2016: 160–165). However, here the primary limitation for the former thinker is that, as an ethnographer, Yaneva necessarily brings a different point of view to these things than that of an architectural designer and theorist, and these distinct points of view need to be respected in terms of their different if co-influential practices. No practice is just like any other. The things so clustered are admixtures of all sorts that constellate as networks of hybrids of the living and the nonliving, which is not to say that we should avoid all attempts to classify the things that compose a world. Taking things and their relations seriously means that we can leap into the midst of their controversies to feel out what is possible, how things might be shifted so as to form assemblages that are less exhausting, and less destructive of environment-worlds.

Notes

1. See https://www.youtube.com/watch?v=yVEZXxEzYqw&t=154s; 'In 2003, Varda was invited by curator Hans Ulrich Obrist to show her visual art at the Venice Biennale'. http://www.lacma.org/sites/default/files/Agnes-Varda-in-Californialand-Advisory-10.2.13.pdf (accessed 30 June 2017).
2. See https://www.youtube.com/watch?v=nrL8DGNyDhY (accessed 30 June 2017).
3. See Agnès Varda, L'ÎLE ET ELLE, 18 June 2006–8 October 2006, https://www.fondationcartier.com/#/en/art-contemporain/26/exhibitions/294/all-the-exhibitions/627/agnes-varda-l-ile-et-elle (accessed 30 June 2017).
4. See https://www.youtube.com/watch?v=nrL8DGNyDhY (accessed 30 June 2017).
5. One of my students at KTH, Stockholm, Sindri Sigurðsson, who is from Iceland, recently explained to me that: 'The word Þing has two meanings in Icelandic. One means a "thing" and the other a "gathering". In the case of the word Alþingi (Althing) the meaning is without a doubt "gathering". Alþingi does not describe a thing or a place, it simply means a "gathering for all" and it was at such a "þing" that the most important leaders (goð) of the country met to decide on legislation and provided justice.' That is to say, there is something of slippage of terms when it comes to Latour's description, in that Althing means a gathering but not a thing, though 'Þing', on the other hand, does do this etymological work of standing for both a thing and a gathering.
6. See https://edinburghuniversitypress.com/series-speculative-realism.html (accessed 20 October 2017).
7. On the role of the preposition in relation to research, see, for instance: Downton (2003); Frayling (1993); Frichot(2016); Rendell (2010: 6–7); Stengers (2011c).
8. A video documentation of Chelle Macnaughtan's PhD defence, which took place in 2010, can be seen at: https://vimeo.com/29078720. Her examiners included Jane Rendell, Linda Marie Walker and Stephen Loo.

4

Thing-power

Object-oriented democracy

In his introduction to *Making Things Public*, where Bruno Latour goes in search of a philosophy of things to accompany what he calls a 'dingpolitik', the philosopher of technology and science who was a key contributor to the formation of Actor Network Theory (ANT) draws attention to two senses of representation, which he argues need to be re-conjoined. On the one hand, there is that form of representation associated with what Latour calls schools of law and political science, which 'designates the ways to gather the legitimate people around some issue' (2005a: 16). This definition describes forms of political representation, suggesting the need of a gathering place or an assembly, with associated, very material, spatial counterparts, such as assembly halls, parliamentary complexes and local community buildings. The second definition of representation, which Latour locates within science and technology studies, 'presents or rather *represents* what is the object of concern to the eyes and ears of those who have assembled around it' (16), that is to say, those who have gathered to study some thing, and to glean some knowledge from it. Latour wants to draw these two definitions of representation together so as to establish a circle or a place that creates an assembly out of *who* is concerned. The *who* so gathered share (or share out, that is to say divide) a *what*, that is, *whatever* it is that is under consideration. Having brought these two definitions of representation into play, Latour then introduces a third sense of representation, one he associates with art, but which can be associated with architecture (though the second definition of representation, as that which is presented to the eyes and ears of those gathered, also pertains to the effects of architecture).

The third definition relates to visual representation achieved via compositional means, and through the use of specific media and rendering techniques. Engraving is the example Latour offers, but for architects these days computational technologies of representation are more relevant. From the point of view of the architect, this supposedly more obscure, third sense of representation is the one most likely to come to mind first in terms of how we represent our projects to our public, our clients and our audience. Latour turns this third sense of representation, so well known to architects, into the problem of the visual puzzle of assembling bodies.

From this he proceeds to remind us that the 'Body Politik' and how it is represented, its political *whos*, its scientific and technological *whats*, its aesthetic renderings or modes of expression (thus the three given definitions of representation), are not simply composed of people, but are 'thick with things' (Latour 2005: 16). This thickness of things includes cities, fields, ships, technologies, cutting across technological or cultural artefacts and natural environments. In his account of a philosophy of things, and its political correlate, which he calls an 'object-oriented democracy' (2005: 16), it is worthwhile noting that Latour at first seems to swing indiscriminately between using the terms 'objects' and 'things'. This indiscrimination is eventually sorted out at the moment of disaster, when the parts formerly cohering between a multifaceted object come undone, are exhausted or are destroyed, so that the object in question loses its objective quality as something coherent and becomes a thing, specifically, a thing around which we gather with our shared yet distinct concerns in order to find out what just happened.

Rather than a broken tool suddenly becoming present-at-hand and thereby corralling the forces of theoretical reflection, Latour takes on a larger event to discuss the transition from a technological object to a thing, and that is the explosion of a space shuttle and its aftermath. In this he draws on an earlier thought-image described by the philosopher Michel Serres, who deliberates on the disintegration of the space shuttle Challenger shortly after its take-off at 11.39 am on 28 January 1986 (Serres 2015: 2). Critiquing Heidegger's strong distinction between privileged things such as jugs and shoes and less beloved technological objects, Latour asks: 'What would happen, I wonder, if we tried to talk about the object of science and technology, the Gegenstand, as if it had the rich and complicated qualities of the celebrated Thing?' (2004: 233). For Latour, the 2003 explosion of the Columbia space shuttle illustrates this transformation from an object to a thing, or rather, not just one thing but a vast range of debris post-explosion. With this example Latour posits an exemplary moment in which a complex technological machine, seemingly circumscribed in its distinctiveness, reveals something else about its composition and the concerns it gathers around it as it becomes another kind of thing altogether.

In architecture, we necessarily develop our modes of communication via an array of *representations*, communicated to the eyes and ears of those who have gathered (the clients, the critical jury, our professional peers), but perhaps these would be better described as *presentations* of the event of sense, including the affects that are caused to thereby circulate and cluster in atmospheres of affect. Architecture through its presentations is more often propositional, presenting worlds that are yet to emerge and presenting possible assemblages or associations of bodies that cannot be logically anticipated in advance and yet are imagined as though they might be possible. Latour argues that, 'each object – each issue – generates a different pattern of emotions and disruptions, of disagreements and agreements … Each object gathers around itself a different assembly of relevant parties. Each object triggers new occasions to passionately differ and dispute' (2005: 15), or rather, each 'thing' offers such opportunities as it comes to be animated amidst an event. These events so procured by architecture arouse atmospheres of affect, which undertake an erasure of the object that is architecture (Frichot 2008). The consideration of a built object cannot exhaust all that is of relevance to an event; rather, a complex assemblage of all manner of actors and things, the circulation of sense and sensation, demands to be mapped. By acknowledging the always complex relations of a built, or even an unbuilt, architectural project (see Runting 2018), the hope is that more ameliorative approaches to local environment-worlds, their global and local intra-actions, can be achieved.

Architectural things

What kinds of things do we habitually associate with architectural activity? The exemplary architectural event appears to be satisfied in the figure of the civic monument, the stories it tells of national and local identity and the future peoples it anticipates through its ritual refrains. The monument appears to be an exterior expression of identity as distinct from an interior expression. But what would allow us to consider architecture less as an object in contradistinction to our selves as subjects and more as a set of relations that inaugurate an event, or a series of events? In *What Is Philosophy?* Deleuze and Guattari suggest that the duration of a monument can vary greatly: 'The young man will smile on the canvas for as long as the canvas lasts. Blood throbs under the skin of this woman's face, the wind shakes a branch, a group of men prepare to leave' (1994: 163). The examples Deleuze and Guattari used to explain their idea of a monument are not conventional ones. In their sparse notes on the monument Deleuze and Guattari draw attention to an indeterminate life at work in things. The architectural monument is not isolated out of time, but is tied up with events, and with temporal unfurlings: 'A monument does not commemorate or celebrate something that happened but confides to the ear of the future the persistent sensations that embody the event: the constantly renewed suffering of men and women, their re-enacted protestations, their constantly resumed struggle' (1994: 176–177). A monument, they add, 'is always in the process of becoming, like those tumuli to which each new traveller adds a stone' (183–184). It is inherently additive, and temporal, and spatial, and material. Latour and Yaneva more recently point out that: 'Everybody knows – and especially architects, of course – that a building is not a static object but a moving project, and that even once it has been built, it ages, it is transformed by its users' (Latour and Yaneva 2008) by future renovations, by disrepair, maintenance and even demolition. Much the same can be said of unbuilt architectures, whether purely speculative, or else failing to be constructed for whatever reason (Runting 2018).

How does the architectural monument as event work? It must be sufficiently durable that it can stand up on its own, even while it manifests as 'morphogenetic movements, displacements of cellular groups, stretchings, folds, migrations, and local variations of potentials' (Deleuze and Guattari 1983: 84), that is to say, the monument enables us to explore multiple and shifting material identities composed of not only who we have been, but who we are perpetually in the midst of becoming. This makes the question of a politics of things something that can never be resolved once and for all. The *Ding* around which concerned parties gather will give way to other things and matters of concern.

Here we could return briefly to Kerez's incidental thing, his grotto, his inscrutable thing, which has been situated by the curator of the Swiss Pavilion as an event (Oehy 2016), assuming when she states this that it can be taken as a thing without relations, standing there as a pre-eminent architectural wonder. Yet events never take place in isolation, and it is not possible to determine in advance what kinds of collectives they will produce. Architectural events take place across shimmering post-human landscapes composed of assemblages of vibrant material things, human and non-human actors entangled in all manner of political and ethical relations. The event pertains equally to material expressions and immaterial forces (Frichot 2005); it is a mobile instant that perpetually eludes the present, bifurcating instead into a past and a future (Deleuze 1990: 151). Although Deleuze claims that the event belongs to language, he stresses that language is what is said of *things* (1990: 22). Events 'raise very complex questions about composition and decomposition, about speed and slowness, about latitude and longitude, about power and affect' (Deleuze 1991: 95). Deleuze stresses the ethical aspect of events, specifically, that we should 'not be unworthy of what happens to us' and even more explicitly that we should aspire to 'become worthy of what happens to us ... to become the offspring of one's own events' (1990: 149). In this formulation, the event comes before the subject and the object; it is rather through a series of events, bursts of materialization, that subjects and objects emerge and distinguish themselves, only to be followed by the slow burning consumption of dematerialization.

There is a paradoxically open determination at work here, what can be called Deleuze's transcendental empiricism. While the outcome of events is inherently unpredictable and never entirely within the subject's control (and the subject in any case is only ever realized retrospectively out of an impersonal or preindividual field, what Deleuze and Guattari call a plane of immanence), there is a necessity embedded in the ongoing upsurge of events. Something will definitely, and determinedly happen, we just cannot be exactly sure what, and when. Doreen Massey, well known for her work on space, place and gender (1994) argues for a crucial understanding of the future as open, and thereby available to be made, that is, as an 'open future of possibilities, of creation' (2005: 32). This is a creative openness that is discussed in the work of philosophers such as Bergson and Whitehead, whom Deleuze closely reads. With Deleuze and his commentators, including Latour and Yaneva's take on architectural things, Massey argues against a focus on 'the discrete at the expense of continua, things at the expense of processes, recognition at the expense of encounter, results at the expense of tendencies' (2005: 20), because all such things are bound up and entangled in processes moving at faster and slower speeds. Necessity and radical contingency work together here: Neither the subject nor the object is established as primary units; the subject and object only arrive much later on the scene, and they come to be formed through time, inside what occurs, expressed via the event.

In his book *The Fold*, which for a time during the 1990s was popular with architects keen to discover new formal possibilities in folding, Deleuze remarks: 'If the status of the object is profoundly changed, so also is that of the subject' (Deleuze 1993). Following my exercise in gleaning things, as attempted so far, many approaches have been made to this perplexing encounter, and the way in which neither objects nor subjects remain stable for long. I have found one of the most useful accounts of these dynamics in the philosopher Michel Serres's book *The Parasite*, in an essay called 'Theory of the Quasi-Object' (2007: 224–134). He opens this essay by asking: 'What living together is. What is the collective. The question fascinates us now' (224), and while he writes from the standpoint of the last millennium, this makes his questioning no less pertinent today. He too ventures an approach to what we call 'we', arguing that it is more than the collective enunciation of the personal pronoun 'I'. The notion, based on mere addition, that 'Everyone carries a stone, and the wall is built. Everyone carries his "I", and the "we" is built', is an idiotic construction, he claims (227). Instead, he asks the reader to consider a ball game, though the ball that is passed from one player to the next could be 'a ring, a button, a thing' to which can be added those units of exchange that constitute money (229). The game works like this: It is composed as a network of passes between players, something is passed, whatever it happens to be. When you grab hold of a thing, a ball, a token or a dollar bill, you enunciate your position. For a moment you are 'it', which may be a momentary privilege, but also places you at risk. You have effectively placed yourself at the centre of attention for the time being. Serres asserts that we do not know whether the quasi-object, the quasi-subject, the ball or the enunciated 'I' are beings or relations, 'tatters of beings or end of relations' (227). Everything takes place on the move, and the thing you hold onto right now can be lost again in the next moment, secured by another. Being is abruptly abolished in lieu of the relation, and yet being, the thing, stubbornly expresses itself all over again in a different formulation. The transmission, the stops and the starts of the throw of the ball from one player to the next produces a choreography of rhythms of sense and sensation.

This emphasis on the elusive, process-oriented aspect of things is what has exasperated thinkers enough to venture a return to obdurate objects as something more solid and more durable, as is evident for instance in Harman's recent retort to a republished version of Latour and Yaneva's essay in *Ardeth* (Harman 2017; Latour and Yaneva 2017). He absolutely refuses the flow and relation of things, asserting at every turn the persistence of isolated objects. Yet the thing is, it is not all about endlessly homogenizing flows for Deleuze and Guattari, nor even for Latour and Yaneva who allow for concrete entities and emphasize 'earthly encounters' (Latour and Yaneva 2008: 88); things are not exhausted by their relations, rather it is by way of a careful study of relations that things can be better apprehended. They simply want to find the analytical means by which to transform the dominant glossy magazine image of the building as static, into an understanding of the building as a project in movement. In obviating flows, attempting to stop up or deny their course, there is something else that goes missing. Daniel Smith points out that when Deleuze and Guattari introduce this concept-movement of flows, which has frustrated many of the aforementioned thinkers and practitioners, in fact they are drawing on economic theory and the idea of *break-flow* (Smith 2012: 165). The game of passing the ball, transferring the dollar bill, as Serres has elucidated, is one that stops and starts. Incoming and outgoing flows facilitate transmission, following a passage from one interceptor to the next. One risk of stopping up the flow, or denying its conceptual power, especially for architects, is to overlook the role of economics when it comes to the commissioning, design, construction and occupation of built projects – to say nothing of social, political, ethical, environmental and labour-related issues.

An entangled web of things

Concepts and things are materially, semiotically entangled, as Donna Haraway and Karen Barad and their readers frequently insist. Entanglement is a specific recurring motif to be found across both Barad's and Haraway's work, as well as in the recent work on matters of care by Maria Puig de la Bellacasa (2017). Entanglement has in its own right become a conceptual leitmotif. A tangle, as in a tangle of weeds, or a tangle of hair, or a tangle of string, presents a compelling non-linear thought–image, even a diagram by which to think our way through the midst of things. Haraway has taken to using the thought–image of the 'cat's cradle', a children's game composed of string that is most satisfying when stretched out between two sets of hands belonging to two players. A loop of string can be configured and reconfigured into many different shapes and constitutes one of the oldest games known to human society, Haraway explains (2016: 13). String figures concoct stories by proposing patterns that are performed; a game of cat's cradle stands in as an apt way of thinking Haraway's material semiotics as that which 'is always situated, someplace and not noplace, entangled and worldly' (2016: 4).

Taking Latour's argument that 'we have never been modern' and that the 'Great Divide' we habitually construct between what counts as nature and what counts as society is deeply questionable, Donna Haraway, celebrated for her feminist cyborg manifesto (1991), similarly suggests that we have never been human. As she proudly announces, 'I love the fact that human genomes can be found in only about 10 percent of all the cells that occupy the mundane space I call my body; the other 90 percent are filled with the genomes of bacteria, fungi, protists, and such' (2008: 3). This is how she frames Part One of her book *When Species Meet*, where she also takes a large critical swipe at Deleuze and Guattari's famous concepts of becoming-animal, and becoming-woman, as having little to do with the situated and material knowledges of either one (Haraway 2008: 27–30). If we have never been human, then we can hardly claim to be post-human, is the implication of such an argument. Thrift insists that what Haraway offers are attempts to forge different relations with the non-human (Thrift 2006: 189), which of course also includes the situation, the different shapes and sizes and material semiotic performances of the human subject. As N. Katherine Hayles explains, the post-human is the concept by which we can better understand the human: 'the posthuman requires taking the human into account' (Hayles 2003: 137). At the same time, our definition of the human must necessarily change, especially when the human actor is resituated amidst assemblages of non-human actors. Caught amidst entangled things, composed of an entanglement of material stuff and relations, our (human creaturely) selves bear witness to the dramatization of the vibrancy, even the 'wildness' of things including our own human bodies.

The wildness of post-human landscapes assumes the smoothing out of erstwhile striated spaces, general unpredictability and the reign of emergent systems without a central human point of command (Kwinter 2008: 186–194). It is where the only apparently striated organization of the city disaggregates as 'sprawling, temporary, shifting shanty towns of nomads and cave dwellers, scrap metal and fabric, patchwork, to which the striations of money, work, or housing are no longer even relevant' (Deleuze and Guattari 1987: 481), though this is by no means a one-way process, and striation can at many points reimpart its forces of organization. We are in fact intimately familiar with post-human landscapes, for they fill our mediatized imaginaries in the form of apocalyptic fantasies and science fiction thrillers. While such visions may haunt us, I suggest that the post-human landscapes we already inhabit are far more mundane, just as Haraway argues from her position. Haraway, who speaks joyfully and humorously from the point of view of her gut bacteria composing the better material part of what she is, frequently insists that it is better to get back down into the slime and keep our distance from the sublime, for 'to be one is always to become with many' (Haraway 2008: 4). Likewise, Bennett has demonstrated that it is necessary to get into the gutter to understand our material cohabitations, whom we share our environment-worlds with. Besides the gut and the gutter, Bennett demonstrates how an understanding of thing-power amidst vibrant material assemblages can assist us to witness the complex infrastructures of everyday life, from obesity epidemics to power grids.

Practice scene: Julieanna hauls mud

She appears by the roadside at regular intervals, each time covered in more filth, each time a little more weighed down, weary under her self-appointed load, nearing exhaustion. Arriving with buckets strapped to a trolley, she mobilizes her load by using the counterweight of her body. She is depositing something part-liquid, part-solid onto the pavement. In exchange, timber pallets are being gathered and returned, one after another to the tidal zone of the river below from which she has been collecting the sludge. A sign on the pavement reads: Free Art. Visitors are invited to participate, but no one offers to give her a hand; instead, they pause to chat as she continues to work, depositing substances unmentionable onto the pavement, matter in the wrong place. She continues in much the same way for two long days.

It is important to acknowledge the gestures of her body performed in relation to the materials she shepherds through her explorations. Her face is downturned and concentrated. She moves slowly, rests often, as though testing the proprioceptive relation of her material body to itself and its surrounds. Sometimes her arms sweep arcs through the air, sometimes her hips sway, sometimes she carries buckets of mud, smears her face with muck, massages stones, as she redistributes the diverse materials of her local environment-world. She expresses bursts of material exuberance. Or else she remains quiet, curled up, exhausted. Her chosen materials are many, and her approach is one that is anti-hylomorphic, that is to say, she refuses to be the architect-designer as mistress form-giver, and chooses instead to follow the materials of the specific situations in which she embeds herself. This has meant the redistribution of materials such as plywood, bales of wool, rolls of duct tape, mud, coal, ice, straw, butter and eggs, her own body. No material in the aforementioned list is strictly 'natural', nor entirely 'artifactual', but arrayed as a material spectrum. Sometimes she has made herself sick in the process, such as when she took on the task of hauling mercury-contaminated mud from the Whau River up to Rosebank Road. Taking material immersion seriously is a risky endeavour; sometimes our body will conjoin with other material bodies to form a greater composition, and sometimes, on the contrary, 'a body or an idea threaten our own coherence' (Deleuze 1988: 19).

Julieanna Preston is a New Zealand academic and creative practitioner of architecture and interiors who insistently asks what can the materials of our environment-worlds do?[1] Who thereby insists through her probing that we will not get to the end of following materials, understanding our deep entanglement with them. This assumes that a lasting and prudent experimentation is required. She moves between site-writing, architecture-writing and performance writing, all of which demand a 1:1 approach based on the immediacy of her encounters. Julieanna's work, conceptual and material, makes a specific contribution to the burgeoning area that has come to be called 'new materialism'.[2] She is informed by a feminist approach to new materialism, drawing on writers such as Jane Bennett, Rosi Braidotti, Elizabeth Grosz and Donna Haraway, each of whom can be identified as holding their own specific relation to the power of precarious material things, including processes of immaterialization, and the mixing of the corporeal and the incorporeal. The contemporary resurgence of feminist practices is a crucial context for Julieanna's work, and many of her tactics have been resituated into the domain of architecture and design from earlier feminist art performances that incorporated processes of materially oriented embodiment.[3] Many of her precedents, more familiar to artists than designers and architects, continue to open up a promising range of approaches, especially in light of the rise of creative practice research and research by design.

In Julieanna's project *Moving Stuff* (2013), a performance that took place between the Whau River estuary edge and Rosebank Road in Auckland,

FIGURE 4.1 *Julieanna Preston,* Moving Stuff, *2013. Photography by Mick Hubertus Mica.*

New Zealand, as part of the Rosebank Art Walk at the Auckland Festival, she aimed to 'dispel artificial boundaries that segregate the natural world from the artificial world, the estuary from the industrial zone, and the ecological from the manufactured'.[4] Mud and water, in brimming bucketfuls, were relocated from the polluted river up to the road's edge, and onto timber pallets, drawing attention to the waterway moving invisibly nearby. Among mud, water and the timber pallets a transaction was performed achieving the transmogrification of bare quasi-biological stuff into the domain of economic industrial manufacture. The timber pallets with which her loads of mud were exchanged are a unit of transport that carry goods through vast journeys across global networks of production and consumption. On her way to Edinburgh, UK, the following year for another performance, the iodine she was carrying in her suitcase as a treatment for the mercury that had contaminated her body from handling the mud leaked everywhere.

In Edinburgh, she performed further acts of material care, arriving with the cleaners each morning to sweep the space where conference delegates would be gathering for the Emptiness and Plenitude symposium on Architectural Research by Design (2013). Here her project *Ground Maintenance* clearly acknowledges the caring labours of her predecessor Mierle Laderman Ukeles,

FIGURE 4.2 *Julieanna Preston*, Moving Stuff, *2013. Photography by Mick Hubertus Mica.*

especially Ukeles's *Maintenance Art Manifesto* of 1969. She is an important precursor, acknowledging the invisible labour of undervalued workers, the cleaners who make good our institutional environments and the garbage truck drivers who shovel our waste out of sight.[5] There is a great deal at stake with respect to the generally undervalued and under-represented material and immaterial labour of creative minorities, intersectionally applicable well beyond the gender assignment 'woman'.

At the Industries of Architecture conference in Newcastle, UK, the eleventh annual Architectural Humanities Research Association (AHRA) event convened by Katie Lloyd Thomas — well known for her collection *Material Matters* (2007) — with her colleagues Tilo Amhoff and Nick Beech, Julieanna performed *A Reconciliation of Carboniferous Accretions*. She invited everyone to join her on a site-writing journey from the entry of Neville Hall progressing upstairs into an abandoned room in the North Eastern Institute of Mining. Each one of us was asked to carry a lump of coal, to be removed from a large sack at the designated meeting place outside on the streets of Newcastle on a Friday night animated with the fervour of wildly drunken youth. Upstairs we were each asked to deposit our lump of coal in the middle of the floor of room 210, in the act acknowledging a long historical seam of coal mining, burning and export that runs through Newcastle's history at least since Roman colonization. The lights were dark and a woman with heft to her hips began to gyrate in a slow dance to music issuing forth from a transistor radio, dancing to the coal. As the lights were switched back on, we were asked to roll the carpet back over the pile of coal that had now accumulated there, bringing it to rest in the Institute of Mining.

The following year in Stockholm, Julieanna took part in another event, the eighth International Deleuze Studies conference, with the delicious title – apt to be copiously misinterpreted – Daughters of Chaos: Practice, Discipline, A Life. Her material performance installation was called *Stirring Stillness: Aesthetic Refinement on a Concrete Plane*. Her palette of materials was particular to her preconceptions of Sweden, a combinatorial list of material associations: eggs, straw, clay, salt, sand, charcoal, butter, ice. These are innocuous materials, usually not found in combination, but here choreographed across the repurposed concrete floors of the former Eriksson factory, now the Konstfack University College of Art, Craft and Design. Over four days, she arrives first thing in the morning with the cleaning staff, and could be mistaken for one of them. An approach similar to the one she took in Edinburgh in 2012. During the conference, delegates accidentally break eggs or scrape charcoal along the floor between the seminar rooms. Outside a large block of ice slowly melts as

FIGURE 4.3 *Julieanna Preston*, A Reconciliation of Carboniferous Accretions, *performance. Industries of Architecture AHRA Conference, NIEMME, Newcastle Upon Tyne, UK, 2014. Photography by Ole Steen.*

mid-summer is upon us and the air is warm. The ice, of course, is an incidental reference to Francis Alÿs's performance *Sometimes Making Something Leads to Nothing* (1997), which involved the artist pushing a large block of ice around Mexico City until it melted. He labours under the warm sun, demonstrating how some acts of creativity lead to naught but the exertion expended in the making.

For Julieanna, creative practice is located at the core of her being, and this being is one that is empathetic intermingling with diverse materials. She writes love poems to bare material stuff, to stones and dirt, acknowledging our wholesale entanglement in environment-worlds, and how we are all apt to decompose, eventually. An entry into Julieanna's body of work requires an acknowledgement of the persistence of utter matter, and that material immersion persists at every turn despite our aptitude for decomposition.

You are in the midst of things, and with these things you form confederations, corpuscular societies, molecular collectives for the meantime, some weaker, some more powerful. A privileged position is a kind of conceit you construct to get by. If you can claim a privileged position, it is only ever temporary, partial and fragmentary. Given Julieanna's keen appreciation of her material relations, and the close or haptic vision this proximity demands, the work draws urgent attention to material relations that are increasingly at risk of becoming exhausted, especially because what a material can do has not yet been given sufficient consideration. For too long mere matter has remained that which has been taken for granted, a situation that Julieanna has already done a great deal to remedy, in that she *follows the material*, rather than imposing pre-established ideas upon it.

Her work has driven her incrementally towards a series of site-specific installations where she explicitly acknowledges that her performing body is one medium amidst many. She has frequently addressed the interior materials of her local institutional environments so as to allow them the opportunity to speak, but she has also ventured further out into less-circumscribed environments to engage, as witnessed earlier, with the mud of toxic rivers. Her engagement with the vibrant matter of her local problematic field is a question of creative resistance. In recognizing the immediate and inextricable condition of material relations and flows, resistance can provide the means by which a claim can be made sufficient to define a project. The challenge is how to act from amidst the flux of material relations and flows, so as to secure some material resilience for the time being. Creative resistance, as Julieanna demonstrates, can quite simply be related to material resilience, how a certain material is resistant to moisture, another to sound, and how resistance at times may also have something to do with yielding.[6] Her creative resistance is an acknowledgement of material relations and the potential, and responsibility, you hold to remake yourself and the present otherwise.

Julieanna goes so far as to demonstrate the material liveliness of the archive, which becomes material she can follow too, because material should not be thought outside its social, political and cultural history. Every material has a story to tell. Julieanna pledges her allegiance to material things. She advocates, as she explains, a 'taking the side of things'.[7] Drawing attention to care as an act of maintenance and repair, a set of connections is construed in that a caretaker not only sees to the needs of children, the ill, and the elderly, but also takes care of a building. Preston cites Virginia Held, who argues, 'care has the capacity to shape new *persons* with ever more advanced understandings of culture and society and morality and ever more advanced abilities to live well and cooperatively with others' (Held 2006: 32). Not just persons, Julieanna also reminds me of things, situations and where I am right now.

Finding ways to develop an ecological sensibility that attends to the horizontal relations between material humans and material things becomes a challenge. To recall the history of feminist practices, it is worthwhile looking more closely at what Donna Haraway has famously called 'situated knowledges', which is about celebrating diverse feminist formations of knowledge where a necessarily partial and fragmentary situation is acknowledged, but one still adequate to make a rich account of a world, at least in a local way (Haraway 1988). Between arguments concerning radical social constructivism, on the one hand, and sometimes over-reaching expressions of positivist science, on the other, Haraway stresses that it remains crucial to find adequate ways to make an account of the world, even if those accounts can only address the very immediate world of your close-at-hand experience. Now, while it might be easy to mistake this for a licence to produce autobiographical meanderings that get stuck on personalogical habits, 'situated knowledges' neither forward a subject-centred approach nor an opportunity to relate pre-packaged stories of your memories, your life, your travels, your dreams, your fantasies (Deleuze 1998b: 2).[8] Instead, your experience, situated for the time being only, constructs you and continues to do so as your field of action contracts and expands as a result of so many micro- and macro-encounters, stirred up amidst material and immaterial forces. It is also important to remember that the things around you do not depend on you to achieve their own significance, neither does this mean that the accounts you hope to offer are merely or only 'constructed', instead, it is a question of a 'radical multiplicity of local knowledges' (1988: 580), as Haraway puts it. In the encounters procured between the subject in formation and her seething environment-world, the power of feminist-situated knowledges emerges. Complementary to situated knowledges, 'situated learning' or rather 'situated material learning' offers yet another way of exploring feminist practices and what they have to offer amidst a multiplicity of ever-transforming local conditions.

Feminist practices, and what Haraway calls 'collective discourses' as exemplified in Julieanna's work, do not constitute a mere special interest group, but contribute to a 'earthwide network of connections, including the ability partially to translate knowledges among very different – and power-differentiated – communities' (1988: 580, 582). It is a question of deploying a feminist objectivity as partial vision, limited location, situated knowledge *and* material learning. The lesson to be learnt here is: A practice is never independent of its environment-world or milieu, and you do not know in advance what a practice can become; it is a matter of experiencing–experimenting.

Onflows, through-flows and things

In *Architecture from the Outside*, the feminist philosopher Elizabeth Grosz dedicates an essay to things, entitled, quite simply, 'The Thing' (2001). The name 'thing', she suggests, is only a recent incarnation among a series of terms, including 'the object, matter, substance, the world, noumena, reality, appearance, and so on' (167). Despite the history of representations of the thing, what needs to be stressed is that the thing has a life of its own, and its own history, and furthermore 'we need to accommodate things, more than they accommodate us … It is matter, the thing, that produces life; it is matter, the thing, which sustains and provides life with its biological organization and orientation; and it is matter, the thing, that requires life to overcome itself, to evolve, to become more' (168). Objects only come to be identified and catalogued afterwards; they are what we make of things and how we frame and attempt to tame a wild profusion of things. What is crucial here is the alignment of things with an emerging reconsideration of matter and processes of materialization, together with an insistence on the perpetual becoming of things. Even though we take up things and actively make objects of them, setting them in relation to ourselves as purportedly human subjects, especially in our attempts to make the world amenable to us and mean something to us, objects are framed out of the chaos of pre-objective assemblages, much as subjects or individuals only emerge fleetingly from pre-subjective or preindividual fields, layered over what can be called a plane of immanence, understood as something that binds, connects and renders things and thinkables possible (see Deleuze and Guattari 1994; Grosz 2017: 135–141; Simondon 1992).

Onflows and through-flows of things, that is to say 'openness, and heterogeneity, and liveliness' (Massey 2005: 19) amidst environment-worlds, assume various emphases: on becoming (Braidotti 1994; Grosz 1999, 2011; Massey 2005), on onflows of everyday life mixed up with maelstroms of affect (Thrift 2008), on vibrant matter and processes of materialization (Bennett 2010; Coole and Frost 2010) intermingling with the shimmering of affect (Seijworth and Gregg 2010), on feminist new materialism (Alaimo and Hekman 2009; Dolphijn and van der Tuin 2012), on material matters in architecture (Lloyd Thomas 2007), on architecture in the space of flows (Smith and Ballantyne 2011), on open dynamic systems in relation to space–time continuums entangled with processes of materialization *and* the incorporeal (Grosz 2017), including the emergence of subjects and objects erupting here and there amidst differentiated and differentiating environment-worlds. These affective becomings, these new conceptualizations and shifts of emphasis from one conceptual frame to the next, most of which maintain a strong desire to break down binary oppositions and be done with the fixed categories that organize the wild profusion of things, risk producing a kind of tedium, an exhaustion in the face of things that keep slipping away, thwarting our desire to grasp hold of them somewhere in the middle. Nevertheless, we must go on.

Attending this theoretical-cum-material momentum there arrives one theoretical, discursive, analytical turn after the next, a departure from the linguistic and the cultural turn towards a material and then a non-human turn, a shift from social and cultural constructivism to the acknowledgement of environmental forces and flows. There is even a swerve away from an emphasis on new materialism towards 'immaterialism' (Harman 2016) and the 'incorporeal' (Grosz 2017) – though caution must be issued immediately, because that is not at all to say that the thinkers concerned (Harman and Grosz) in any way share a project. A conceit attends the vertiginous effect of so many turns, a conceit which assumes that a theorist or a practitioner must use and then discard one theoretical tendency after the next, including each theoretical tendency's respective toolbox of concepts. With a tired yet persistent voice, the late Doreen Massey suggests that our arguments about openness risk being 'recited to the point of tedium' (2005: 33). A certain theory fatigue settles in. Nevertheless, the flow of voices by no means dries up; instead, it continues to proliferate. It is no wonder that attention momentarily alights on those who call for a return to objects as discrete and irreducible. It is unsurprising to read of the fatigue expressed by architectural theorists like David Gissen who situates his book *Subnatures* as an 'alternative to the emerging "vitalist" discourse on "flow" as the dominant effect of nature in architecture' (2009: 23). Vitalist flows of matter become all the more evident in the years following his publication, as is evident from the publication dates of many of the volumes cited earlier – vitalist flows that architects like Wiscombe, Gannon and Ruy bitterly complain about (2015).

Diana Coole and Samantha Frost's project makes an urgent call for a radical return to materialism, specifically because 'unprecedented things are currently being done with and to matter, nature, life, production and reproduction' (2010: 2). Without an engagement in materialism – and this is something Levi Bryant likewise stresses (2014) – we have no way of grappling with issues concerning climate change, environmental devastation and the material world that presses in on our daily lives and embodied practices: A vibrant material life that cannot be explained away. This includes a renewal of materialist feminisms. Towards this end, Coole and Frost include essays from important feminist thinkers such as Elizabeth Grosz, Sara Ahmed and Rosi Braidotti, the last often cited as one of the key signatories to this reorientation towards new materialism (Dolphijn and van der Tuin 2012). Likewise, Stacy Alaimo and Susan Hekman directly address the importance of thinking material feminisms in a book of the same name (2009). What is suggested in the turn towards materialism is the exhaustion of the linguistic paradigm, where explanatory models base themselves in textual practices and play, sometimes following a delirious discursive drift, or else calling on social and cultural constructivism. What Thrift, and Coole and Frost share is a desire to problematize forms of social and cultural constructivism and instead impress upon us an urgent political re-engagement with the politics of affect and new materialisms, respectively. Still, there is a risk that important processes of learning how to cope in a world are being too quickly discarded. Coole and Frost cautiously point out that a great deal has been learnt from social constructivism; it has provided researchers with valuable tools. Similar restraint can be recommended where a delicate attention to textuality remains beneficial, including the material expressions and entanglements of composing a text, such as the one I am laboriously working on now. Amidst a certain theory fatigue, how can we nonetheless be sustainable with our methods and concepts?

Zoë Sofoulis, in what she calls an 'ethic of reuse' (2009), asks, tongue in cheek, whether it is worth another turn through notions of constructivism. Although social constructivism now seems rather like a 'repetitive and unconvincing grumpy old woman' (Sofoulis 2009), on the verge of exhaustion, does that mean we need to entirely dispense with the lessons she has offered us? Sofoulis progresses from Karen Barad's concept of intra-action to Bruno Latour's ANT to do this work, reminding the reader that Latour's project commenced out of social constructivist research 'with non-humans included in the social domain, and society understood as a heterogeneous assemblage of humans, plants, animals, technologies, infrastructures, natural entities and contingent events' (Sofoulis 2009). Unlike Harman, Sofoulis does not see that Latour has done away with things, only re-oriented our modes of synthetic analysis. Latour attempts his own rescue operation of social constructivism in *Reassembling of the Social*, insisting that the social must be taken to mean all those things that gather and thereby form associations, the necessity of which cannot be determined in advance, all the while drawing attention to 'heterogeneous realities entering into the fabrication of some state of affairs' (2005b: 92). Latour issues warnings, though, about what we take to be material, arguing that we cannot place material processes and objects on the one side and social relations and human subjects on the other. He warns that we should be wary of distinguishing human action from material causality, which is to reinstate, yet again, a mind-and-body divide (Latour 2005b: 85). Instead, Latour requires an extended sense of matter and material objects, which should be understood in association with each other and embedded in the midst of a situated gathering (2005b: 194). Sofoulis explains that 'the idea of "social construction" can be unfolded to encompass a more complex set of processes, and a more diverse set of actors and practices, than sociologists and cultural researchers conventionally consider' (2009: 46). Sofoulis, like Latour, aims to rescue the useful lessons of constructivism and offers an opening to thinking of constructivism as much like building construction, procuring 'intentional processes of design, planning, coordinating, assembling and finishing' with the proviso that there is no master builder, that intentions are delimited, and more usually de-coupled from artefacts and things (2009). She offers an adapted concept, 'co-construction', and aligns this with co-evolution and a shaping of things and relations over time, suggesting an iterative process of interactions between humans and non-humans.

When we hesitate in awe before an apprehension of a human and non-human traffic in things, including what has come to be called the Internet of Things, what we bear witness to are 'logistical worlds'. These are often worlds in which human actors play increasingly marginal roles. As Ned Rossiter explains: 'Infrastructure provides an underlying system of elements, categories, standards, protocols, and operations that, as many note, are only revealed in its moment of failure and breakdown. Logistical media stitch these various components into a relation that makes the world' (2016: 5). He goes on to ask: 'But where, exactly, is the infrastructure that makes these planetary-scale economies, biopolitical regimes, and social lives possible? We see or become aware of infrastructure only when it no longer works' (5), which is yet another take on the tool as a systemic technology writ large, an infrastructural conglomeration oscillating between being ready-to-hand and present-at-hand.

Sofoulis's specific infrastructural problem in which she situates her concepts concerns water utility networks, water being a big issue in a dry continent like Australia where she lives and works. Where Bennett talks about the electricity grid, Sofoulis speaks about water and explains how we (human actors) are shaped by technologies and infrastructures as well as by our fellow creatures and how 'we, our technologies and infrastructures need to co-evolve into different configurations in order to mitigate climate change and other forms of environmental instability' (2009: 90). Her story of co-construction of water–human infrastructural assemblages is one that demonstrates how the complex network of water infrastructure needs to be engaged, and that the 'purification' (Latour's term) of human habits of water consumption from technical systems means that, where one part of the 'network' is attended to, another will end up failing. A co-constructive or co-evolutionary model instead negotiates changes in the technical specifications of water systems at the same time as aiming to shift consumer norms. Critical invention, experimentation and reconstruction suggest other strategies for the human and non-human players in the field of water management with the aim of making a world a little more liveable.

Part Two of this book, which has been dedicated to things, has been an exercise in gleaning, picking up references here and there with a focus on urgent contemporary discourses and their intersections with creative practices. More could have been said about Appadurai's social life of things (1986, 2006), or a return to architect and theorist Stan Allen's influential essay 'From Object to Field' (1998) might have been discussed so as to foreground the importance of field conditions and background the presumed objecthood of architecture, or an account of Lucy Lippard's dematerialization of the art object (1997) and the subsequent return to a fascination of objects in art theory and practice might have been discussed (Hudek 2014). The theoretical ball might have been passed through a series of different players' hands, and a somewhat different game might have been played. Or rather, to mix my mobile metaphors, what I hope is that I have left things behind that might be gleaned by other thinkers and practitioners, for what a sad state of affairs would remain if more work could not be done, with our heads turned towards the ground that we cover.

I conclude in the section that follows amidst a jumble of mute things, in a storehouse of obsolescent furnishings, with the hope that we might reanimate our relations with things; and so I make a plea for things, however slippery, and their relations and non-relations towards a participation in more sustainable architectural ecologies, addressed across the three ecosophical registers: subjective, social and environmental.

Exhaustion: of things

> Fallen pieces, waste, wreckage, jagged bits, remains,
> inner organs of slaughtered beasts, shreds, filth, and excrement,
> on which contemporary art – *trash art* – gorges itself
> Jean-Luc Nancy, *The Sense of the World* (1997: 132).

D. H. Lawrence tells a short story entitled *Things*, about a young couple and their accumulation of many precious things. Their things seem to promise a means to punctuate and register the otherwise ungraspable passage of time as they inexorably age, reifying significant events and the different places they have visited. The Melvilles, who are first presented by Lawrence as youthful, idealistic and engaged in alternative belief systems, specifically Buddhism, depart the new world for the old, leaving behind North America to sail for Europe in search of something authentic. At first their shared life is relatively unfettered by things, but then they grow attached to certain domestic artefacts, which collect the weight of significance like so much dust, and which slow them down: 'Oh, they had been picking things up since the first day they landed in Europe. And they were still at it' (Lawrence 1987: 169). *Things*, set during the opening decades of the twentieth century, is a morality tale that attends to new expressions of modernity where previously unimaginable forms of life, novel subjectivities and globalized trajectories of mobilization and consumption were becoming increasingly available, at least to industrialized and educated Westerners.

The idealistic Mr and Mrs Melville are in pursuit of what they have very vaguely, and in a rather abstract fashion denominated 'freedom' and 'beauty' (Lawrence 1987: 165). Along the way they collect some things: *objets d'art*, knick-knacks, eclectic items of furniture, a 'Bologna cupboard', a Venetian bookcase', 'Sienna curtains and bronzes'. They arrange all their 'things' in one apartment after another, now in France, now in Italy, dwellings that provide a suitable backdrop or setting for their collected things, all of which are suffused with meaning. Having finally decided that they have exhausted Europe, they return to America loaded down now with all their things. Where in their youth the Melvilles imagine that the beauty of things will secure their liberation, by increments they instead become entrapped as things solidify around them, weighing them down.

Lawrence's morality tale shows us a couple entrapped by their things, and reduced to limited subjectivities that in some ways become indiscernible from the inanimate objects they have collected. The Melvilles gloat over the rarity of their things: silk curtains that remind Mrs Melville of Chartres and Mr Melville's sixteenth-century Venetian bookshelf displaying a choice selection of books less for erudition than to impress visitors. These things after which the Melvilles avidly hunt separate them out from their everyday and singular existences and close off their possible affective relations and becomings-with in a local environment-world. As Michel Foucault argues, '*Homo oeconomicus* is not the human being who represents his own needs to himself, and the objects capable of satisfying them; he is the human being who spends, wears out, and wastes his life in evading the imminence of death' (Foucault 1970: 257). Their pursuit of things is as exhausting as it is exhaustive, causing them to race around in circles in search of something that is not of this world: 'But like images the things no longer form anything but a sequence of intensive states, a ladder or a circuit for intensities, that one can make race around in one sense or another, from high to low, or from low to high' (Deleuze and Guattari 1986: 21–22).

The Melvilles know the power of atmospheres of affect well, but also the precariousness of the power relations that participate in the circulation of affects. They curate their architectural interiors to maximum effect, arousing affects that produce emotions of envy, desire and delight in their visitors. When the visitors leave, something curious occurs, 'the halo dies from around the furniture, and the things became things, lumps of matter that stood or hung there, ad infinitum, and said nothing: and Valerie and Erasmus almost hated them' (Lawrence 1987: 170). The Melvilles produce an atmosphere of affect within their cold rented Palazzo in Venice, but in the absence of visitors, life drains out of things, and matter returns to muteness, and a post or pre-human, or more-than-human landscape can be fleetingly witnessed persisting despite them.

On their return to the United States, their economic situation is much diminished. The Melvilles discover that they do not have enough money for the lease of a sufficiently voluminous residence in which to curate an arrangement of their things; instead they are obliged to store their worldly possessions in a warehouse for fifty dollars a month. Their avarice, the way Valerie Melville 'burns' for her things, produces an after-image that fast forwards us into an everyday life of things enjoyed today. Their avid dedication to things anticipates the astonishing speed and volume of the circulation of goods we currently witness, facilitated by an Internet of Things and a global infrastructure of warehouses through which a seemingly inexhaustible supply of objects passes, Global Positioning System-tracked through every micro-moment of their travel. As Rossiter explains, tirelessly generating data from the movement of peoples and things, 'The Internet of Things (IoT) integrates ubiquitous computing within urban settings, producing a city of calculation and measure' (2016: 54).

By the conclusion of the tale Mr Melville must take measure of his life and his dwindling means. He must resort to giving up his freedom and his beautiful life to take up a teaching position at Cleveland University. Yes, he will be obliged to work for his living, but now all their things could be unpacked and arranged in a modern 'up-to-date' little house on the university campus. Extracted from their cultural context, the cupboards, book shelves, curtains and side tables all look 'perfectly out of keeping' (Lawrence 1987: 175). Yet this stark contrast between the spoils of the old world and the interior styling of the new provides an apt backdrop when the gawking guests arrive and the Melvilles can commence their performance of regaling them with their European experience. Furthermore, the local landscape features the impressive furnace stacks of industry as distinct from the old spires of cathedrals.

Mr Melville feels trapped now, like a rat in its cage, but at least he feels safe, he reflects to himself. Through the final pages of the story he takes on the sinister demeanour of a rat watching over his life and his things with selfish anxiety (Lawrence 1987: 173–175). This metamorphosis suggests that the accumulation of things not only represents how we hope to be perceived, but threatens to transform us in disturbing ways; and the moral of this tale would appear to be that 'things' entrance us only to become a burden that imprisons us. Yet equally as interesting as the environmental transformation of subjectivity is the journey that is taken through this series of encounters with things, places and ideas.

Lawrence's tale concatenates near-exhaustive combinatorials of things, places and ideas, of 'any-thing-whatever'. The furniture and the knick-knacks, the place names such as Paris, France, Venice, Italy and even California, compose long inventories of things and locales that are accompanied by a series of 'ideals', such as freedom (to live one's life as one wishes), and beauty. As Lawrence points out, while the Melvilles' ideals were lofty, their passions moved according to another axis, 'the lives of the idealists had been running with fierce swiftness horizontally' (1987: 169). The onflows and through-flows of things gather, accumulate and coagulate, and finally the Melvilles realize that they have succeeded in exhausting the possible by 'forming an exhaustive series of things' (Deleuze 1998a: 161).

Notes

1 I have previously discussed Julieanna Preston's work across a series of essays, including: 'Introduction: Following the Material, or Materially Situated Learning', in *Performing Matter: Interior Surface and Feminist Actions*, edited by Julieanna Preston (Baunach, Germany: AADR (Art Architecture Design Research) Spurbuchverlag, 2014); 'Five Lessons in a Ficto-Critical Approach to Design Practice Research', in *Drawing-On: Journal of Architectural Research By Design*, Edinburgh, 2015, http://drawingon.org; Hélène Frichot, *How to Make Yourself a Feminist Design Power Tool* (Baunach, Germany: AADR (Art Architecture Design Research) Spurbuchverlag, 2016). We have also collaborated on performative papers, such as 'Tabling Femininities: Two (or more) voices on Still Life', *Writing Place: conference on literary methods in architectural research and design*, Faculty of Architecture TU Delft, 25–27 November 2013, and we have further collaborated with Katja Grillner on the essay 'Writing around the Kitchen Table: Feminist Practices in Architecture-Writing' in *Feminist Futures of Spatial Practice*, edited by Meike Schalk, Thérèse Kristiansson and Ramia Mazé (Baunach, Germany: AADR, 2017).

2 See the following collections, all of which discuss the rise of 'new materialism': Diana Coole and Samantha Frost, eds, *New Materialisms:*

Ontology, Agency and Politics (Durham and London: Duke University Press, 2010); Katie Lloyd Thomas, ed., *Material Matters: Architecture and Material Practice* (London: Routledge, 2007); Rick Dolphijn and Iris van der Tuin, eds, *New Materialism: Interviews and Cartographies* (Ann Arbor: Open Humanities Press, 2012). See also Jane Bennett, *Vibrant Matter: A Political Ecology of Things* (Durham and London: Duke University Press, 2010).

3   Lebovici offers an account of how women have taken up their own bodies in art practice as a means of manifesting female agency through practices of embodiment. See Elizabeth Lebovici, 'This is not my Body', in *Spheres of Action: Art and Politics*, edited by Éric Alliez and Peter Osborne (London: Tate Publishing, 2013), 65–77.

4   Julieanna Preston, *Moving Stuff*, Auckland, New Zealand (2013). http://www.julieannapreston.space/#/moving-stuff-2013

5   See Gunnar Sandin, 'Modes of Transgression in Institutional Critique', in *Transgression: Towards an Expanded Field of Architecture, AHRA Critiques: Critical Studies in Architectural Humanities*, edited by Louis Rice and David Littlefield (Abingdon Oxon and New York: Routledge, 2015).

6   See Julieanna Preston's works *SHEET GOODS*, 2008–2010, discussed in Chapter 2: The Yield Principle, an antigen to rigor mortis. Preston, *Performing Matter*.

7   Julieanna Preston, Lecture, Regensburg, Germany, 2017.

8   In 'Literature and Life', Gilles Deleuze insists: 'To write is not to recount one's memories and travels, one's loves and griefs, one's dreams and fantasies', instead to write is about following the power of the impersonal, whereupon all these acquisitive, personal and possessive qualities take flight.

PART THREE

Thinkables

5

Noology

How do we arrive at what I have called thinkables, having travelled through these concept-situations of environment-worlds and things? You might want to hesitate and ask: Who are you to tell me how to think anyway? Philosophical training offers neither universal licence nor the right to claim that I am the privileged thinker. There is no guarantee that we can begin with the Cartesian assertion, the famous cogito: I think therefore I am. Because, in any case, the two statements simply reveal a chasm, as thinking and being express themselves out of step, operating disjunctively. In any case, as Deleuze and Guattari argue, no one needs a philosopher to think, reflect and contemplate for them, and especially not on their behalf (1994). Instead, when it comes to the activity of thinking, during those rare moments when it takes us out of the habitual circuits of common and good sense, thinking turns out to be profoundly creative. Shocking us, startling us out of our comfort zones, even allowing us to entertain a becoming-imperceptible with our local environment-worlds by thinking-with.

Story three: Zoë Sofia (Sofoulis) – unthinkables

In the spring of 2000, nearly eighteen years ago now, an essay appeared in the feminist journal *Hypatia* called 'Container Technologies', addressing the spectre of resourcelessness and figuring facilitative environments as mixed compositions of complex infrastructures and increasingly scarce resources, for instance, water. *Hypatia* is a journal dedicated to feminist theory, named in acknowledgement of the Alexandrian mathematician and philosopher infamously murdered by a Christian mob for her atheism. The name of the article's author was given as Zoë Sofia, though this turned out to be a pseudonym, in part born from a father's disapproval of some of the author's research themes and provocative essay titles. Where Zoë means life, Sofia means wisdom, which when conjoined with philo (*philo-sophia*) describes the philosophical love of wisdom. Zoë Sofia, aka Sofoulis, is an Australian academic – retired now – who undertook her doctoral research in the History of Consciousness program at the University of California, Santa Cruz, with Donna Haraway as her adviser. Haraway, it should be noted, cites Sofia (Sofoulis) when she constructs her argument for situated knowledges, specifically where Haraway challenges the conceit of an all-seeing masculinist objectivity, warning that 'vision in this technological feast becomes unregulated gluttony' (1988: 581), thereby drawing a direct connection between exclusive knowledge practices and habits of overconsumption that threaten a world. A young woman at the time, in 1980, Sofoulis travelled the great distance from Perth, Western Australia (the most geographically isolated city on the planet), to Santa Cruz, California, funded by a Fulbright Scholarship, and further supported by an Australian Caltex grant. Caltex is a petroleum brand, and the irony of using grant money from this company to speculate on extinction and the 'two-faced character of modern technology' (Sofia 1984: 48) must have surely aroused a wry smile at the time. In her early 1984 essay 'Exterminating Fetuses: Abortion, Disarmament and the Sexo-Semiotics of Extraterrestrialism', Sofia critically addresses the threat of extinction, writing: 'The unthinkable has never been innocently unthought' (47), going on to argue that extinction, the unthinkable, is an issue that has been displaced onto other concerns and symbols, for instance, pro-life anti-abortion debates. The non-innocent unthinking of the unthinkable is the means by which present and looming crises are pushed into the background of our considerations, she argues.

Extinction is a theme that Claire Colebrook, another Australian thinker, has subsequently picked up, and it is interesting to note that in putting forward what she calls 'extinct theory', Colebrook cites an essay by Jacques Derrida that appears in the same issue of *Diacritics* as Sofia's provocatively titled early article. Colebrook likewise takes up the unthinkable by speculating on theory beyond *theoria*, asking: 'How would theory confront the absence of theoria: "life" without the human look? Life without praxis, life without meaningful action, life without production or labour: such would be theory after theory, or theory that opened itself to the thought of extinction' (Colebrook 2014a: 38). Who are the thinkers who have assisted us to think the unthinkable? Today they can be named, and include (feminist) philosophers of science Donna Haraway and Isabelle Stengers, to which I would add Zoë Sofoulis and a chorus of thinkers helping us to confront how to maintain arts of living on a damaged planet, as Anna Tsing and her co-editors describe the task before us.

We suffer erasures, sublimations, displacements and a generalized forgetfulness, as we get on with being 'busy people' (Kierkegaard), crazy-busy, exhausted people. It is a complaint too often heard within and beyond institutional settings – a displacement, a forgetting, as I have argued in Part One of this book, that is persistent and insidious. We continue to forget the environmental crises and climate events in which we all the while find ourselves, some of us more vulnerable than others. We imagine we stand outside a situation, on safe ground, despite bearing witness to sophisticated animated graphics demonstrating the likely inundation of coastal cities and settlements due to global warming, and rising sea levels, and storms, political as well as those of wild winds and rains, coming our way.

As will have become clear by now, the three stories that I use to help me enter the three parts of the book have been dedicated to older women and the trails they blaze in order to show other ways into uncertain futures, other possibilities for those who feel their voices have been marginalized or even oppressed. There is, of course, the risk that these stories veer into a kind of hagiography, upholding certain thinkers and practitioners as something like secular saints. What I intend is simply an acknowledgement of those who have helped us to think differently, those who may have helped us to be sufficiently sensitive to a shock to thought when it comes our way. This requires that readers must propose where their own debts are owed, debts they are happy to acknowledge in relation to their own precursors. Rather than merely offering commentary, somewhere between construction and destruction, it may also be possible to 'restore an incommunicable novelty to our predecessors' (Deleuze and Guattari 1994: 204).

It is Sofia's essay 'Container Technologies' (2000) to which I find myself returning again and again, especially today as we witness its coming of age. Sofia undertakes a reorientation of thinking around technology that is invaluable. Like her mentor Haraway, Sofia's approach to technology embraces neither technophobia nor technophilia, but accepts our profound imbrication amidst simple and complex technologies, from tools to apparatuses to complex communication infrastructures. Well in advance of the recent wave of (feminist) new materialisms, Sofia argues for a take on spatialized matter that refuses its inert qualities and its attribution to the feminine where the feminine is assumed to be passive, a mere receptacle through which life passes. Where we habitually associate technology with projectile force, with speed, noise and smooth machined forms, Sofia draws our attention to the container, the bowl, the humble jar and the woven basket, arguing that without these technologies of containment, *Homo sapiens* could hardly have settled down into the sedentary existences we hold so dear today, cossetted as we are by our dressed interiors and our favourite knick-knacks, at least for those privileged ones who are so fortunate. The storage rendered possible through container technologies means that subsistence modes of survival could be displaced by the safe-keeping, even the hoarding, of supplies.

Sofia's focus is on facilitating environments and their capacity to support containment and supply, or what she calls re-sourcing. She argues that: 'Artifacts for containment and supply are not only readily interpreted as metaphorically feminine, they are also historically associated with women's traditional labors' (Sofia 2000: 182). Here we might recall the way Agnès Varda's rural gleaners swept up their skirts and aprons, turning them into flexible cloth containers for the collection of food stuffs. Drawing on Lewis Mumford, Sofia points out that container technologies form a series of things, from utensils such as pots and baskets to apparatuses such as dying vats and kilns, to utilities and infrastructures such as reservoirs, aqueducts and buildings (186). The container, usually neglected in histories of technology, is a 'structurally necessary but frequently unacknowledged precondition of becoming' (188). No doubt architects should be paying special heed here, because the buildings we construct are likewise a container technology of a special kind that shelters the human creature, as a 'body-holding' technology.

Sofia also draws on Gregory Bateson's organism–environment ensemble, pointing out that 'the environment itself is a bearer of intelligence' (182). This intelligence follows the whole series of forms of containment, and once Sofia arrives at her conclusion she places us with her in the domestic space of her kitchen to argue her point. She brings us home with her. A simple survey will suffice, she argues. Just look around and take in the forms of containment that shelter you, that supply you with sustenance: 'so many containers for channeling dynamic flows and ensuring supply, unobtrusively linking this domicile to vast grids of energetic and institutional power (as long as I keep paying the bills)' (190).

The unthinkable that must all the while be thought is the impossibility of extracting our human embodied selves from such intricately woven latticeworks of containment and supply. Whether or not we hesitate to speculate on an unthinkable world that leaves behind the embroilments of human life, language and labour, will no doubt impact on what we do about our practices today. If we feel we have no choice but to give up when faced with the unthinkable, on confronting the wholesale exhaustion of our material and mental resources, then surely this lack of belief in the slim possibilities of our local environment-worlds can only mean the destruction of what ecologies of creative practices we have left to us. Instead, surely, it is necessary to find some way to continue from amidst our worldly exhaustions.

Thinkables

> We live with a particular image of thought, that is to say, before we begin to think, we have a vague idea of what it means to think, its means and ends.
> Gilles Deleuze, *Desert Islands and Other Texts 1953–1974* (2002a: 139)

There is a great deal that constrains thinking, making the encounter with what I call a 'thinkable' extremely rare. The thinkable is that which erupts out of the unthinkable. What do we engage in, what do we do when we encounter a thought? Do we encounter a thought as a violent excitation to the system, or as a slow pleasurable swoon? Isabelle Stengers argues that we are suffering a disaster of thought, and it is this that has contributed to the exhaustion of our environment-worlds today. Bad habits, in thought and in practice, are hard to shake. In the news media and across Web 2.0 feeds, plugged-in readers bear witness to the plague of 'alternative facts' and 'fake news'; readers become prey to misinformation. As Bruno Latour has pointed out, if fundamental extremists are deconstructing facts according to a well-exercised logic of social constructivism, in effect redeploying the arguments of critical thinkers, what are we to do (Latour 2004: 227)? How do we disentangle an assertive matter of fact from an ideological miasma in order to gather around our cares and concerns? Can we fight critique with yet more critique? If so, how might we better hone our critical concept-tools? The job of criticism has been to challenge the myth of a stable ground, but this thought becomes a weapon that can be trained towards the most dangerous ends. At the same time, we cannot reserve thinking for the initiated or those with higher degrees and special qualifications. We should be extremely wary of any claim that critical thinking should be reserved for the 'guardians' of knowledge alone.

Deleuze and Guattari tell us what we already know so well: 'we constantly lose our ideas. That is why we want to hang onto fixed opinions so much. We ask only that our ideas are linked according to a minimum of constant rules' (1994: 201). We can also assume that there would not be this minimum order in ideas if there were not some semblance of order in things and states of affairs. It is a significant challenge, which could be described as: 'how to create a structure of life that is not an apparatus of life' (Pelbart 2015: 18–19). We need some minimal rules lest thinking fly off in all directions, we need somehow to make thinkables sufficiently durable in relation to our concrete problems; but we also need to maintain a critical awareness lest thinkables become the kinds of universal concepts that impose themselves as dogma. At the time of writing, I am happy to report that rousing thinkers, like Rosi Braidotti with her newly launched series simply called *Theory*, are arguing again for the benefits of practicing critical theory exactly in the face of a content exhausted world, even as a necessary means of coping with an excess of access to information. She claims that, 'the vitality of critical thinking in the world today is palpable, as is a spirit of insurgency that sustains it' (2017: xiv–xv).[1]

This third part of the book will travel through a series of concepts, again concatenated as something of an incremental series, from noology to noopolitics to noourbanography, via a discussion of the Image of Thought, and thence onto thinkables, and finally concept-tools. Two practice scenes will be presented, and Part Three will conclude with a reflection on the exhaustion of concepts.

Noology

Noology is a concept that names the logic of mind (noo; Gr. *nous*),[2] but without getting caught up in a philosophy of mind, two things need to be kept in mind when it comes to noology: That mind is necessarily embodied and thereby situated, somewhere, sometime, but at the same time it is distributed and interconnected, producing something of a collective intelligence, or else, a collective stupidity, as the case may be. 'Nous,' for those with an Anglophone heritage, is another word for common sense, which will become relevant later when I discuss the postulates and theses associated with the Image of Thought, where noology is captured and stabilized creating normative frames of reference and habits of thought, the result of which is often poorly posed problems. Where maintaining its mobility and capacity for change, the *nous* of noology, the logic of mind, comes to operate across concrete problematic fields, in situ, where you are right now, that is to say, immanently. Common sense, where it best practises its know-how, can work for or against us.

The special object of noology, Deleuze and Guattari explain, is the Image of Thought, which covers and controls all of thought (1987: 374). Today, it would be pertinent to propose that noology leads us to a contemporary Image of Thought that captures a global situation of information and communication overload and exhaustion, a near-complete saturation amidst a global environmental milieu in which well over 50 per cent of the world's population inhabits urban contexts of increasing density. Yet, at the same time as achieving greater material proximity, we are more likely than not to communicate remotely, so that a curious situation of proximal distance is procured, what Peter Sloterdijk has called ego-spherical 'co-isolation' (2007b) and what Lieven De Cauter has identified as our capsular civilization, where 'people seem to have given up on the street, on the world outside' (2004: 16). Noology registers a logic of thinking that materializes in both affirmative socio-political relations and oppressive ones, depending on the practices of thought rendered material in everyday spaces. Where noology as a logic of a thinking embodied *and* distributed mind, singular *and* collective, is ever at risk of being overdetermined by an Image of Thought, noopolitics pertains to the capacity, so easily abused, of the collaboration of minds working together, whether wittingly or not, across a local context plugged into a global network. If we can assume that noopolitics plays out by producing local environmental effects, then something like a noourbanography suggests ways of mapping the material and spatial impacts of how populations think together. We are by now familiar with geopolitical tales of how our collectively produced data are sold by service providers to government organizations, boosting global surveillance programs (Savage and Mazzetti 2013), and more recently how false accounts on sites like Twitter have purportedly contributed to the outcome of what were meant to be democratic election processes.

Noology, following Deleuze and Guattari, can be defined as distinct from 'ideology', and from 'phenomenology', because it neither assumes an external thought imposed upon a subject (ideology) nor a stable consciousness that thinks (phenomenology); it comes neither from without nor within, neither from object nor subject (1987: 376; Colebrook 2005). Instead, noology tracks what stirs on the level of the pre-subjective or pre-objective, and in this way can also be related to discussions concerning pre-personal 'affect' and 'percept'. Rather than percepts belonging to perceiving subjects, and affects belonging to affected or affecting subjects, there is first a slow or more rapid arousal of subjective capacities. In his seminal essay 'The Autonomy of Affect', Brian Massumi argues how the emergence of affect follows trajectories that cannot be anticipated in advance. Melissa Gregg and Gregory Seijworth speak of affect in terms of variations, passages, intensities, resonances, accretions of force relations and happenings taking place *beside* and *in-between*, but never belonging to subjects or objects (2010). Quasi-subjects exchanging places with quasi-objects instead pass into and out of existence, pausing momentarily in more or less stable compositions. This mobility of affects and percepts, their varying speeds and slownesses, and how they coagulate amidst what we habitually call subjects and objects, is indicative of the utter permeability of processes of subjectivation in terms of how influences are enfolded, and actions unfolded into local environment-worlds – hence the great importance of grasping hold, as far as possible, of local occasions of noological expression, and of telling a story in terms of its local impact.

On the one hand, noology shows that such a thing as a counter-thought can enable an escape from a dogmatic Image of Thought. On the other hand, noology gets tied up with the concrete, empirical situation of a noopolitics, and the insistence of a contemporary Image of Thought from which it is extremely difficult to escape. Most often it would appear that the Image of Thought is that which must be destroyed, exactly so as to liberate a counter-thought, but sometimes it could be that constructing new images and contributing to an alternative Image of Thought may prove beneficial. One way or another, and as Deleuze and Guattari stress, 'the less people take thought seriously, the more they think in conformity with what the State wants' (1987: 376). State here might be replaced with the name of a multinational corporation, Google, or Facebook, or else, the name of a multinational bank, or a successful advertising agency, where marketing executives have taken over the task of constructing 'concepts'.

To counter an Image of Thought there is the violence of 'counter thoughts', arriving from outside thought, that is, a thought from an outside understood as generative chaos. Order and chaos, as Isabelle Stengers and Ilya Prigogine have argued, are co-present and co-productive: 'The natural contains essential elements of randomness and irreversibility. This leads to a new view of matter in which matter is no longer the passive substance described in the mechanistic world view but is associated with spontaneous activity' (Prigogine and Stengers 1984: 9). Out of chaos order emerges, and back into chaos ordered structures plunge again. It is important not to mistake chaos for complete disorder. As Deleuze and Guattari elaborate, 'chaos is characterized less by the absence of determinations than by the infinite speed with which they take shape and vanish' (1994: 42). Across whatever this outside of thought is, which Deleuze and Guattari call chaos, contours take shape marking out regions of consistency that different disciplines subsequently claim and territorialize.

In all likelihood, right now you are in the midst of either thinking alone or with others, and most likely you are thinking through complex means of technological augmentation, including laptops and tablets, smartphones, and do not forget your more basic technologies of pencil, paper, table and eye glasses. In all probability you are keen to keep chaos, and anything that threatens to disorder the required rectitude of thought, at bay. You will find that usually something has drawn you, alone or collectively, into the orbit of some matter of concern, around which you are likely to gather with others in order to discuss some problem, some crisis, and this matter of concern or care around which you gather in turn procures a noopolitics. In noology we have an operational logic of thought, and an expanded definition of mind and brain, and in noopolitics there are the social and political implications of how noology manifests amidst different concrete occasions, mixing peoples, places, things and political events.

Noopolitics

Complex relationships of image and text together procure noopolitical effects by way of a meta-Image, that is, the Image of Thought. The establishment of an Image of Thought can be mapped according to a diagram of power, designating a tremulous site of battle that pertains to language, labour and life (Foucault 1970); how life is defined and how it continues to transform in societies of control where noopolitics and biopolitics are intimately intertwined (Hauptman and Neidich 2010; Lazzarato 2006). If you want to understand what a society of control is, simply consider all the devices and social media channels you plug into every day, and how they offer you feedback on your mood while telling you what you might like to buy; how far apps such as Twitter have become political devices; how data is corralled and sold off and how hacking shifts the board game of political power. These days noology, where it becomes fixed in place as a dogmatic Image of Thought, might just be a fancy name for the collation, at the scale of populations, of Big Data, a treasure trove of images and ideas and their circulation.

Returning briefly to Deleuze on exhaustion, what he calls *Language I*, the first level of the methodology of exhaustion, operates according to serial combinatorials of images, concepts, things and anything whatsoever – those things, locales and grand ideas collected by the Melvilles, for instance. At this level of exhaustion, that which comes to be collected in concatenating series belongs to a shadowy domain of inadequate sensations and ideas where one thing after another is collected before sense can secure some direction forward. What we have is a merely additive, asignifying process, that relies minimally on vague notions of resemblance, on occasions of contiguity, on the simple sequence of one image after the next. As Deleuze has stressed, no preference is expressed whatsoever, nor any inclination; any choice is as good as any other, until we arrive at a point of exhaustion wherein we discover, after all, that we have no choice at all. This begins to sound very much like consumption for the sake of rampant consumption expressed, for instance, in such events as Black Friday and Cyber Monday, forms of collective, mass consumption. The Image of Thought and its own method of exhaustion speaks volumes for the neo-liberal capitalist market place of images, concepts and things and the logic of accumulation for the sake of surplus.

A great deal of labour must be invested in the amassing of such vapid combinatorials. 'Immaterial' or 'cognitive' labour, as Maurizio Lazzarato explains, is that labour which produces the informational and cultural content of a commodity, and which is dedicated to fixing aesthetic norms, tastes, fashions, consumer norms and thence opinion (1996: 133). This describes the contemporary situation in which architectural images are circulated, received and consumed, following much the same circuits as advertising imagery, increasingly populating our Web 2.0 online platforms. Emerging networks of information and communication generate new logics of representation-at-a-distance that operate as noopolitical apparatuses of capture. While the idea of a collaboration of minds (and their collectivized images) might seem a powerful and even a politically emancipatory one, the risk is that our brainpower comes to be resourced so as to better track, map and analyse consumer demand in order to stimulate ever greater demand, not to mention more nefarious ends within what has come to be called our societies of control (Deleuze 1995b). Such imagery populates our existential territories as we, in turn, become increasingly sophisticated and adept in our image literacy, but what cannot be underestimated is the power of the circulation of affect produced through imagery, and its resultant politics. The affective atmospheres procured by way of both architectural and advertising imagery contribute to a 'noopolitics' that results in the insatiable overconsumption of our local and global environment-worlds.

Noourbanography

If noology informs the taking place of a noopolitics, and noopolitics is always situated in some space, time or place, this means that something like noourbanography can become a useful methodology when it comes to surveying the impact of collective thinking on an urban scale.[3] 'Noology is the study of images of thought and their historicity,' Deleuze and Guattari explain (1987: 376), which in turn suggests powerful political implications pertaining to the way we construct worlds. As Claire Colebrook argues, 'noology assumes that if images of thought can be created, they can always be recreated, with the ideal of liberation from some proper image of thought' (2005: 193–194), which further suggests that with enough effort, a more positive way of thinking can impact on the material admixtures of local environment-worlds. Noourbanography offers the possibility of mapping and diagramming the impact of thinking, together and apart, and the spatial and material power relations of how modes of thought procure real material effects. This requires discovering the means to map mood at the scale of an urban context, and how a taste for certain ways of curating one's environment-world takes hold across a populace.

Deborah Hauptman uses another term to describe the taking place of noopolitics, and that is the noosensorium, where sensation, affect, perception, memory and experience affect space and emerging temporalities too (Hauptman and Neidich 2010: 29). Likewise, Jussi Parikka, reading N. Katherine Hayles and Nigel Thrift, draws attention to how a technological unconscious or non-conscious contributes to a 'massive conditioning of gestures, perceptions, memory, and other human characteristics in software embedded environments' (2013). This conditioning can take place at a distance, as Lazzarato argues, citing Gabriel Tarde. With the emergence of the newspaper, a public is produced, one that has substantially metamorphosed today, but what is shared nevertheless is how 'the influence of minds [esprit] on one another has become action at a distance' (Hauptman and Niedich 2010: 12; Tarde cited in Lazzarato 2006: 179). Information travels at greater speeds, producing more immediate impacts; this can lead to either the election of questionable political representatives or the generalized condemnation of predatory sexual behaviour. Hauptman and Neidich stress that, 'architecture and urbanism inhabit the same spaces and temporalities that characterize these new modes and relations; their presence also possesses the potential to bend and contort the very systems in which they operate' (2010: 12).

When it comes to collective intelligence, supported through the ubiquity of computational means, this is something designers have a vested interest in as they search for positive applications. Christopher Hight and Chris Perry emphasize the potential of collective intelligence facilitated across new communication technology platforms and relate this potential to Michael Hardt and Antonio Negri's notion of the 'multitude' as an activated, collective political body. At the same time, Hight and Perry acknowledge that, '[s]ocial relations shape machines as much as machines or new forms of technology shape social relations' (2006: 9). Since the time of their writing, the sophistication of communication technology platforms has become all the more honed and, given this affective reciprocity, the activated political body can be encouraged to swerve across the political spectrum in unexpected ways. In their edited collection *Cognitive Architecture*, Hauptman and Neidich remain more wary, but likewise draw attention to the powers exerted over the 'life of the mind, including perception, attention, and memory' in our communication and information age (2010: 11). Of course, it becomes risky to make sweeping statements, because what needs to be mapped are specific instances where collective intelligence and cognitive architectures play out, creating liberatory or oppressive situations, including some, excluding others.

One simple noourbanographical test I have undertaken with my colleague Helen Runting involved an image survey of the Swedish real-estate site and app Hemnet.se, a site that purports to have 2.6 million viewers a week in a country of just under 10 million.[4] Having surveyed images in an informal way over many months across real-estate apps and in the real-estate pages of local newspapers, Helen sat down to the task of reducing her survey to one sample set, confined to the rapidly gentrifying inner Stockholm island of Södermalm. She studied 132 apartments available for purchase on a given day, and discovered that the primary advertising image depicted a preponderance of white, white walls, furniture, designer features (49 per cent), and that supplementary images were also dominantly white (52 per cent). In our co-written essay she explains: 'Of the images that do not show totally white walls, in 26% of cases this is the result of a wall or section of wall covered with patterned wallpaper, and in a further 22% photographs deviate from "all white" because of a grey wall (or walls). Exposed brick and then marble (mainly in bathrooms) made up the majority of remaining deviations' (Runting and Frichot 2016: 234–235).[5] White, we have argued in this essay and elsewhere, achieves a number of things: Primary among them is the interchangeability of the spatial commodity that is the Stockholm apartment, contributing to the imposition of an increasingly homogenized taste regime that impacts on neighbourhoods in so far as such marketing strategies assist in pushing up the prices of apartments at a time when Stockholm is suffering a housing crisis (Runting 2018; Runting and Frichot 2016). In brief, our noourbanographical argument is that the circulation of images of domestic interiors has a correlate impact in the way a neighbourhood is rendered increasingly inaccessible to those who can no longer afford to buy these styled and sought-after apartments. This, as I will explain in the next chapter, procures a dogmatic Image of Thought that circumscribes the way we curate our urban habitat.

Practice scene: Michelle Hamer follows one stitch at a time

When I first met Michelle Hamer over six years ago to talk about her forthcoming exhibition, *Dangling Carrots* at Craft Victoria, Melbourne, she asked me not to discuss her illness.[6] Michelle made the disciplinary move from architecture to art as part of her personal experience with corporeal exhaustion. She did not want to be known as 'that sick girl' artist. So while I discussed exhaustion at length in the review I subsequently wrote in engagement with her work, drawing on what I call Deleuze's methodology of exhaustion, I downplayed the fact that Michelle was suffering from a chronic illness. Instead, I discussed her work in terms of exhaustive series and the exhaustion peculiar to the subject matter the artist treats, which for Michelle included flickering freeway signage coordinating traffic networks across the vast suburban sprawl of Melbourne; failed housing estates at the peri-urban fringe; warning signs posted at the dead end of the road, all of which could be set against the backdrop of the economic exhaustion suffered in the wake of the global financial crisis of 2007–2008 and the American sub-prime mortgage disaster. Even though Michelle's development of her modes of aesthetic expression emerged in partial response to a chronic illness, there remains the risk that the work will not be appraised in its own right if the artist's condition is foregrounded, and her identity fixed in place. Yet, it is from exhaustion that her work emerges, as well as suggesting themes of exhaustion throughout her serial investigations. From the vantage point of her couch, Michelle took to stitching tapestries, which allowed her to maintain a comfortable supine position. She explains that one of the hardest things is to hold her neck upright, and so to work with her exhaustion she must find postures, specifically lying down, in which she can still create. One of her tapestries is called *My Vice Is Being Upright*, where she comments on the limitations of an exhausted body. Moving through her exhaustion she slowly expanded her local environment-world, progressing from the couch to the car, to funded international research field trips in search of other boundary conditions beyond her own corporeal and existential exhaustion.

Michelle's work commenced partially by happenstance. A friend insisted that she get up and come with her to a local art-and-craft supplies store, though this is not to suggest that she was not making the greatest efforts to lift herself up already. Here, somewhere on a back shelf dedicated to craft, Michelle discovered the industrially produced plastic grids that remain part of her body of work to the present day. These are industrial off-the-shelf products available to a Do It Yourself (DIY) craft market that Michelle explains were on an unmarked shelf. While their intended use remained unexplained, their structure immediately suggested purpose to her. Following this material encounter, and its suggestiveness, Michelle commenced with a

FIGURE 5.1 *Michelle Hamer,* Fatigue Kills, *tapestry thread on plastic grid, 2005.*

series called *Life in the Fast Lane*, a commentary on the contrast between speed and slowness witnessed amidst the infrastructural milieu that is the freeway.

Her next theme was closer to home and dedicated to her own body. Using the plastic grids, needle and tapestry thread, and scans and images she had of her body, she began to weave directly into the grids, trusting her hand–eye coordination. Transferring digital imagery directly into the pixel that each stitch constitutes, she mixed new and old technologies. Because it was never just about a personal problem, she soon followed this second series with one dedicated to weather systems, creating connections between bodies of different scales, placing an exhausted female body and a body of weather beside one another. Later she explained to me that she always seemed to be getting caught up in big weather events. She experienced a category five cyclone in Broome, north-western Australia, and she was in New York for Hurricane Irene in 2011, which made landfall at Coney Island. Though the Hudson River did not experience the expected flood surge, the New York subway was closed. Cyclone Irene turned out to be far less violent than Cyclone Sandy the following year.

Returning to the labour of her weaving one stitch at a time, what is demonstrated is the mixing of old and new technologies. Hamer is acutely aware of the proximity between hand-stitching and computation, remarking that each stitch operates as a pixel and that the multiple adjacencies between her seemingly endless stitches enable an image to slowly emerge. Slowness is an appropriate comportment for an exhausted body. It is worth remembering that the exemplary weaving machine, the Jacquard loom and its novel use of punched cards to determine complex patterns through neat algorithmic iterations, was a precursor to the early computer. Each stitch becomes a remark upon the digitization of the world and the broadening reign of Big Data. The personal computer has further expanded, to the point of exhaustion, our relation to space, as well as many if not all of our personal relations, which we increasingly claim at a distance. The weaver's hand plunges straight into a world of bits and pulls the thread through to the other side.

As I explained in my original review of her work, when Michelle was able to raise herself to a seated position she took to her car, projecting her exhaustion beyond a care for the embodied self to the world outside. Prior to the juxtaposed images of an ailing body and weather events, her first fascination was the ubiquitous LED freeway sign, warning of poor traffic, road closures, accidents and speed limits, inspiring a series called *Life in the Fast Lane*. At this time she was driving back and forth along Melbourne's Eastern Freeway in an attempt to liberate herself from her exhaustion and move towards better health. Eventually, leaving behind the arterial logic of freeways, she entered fringe suburbia where she discovered the dead end of the 'no road' sign, alongside the empty promises of billboards advertising new-home loans and forthcoming housing developments.

The tapestry works are collected into a number of suites, each of which can be considered open works in that Hamer could return to any one of the suites and add further images to the series. Although there is a sense in which she may add further tapestry works to any one of these suites, and further extend the series she has constructed, there isn't an infinite number of permutations. She must grapple with the finitude of the situation, which may extend to a large number of combinations of factors; yet it is not possible to go all the way to infinity, so to speak. She must recognize the inherent limits of the material, her stamina and how many variations on a theme are really possible. Deleuze argues that, 'the aporia [of where to locate the limit of a series] will be solved if one considers that the limit of the series does not lie at the infinity of the terms but can be anywhere in the flow … a point that is already reached well before one knows that the series is exhausted' (Deleuze 1998a: 157). Quite abruptly, it becomes time to stop work, leaving tasks to be taken up at a later point. There is no definitive moment in which it is possible to proclaim that enough is enough, for the concrete reality of exhausted hinterlands can be endlessly prospected. Much like Agnès Varda's stories of the gleaners, Michelle listens in to the drying up of voices that live this life at the periphery, extending her empathy towards their spatial stories.

Most recently, she has turned her attention to boundary conditions, making field trips to highly publicized geopolitical walls, such as the one between the United States and Mexico, as well as the walls constructed between Israel and the Palestinian territories. She had planned a visit to Cyprus, but timing and her health worked against her. It goes without saying that the wall is a fundamental architectural gesture of differentiation between interior and exterior conditions. Contributing to the basic conditions of shelter, it designates an environmental technology required for human survival. The boundary wall delineates a site of struggle, whether between one's own quasi-porous corporeal envelope and its immediate environment, or as the barrier that keeps people on the inside or on the outside. As Michelle demonstrates, the wall is a reversible condition, because those peoples and things located on either side of the wall can end up being protected or imprisoned, depending on your point of view and situation.

With this shift in scale, she took to creating larger pieces, using construction mesh and barrier tape. In effect, her smaller tapestries expand to become barrier conditions, a flexible fabric wall. Months after her visit to the border between the United States and Mexico, she retrospectively observed: *You already have a wall!* All this chanting, all this fear packed into the empty refrain: 'Build a Wall! Make them Pay!' when in fact much of the border already

FIGURE 5.2 *Michelle Hamer,* When War Is Over, *tapestry thread on plastic grid, 2017.*

has a wall. At the same time, there are those on both sides hoping to stitch together their relations. Michelle speaks of a city councillor she met in El Paso on the US side of the border, wanting to set up a trolley car connection with Juarez, on the Mexican side. When you hit the wall, it is a matter of finding other ways through or around it.

With the boundary walls series, Michelle collected over 5,000 images. The history of her work can be mapped as a history of the organization and reorganization of makeshift taxonomical categories as her exhaustive arrays of images accrete. The grid of the taxonomic chart is not fixed but flexible, and she shifts images from folder to folder as she wades through all the material she has collected. The volumes of digital photographs that feed her series are further supplemented by the photographs that are sent to her by those who have been infected by her visions. Her series of tapestries render points of view on mundane urban scenarios visible, drawing attention to everyday environment-worlds in such a way that now everyone sees what she has seen. *Once the work is on the wall it is no longer mine*, she tells me, *and it is not my place to tell someone else how to experience it. I've given it up to the world; I can explain my position, but I cannot impose it on others.*

Remaining upright is still an issue for Michelle. It is possible to stitch tapestries from a partially reclined position, with the plastic grid held close to her face. Tapestry requires a coordination from eye to hand and back again. It is a slow craft, taking the time that it demands. This means that Michelle must always be prepared. *I know I can't count on my body*, she explains, *I must always prepare in advance*. Remembering the now anachronistic pleasures of the Rotring ink pen, once used to draft a final architectural plan or section, Michelle realized she could repurpose her plastic off-the-shelf grids in order to experiment with what looks like pixelated drawings. Gallery visitors mistook the immaculately drafted drawings for another anachronistic technology, the old dot matrix printer. But the drawings ended up tiring her more than the tapestries. You have to choose your media in such a way that you can best negotiate your body's limits. Tapestry is a slow medium, and it suits the speeds and slownesses of her body, one stitch at a time, stitching her way through fatigue.

The way I see, she explains, *is like an architect sees, as that is how I was trained*. Art, she has discovered, turns out to be a more solitary work than architecture, and more exposed to public critique. In architecture she worked collectively, in a team; with her art practice, she explains that she feels more emotionally tied up in things. *I'm connected in a personal way and yet I must give my work up once it's done*.

Moving from the couch to the freeway, towards suburban and peri-urban dead-end roads, to the large-scale walls that seek to divide one nation state from another, she ventures further from home, with each step challenging the limits of exhaustion, and paradoxically finding strength there. *I can't go on, I must go on, I will go on*.

We could read Michelle's work according to Deleuze's methodology of exhaustion: First, she collects open-ended combinatorials of digital images, one image after the next, collecting first and then deciding upon a selection next as she begins to organize her taxonomy of images. Second, she listens in to the drying up of voices at the periphery, rendering visible the carriers of significance of a peri-urban fringe and other boundary conditions that are too often overlooked. Third, Hamer's suites and series of tapestries critically address the extenuating circumstances, the partial excuses made to justify the sprawl of the outer suburbs, exhaustion at the peri-urban fringe and the installation of boundary conditions. The exhaustion of the potentialities of space, the third of Deleuze's methodologies of exhaustion (what I have called Language IIIa) is what the philosopher names the 'any-space-whatever'. He quotes Beckett to get at what he means: 'neither here nor there where all the footsteps ever fell can never fare nearer to anywhere nor from anywhere further away'.[7] Such spaces are well trodden and populated, covered in the dusty tracks of weary wandering feet, indefinite as well as completely determined. Recall the rhythm of footfalls that compose Beckett's television play *Quad*, where the organization of the space, including the gestures and gait of the performers, is highly constrained ... and yet where is this space? It is nowhere in particular, it is an 'any-space-whatever'. There are always mitigating circumstances in reference to the indefinite expanses of suburban space, excuses that can be made, claims ventured about a place to call home. After all, in the new world we are intimately familiar with suburban sprawl, it has been so thoroughly integrated into our existences but we barely see it. Hamer draws our attention back to its weary, exhausted spaces, offering a lament of sorts in response to platitudes about the home. Fourth, she dissipates the power of the image, again through repetition and the distinction of minor differentiations. More importantly, the image is exhausted in that it can no longer wield its former power over us. Instead we find ourselves asking questions about advertising billboards, and road signage, the ephemera of daily commuting existence that had once only been background noise. Perhaps we even pause to ask questions about the seemingly unstoppable consumption and development of land at the urban periphery, until finally we hit the wall.

In the end, not even technology will suffice to save us. The only small hope is that once we have managed to exhaust the possible, some new mode of expression will emerge. Through her needle-work Hamer extends her sympathy towards the end of the road, which is to extend the self tentatively towards the other, reaching across the boundary conditions we daily install.

Notes

1 I want to thank Vasily Sitnikov for drawing my attention to this series, and specifically the book *General Ecology: The New Ecological Paradigm*.
2 The 'noo' of noology, noopolitics and noourbanography intersects with the thought of late-nineteenth-century Soviet geochemist Vladimir Vernadsky who speculated on the powerful role of human agency working not from a privileged vantage point outside a situation, but from within 'nature'. The noosphere, a concept he developed later in his career, describes the sphere of human cognition and activity, specifically in connection with how human activity is dedicated to generating sources of energy. See Heinz Kautzleben and Axel Müller, 'Vladimir Ivanovich Vernadsky (1863–1945) – From mineral to noosphere.' *Journal of Geochemical Exploration*, 147 (2014): 6.
3 The concept of noourbanography was introduced to me by the Australian philosopher Jon Roffe, during the development stages of *Deleuze and the City* (2016).
4 'Om hemnet', Hemnet, accessed 17 February 2016, at http://www.hemnet.se/om.

5   Helen's analysis for our essay was undertaken using data from hemnet.se gathered on 17 February 2016, by searching 'apartments for sale' in 'Södermalm'. Each advertisement was logged as to the colour of walls in the cover image and the colour of walls in all the images. Ten advertisements were excluded from the initial sample of 142 due to being visualizations, construction photographs or because the ads had been removed at the time of being logged, leaving a sample of 132 advertisements.

6   The catalogue essay I wrote for Hamer's exhibition was subsequently revised and published: Hélène Frichot, 'Michelle Hamer: One Stitch at a Time', in Louis Mannie Leoni, ed. *05401*, 01 (2012): 17–19, 25–26.

7   Beckett cited in Deleuze, 'The Exhausted', 160.

6

Concept-tools

Image of Thought

The affective labour of images, and how they operate in a reciprocal, if disjunctive relation with the concepts and discursive statements architects enunciate, produces a disciplinary Image of Thought that has been vastly facilitated by the speed and efficiency of new media platforms. This has less to do with the representational quality of imagery, or 'representation' per se, than the power of images to procure affects, and how a politics of affect needs to be considered when addressing architectural projects, built and unbuilt. It is important to understand that images do not stand by themselves in isolation, and there is no such thing as a glossy architectural image that can be taken as a thing in itself, because images operate within animated networks or assemblages involving complex matrices of things and relations: 'The image is not an object but a "process"', Deleuze remarks (1998a: 159). That is to say, the power of the image is in its production and circulation and the processes of subjectification it affects. The risk I identify is how easily quasi-architectural images prescribe realities, foreclosing how future peoples, places, things and their admixtures might express themselves.

A commonplace observation I have frequently remarked upon across a series of essays (2014, 2017), many of which have been co-written with my colleague Helen Runting (2015, 2016, 2018a, 2018b) and with Jonathan Metzger (2016), concerns the relationship of near indiscernibility that can be posited between images of desire composed to portray the privileged point of view of an architectural project and images dedicated to the commodification of worlds through branding and marketing strategies, especially in the domain of real estate. Less than their representational power, the images that circulate, amidst assemblages that collapse the distinction, for instance, between architecture and advertising, operate through the production of affective atmospheres. Rather than an *exhaustion* of the image, an increasingly insatiable thirst is generated towards the ever more rapacious consumption of images. The result is *exhaustive* combinatorials of images, each in turn depending on the fact that previous images in a series of consumption are only partially recalled. Through a serial amnesia of forgetfulness and distraction, or an inbuilt redundancy of the image, every image is obliged to give way to the next image. This furious circulation and exchange of perceptual and affective stimuli inform the remarkable technology of thinking together (Deleuze 1990: 8; Lazzarato 1996).

Depending on your situation; your cultural, social and political baggage; and your sex, gender, class and race, where you are right now, and the problems with which you are grappling, you are apt to be captivated by a dominant Image of Thought. Feminist theorists often describe this as the implicit bias (Saul 2013), unconscious or ingrained schema that determine our behaviour before we even know we have acted, making selections and decisions, inclusions and exclusions, based on a presumed normative standard. For instance, who fits our preconceived image of the architect and who does not? What compositions based on 'good taste' serve to distribute the sensible amidst the commodity form we once called home? The Image of Thought contributes to formations of subjectivity, both singular and collective, informing processes of subjectification, which can easily devolve into an unwitting subjection to norms including the way in which we dress our interiors, which reciprocally dress us, turning us into subjects of a specific kind. What is important here, as Michel Foucault once argued, is that there is nothing essential to the subject or the (architectural) space that imposes liberty or oppression; instead we should be concerned with the practices that are facilitated in a given material space, the environment-world of a residential interior, for instance. Foucault argues that architectural space is something like 'an element of support to ensure a certain allocation of people in space, a *canalization* of their circulation, as well as their reciprocal relations' (2000: 361, emphasis in original). Such an account demands to be supplemented with another kind of circulation, and that is the circulation of architectural images and how they likewise impact upon the practices of (human) subjects in search of a place to call home.

What is this process of subjectification? It is a question I have preliminarily addressed in the first part of this book, Environment-worlds, where I discussed how subjects emerge in light of the situation in which they find themselves, discovering their position retrospectively, continuing to find (and lose) themselves, subsequently revising their position depending on the kinds of encounters they have and the relations they enter into, forming more or less resilient compositions. I have returned to it again in discussing Serres's concept of the interplay between the quasi-subject and the quasi-object in the second part of this book dedicated to things. A subject is less a fixed position than a something in process, though this is not to say processes of subjectification are by any means a free-for-all, or an existential ability to shape oneself as one wishes.

Peter Pàl Pelbart explains that subjection concerns the attribution of roles, functions, places, via sex, nationality, race (2015: 90), and we could add, class. This is a process whereby an illusion is constructed of autonomy and self-domination, where instead subjection and processes of subjectification operate as a restricted interplay of constraint and release. The (human) subject, ever in formation, suffers and enjoys encounters and more or less enduring relations. After Deleuze and Guattari, we could say:

> We are dealing here with a problem concerning the plurality of subjects, their relationship, and their reciprocal presentation. Of course, everything changes if we think that we discover another problem: what is the nature of the other person's position that the other subject comes to 'occupy' only when it appears to me as a special object, and that I in turn come to occupy as special object when I appear to the other subject? (1994: 16)

The position of the subject is both unstable and constrained, and from one moment to the next you may discover yourself as now an object, now a subject, now a mere figure exposed as bare life, now a capacitated actor mobilizing those around you.

Here it is worthwhile returning to Guattari's argument about mental ecology, and its entanglement with social and environmental ecologies. The subject can be taken as a unit or an individual, which requires a problematic abstraction of a process of subjectivation from an environmental milieu. At an informational limit the individual becomes a 'dividual', merely a node through which information passes, a piece played in a global board game where the players themselves cannot always be identified; a piece multiplied and organized according to what Pelbart as well as Lazzarato, drawing on Guattari, call 'machinic servitude' (Lazzarato 2014; Pelbart 2015). The machinically coordinated 'dividual' feeds statistics and Big Data by expressing their consumer habits, interests and personal and professional relations. Importantly though, this machinic affect is pre-conscious, in other words, as Pelbart explains, it is 'no longer influenced by ideological or political content, signification or meaning'; instead the 'dividual' as stripped-back subjective drive is 'affected by asignifying signs (algorithms, equations, graphics) that are not directed to consciousness or to the will, but are imposed as modes of semiotisation in a pre-subjective plane' (Pelbart 2015: 90). Hence, there is an uncanny sense of Google knowing in advance what kinds of products it can advertise to me in the margins of my electronic mail; Instagram selling me images of the products and experiences that it thinks might enthral me; Wordpress.com, free to get started, but requiring payment if I do not want goods, services and experiences advertised on my weblogs; and I am not on Facebook, but I hear things are similar there.

Before we begin to think, we must acknowledge that thinking is constrained. Thinking requires constraints of some kind in order to delimit its survey. The critical and clinical question is how oppressive or liberatory are these constraints, and how can creative resistance be instigated where constraints have entirely overdetermined a thinker's capacity for critically engaging in his or her local environment-world? Pelbart explains that Guattari's way out, his mode of creative resistance and his 'retaliations' were expressed in 'a-signifying ruptures, in a-subjective deterritorialisations' (91). Deleuze likewise argues that creative resistance erupts through vacuoles of non-communication, or as circuit breakers that disrupt control (1995a: 175). Nevertheless, the thing is that modes of oppression and modes of liberation use much the same tools; and critical theory, as Eyal Weizman has demonstrated, can be instrumentalized as an architectural methodology dedicated to facilitating developments in war craft (Weizman 2006), much as critical theory can be used to question the facts of climate change (Latour 2004).

To further pursue the deep ambivalence embedded in theory, which can be applied to all manner of problems, this chapter will expand in more detail on Deleuze's challenging concept of the 'Image of Thought'. The Image of Thought is an ambivalent concept in Deleuze's, and Deleuze and Guattari's lexicon. The destruction of a dogmatic Image of Thought either enables the installation of yet another hegemonic order or opens the way for the production of a new Image of Thought that, hopefully, enables more liberatory practices. As Deleuze and Guattari explain: 'The classical image of thought, and the striating of mental space it effects, aspired to universality' (1987: 379), but a new Image of Thought may promise other possibilities that do not overdetermine mental space, its structuration and associated habits of thought. The question of whether, with enough effort, a dogmatic Image of Thought can be destroyed and replaced with a new Image of Thought that is less oppressive, will be raised. When a dogmatic Image of Thought is dismantled, is it possible to think outside an Image of Thought, or outside that which constrains thinking? What is thinking without an Image of Thought? And where an Image of Thought becomes oppressive, what modes of creative resistance are possible?

The Image of Thought as conceptual construct is discussed at length in Deleuze's books *Nietzsche and Philosophy* (1983), *Difference and Repetition* (1994), *Proust and Signs* (2000) and in an essay included in the collection *Desert Islands* (2004). Deleuze and Guattari together discuss the concept of the Image of Thought in *What Is Philosophy?* (1994). As they explain, thought needs at least a minimum of rules in order to carry out the activity of thinking, and a minimum of rules tends to be coordinated with a minimum of sense available in the organization of an environment-world.

In both *What Is Philosophy?* and *Nietzsche and Philosophy*, there is the glimmer of a new Image of Thought able to counter dogmatism. Likewise, I argue, in Deleuze's essay 'The Exhausted' an Image of Thought flashes up briefly and ambiguously; it is an allusive opening that glimmers, appearing to offer fleeting refuge, or else some promise of a much-needed shock to established thought (Deleuze 1989: 166; 1998a: 169). The image in question 'is precisely not a representation of an object but a movement in the world of the mind' (Deleuze 1998a: 169). Deleuze argues in 'The Exhausted' that 'what matters is no longer the any-space-whatever but the mental image to which it leads' (169), by which he either means a new Image of Thought, or perhaps instead a 'thinkable' that destabilizes what we thought we already knew so well. It remains unclear in this context whether the image about which Deleuze speaks is, strictly speaking, an Image of Thought. Still, this 'mental image' leads to an encounter with a dogmatic Image of Thought and the promise, as I have suggested, of a new Image of Thought that suffices to shake up the status quo. Crucially, the 'subject' in this equation always follows *after* the idea, after the encounter, the (human) subject is not the unique source of an idea, instead they become a 'seer' who bears witness to something intolerable from which they seek a line of escape (Deleuze 1989: 169). Likewise, in his book *Spinoza: A Practical Philosophy*, Deleuze explains that 'knowledge is not the operation of a subject but the affirmation of an idea in the mind' (1988b: 81).

At the risk of being overly didactic, I now proceed in more detail through the eight postulates pertaining to the dogmatic Image of Thought. There is not one definition that exhausts the role of the Image of Thought, and as with so many of Deleuze's, and also Deleuze and Guattari's concepts, 'even *within* a single work or project [such as *Anti-Oedipus* or *A Thousand Plateaus*], [they] do not have an identity that would be reducible to a simple definition' (Smith 2012: 124). Each time the concept of the Image of Thought is raised across Deleuze's oeuvre, it grapples with a different problem, and each time it proposes another way out, another line of escape. Much as Deleuze and Guattari are wary of imposing concepts as universally applicable, likewise, something like the concept-tool that is the Image of Thought must be defined again each time in relation to its specific use and situation. This is no reason to throw up one's arms in frustration and assume, therefore, that their work is either inaccessible, or pure nonsense. What is demanded instead is a close attention to situations and how concepts are created and deployed. I will return to this discussion of the function of the concept-tool in what follows.

So as to better grasp the postulates concerning the Image of Thought, some problem needs to be addressed, the outline of which is determined by a contemporary Image of Thought. A project of increasingly urgent contemporary relevance that I have been working on addresses the 'real estate Image of Thought' in relation to the circulation and composition of images of elegantly appointed residential interiors. This is where a relationship of near indiscernibility can be posited between images composed to portray the privileged point of view of an architectural project and images dedicated to the commodification of worlds through branding and marketing strategies. In the following discussion, each postulate will be passed through this contemporary problem – specifically, how we package the home as a spatial commodity and how this impacts on neighbourhoods and cities in terms of processes of gentrification and social cleansing.

The issue of housing has become ever more acute in global cities. The city in question here is Stockholm, Sweden, where I live and work, and where the housing market has been rapidly de-regulated. As the economic geographer Eric Clark argues, Sweden has opened its arms to radical neo-liberalization, taking housing as its first project of privatization, followed promptly by education and healthcare (Clark 2014). All of this is to say that the neo-liberal diagram has fundamentally transformed what it means to be at home, and one compelling symptom of this change can be discovered in the emergence of the affectively composed real-estate image. Helen Runting describes the situation in this urbane northern city, known for its history of humane (if somewhat over-engineered) social policies, and its attention to issues of gender, equity and diversity in terms of how a shift towards comprehensively planned renewal has resulted in pushing the socio-economically disadvantaged ever further from the centre of the city, beyond the gates or 'tolls' (Runting 2018). Formerly working-class neighbourhoods such as Hornstull on Södermalm, once referred to as 'the knife south' (*knivsöder*), are today described as 'knife and fork south', social cleansing having cleared the way for fine dining. Participating in these processes are the serially produced and consumed images of real estate available via online real-estate sites and apps like booli.com and hemnet.com, in the windows of real-estate boutiques, and across a range of media. It is important, then, to proceed through these postulates with this specific image of a city in mind.

1 **Good Sense:** Assumes the good will of the thinker and the concomitant good nature of thought. Good sense is supposed to be structurally sound, upright and evenly distributed, manifesting situations of homogeneity and a worrying consensus that discourages differences of opinion and the acknowledgement of one's specific

situation. Who would want to argue with good sense? It is presumed, as François Zourabichvili writes, that 'we think naturally' (2012: 45–46) and that in thinking we express a good will, as though this were an inevitable orientation of thought headed along the path of the good. Hence, the ease with which moral judgement is expressed as good sense, which easily translates into the specific domain of 'good design', the morality of design, including the fixing of aesthetic norms, tastes, fashions, consumer habits and thence opinions (Lazzarato 1996: 133).

2 **Common Sense:** The ideal of common sense is guaranteed by the even distribution of good sense in all thinkers. Common sense obliges us to agree with our local taste community, because it makes sense, and because this is how we will secure the best 'resale value' for our real-estate product. Common sense feeds common notions, which concern agreeable encounters between bodies. Still, we must be wary of habitually relying on common sense, as what is immediately agreeable between bodies may later lead to the breakdown of an organic body (human, architectural, environmental). While common sense, understood as consensual habits of thought, can prove invaluable when getting along day by day, it proves dangerous where these habits operate as unconscious bias that begins to determine how we 'curate' the environment-worlds in which we live and work.

3 **Recognition:** It is located in the expression 'it looks like …' and if it looks like a contemporary, or even a 'modern' architectural precedent (or choose your preferred style here), then we think it must be okay. We can subsequently progress from the 'it looks like' to the 'this will be alright for me too'. Recognition is comforting, it is non-confrontational, and it draws on normative criteria creating a spatial sense of permanence. In real-estate imagery, it emerges in the repetition of motifs, signature furniture pieces by Charles and Ray Eames or by the Swedish designer Bruno Mathsson (for the Swedish audience). It rests on pre-established methods that depend on what we already feel we know: This is what Zourabichvili calls the 'screen of the Same' (2012: 47). As Deleuze argues in *The Logic of Sensation*, the artist (or the architect) never begins with an empty canvas, but one packed full of habit, opinion and cliché, with received ideas and images that must first be cleaned away as much as one is able to (2002b: 10–12). If we want to break free of what we think we already know, this means that one of the first challenges is to go into battle with recognition.

4 **Representation:** It follows closely on the tail of recognition, presenting yet again what we have already seen, heard and known. 'Recognition is located as a first step toward representation, the recapitulation and security of the same in identity (ad nauseum)' (Deleuze 1994: 138). Representation functions according to analogy, similitude, identity and simple opposition, rather than venturing an ethos of difference and transformative becomings (142). To counter representation, Deleuze proffers the difficult concept of 'intensity', difference in itself, the unthinkable (144), which turns out to be a matter of letting thought come to us, rather than imposing something pregiven upon it. We are so habituated to what we identify as aesthetic forms of 'representation' in architectural design, for instance, that it is hard to think beyond its conventions. We are in the habit, as Latour and Yaneva point out, of imagining that perspectival representations of architecture depict the reality of a spatial situation, when what they communicate are conventional notational representations that render an architectural project static (2008).

5 **Error:** It is presumed to be a result of external factors leading the good thinker-practitioner astray, and not some more immediate stupor of thought. Error assumes that an answer to what thought is dedicated to thinking about is already available, and it is just a matter of getting to it, of enriching our knowledge. If we do not arrive, then it is because we are in error or have been misled on the path towards the good. Error requires that thought operates according to a negative function, that we never have enough knowledge or that we have mis-recognized the signposts along the way. Deleuze instead insists that error is merely a question of stupidity and distractedness, petty values and base thought that is mired in reactive forces (1994: 105). Stengers further explains that Deleuze historically situated this problem of error – how can we avoid error? – with philosophers of the seventeenth century, while illusion became the problem of the eighteenth century, and stupidity, to which I will return, a problem of the nineteenth century (2015: 120). Though this is not to say that permutations of the problems of error, illusion and stupidity do not also haunt the present.

6 **The Proposition:** It operates as an abstract logical function, which risks overlooking the sensory material milieu, the problematic fields in which we find ourselves. Abstract reason circulates as so much good and common sense, having forgotten exactly where the good and the common of sense have been derived from. Deleuze advises a reverse approach; the proposition should follow after the difficult things we

have sensed and encountered in a world, because: 'We only find truths where they are, at their time and in their element. Every truth is truth of an element, of a time and a place' (Deleuze 1983: 110). This further means that we must venture into extreme places and times, 'where the highest and the deepest truths live and rise up' (110). Yet, 'the philosopher creates concepts that are neither eternal nor historical but untimely and not of the present' and this is how creative-critical thinking is undertaken (1994: 107), that is to say, as a speculative gesture 'in favour of a time to come' (107). How do we plan our local environment-worlds in anticipation of future peoples?

7 **Solutions:** They are what are presumed when propositions are pre-emptively set forth. If we can forward a proposition in relation to a problem, it means that we can articulate a solution. Here problems are assumed to be traced from abstract propositions, leaving out the role of sense and expression as it is aroused amidst embodied encounters. Design solutions directed at styling residential interiors in advance of their sale assume a one-size-fits-all approach: Decluttering and reduction of personal items, especially family photographs; mirrors strategically placed and off-white walls to create the illusion of spaciousness; signature furniture pieces; and the use of wide-angle lens photography to exaggerate spaciousness produce images to be uploaded onto the real-estate sites or displayed in real-estate boutique windows (Runting and Frichot 2016). The idiosyncratic specificity of interior spaces is erased in favour of the generalized constraint of expressions of taste.

8 **The Result:** The result or the end product is how we fix good design 'knowledge', the result of which is a subordination or a devaluation of processes of learning to established knowledge (Deleuze 1994: 167). The pedagogical design exercise, for instance, is generally assessed based on outcome, and less on process. In response to this demand, the student of architecture quickly learns that the best way forward is through the composition of an affective image and what the image can be made to arouse in a critic: Recognition leads to established styles of representation establishing the presumed good and common sense of design. Recognizable design precedents become a must, so that critics can be reassured by what they recognize. The emphasis on a result is likewise a problem when it comes to the home front, which can never maintain its uncluttered, curated interiors, because home is an unending project that thwarts all attempts to achieve an end result, but this too is related to our societies of control, where we are never supposed to graduate or succeed from one segment to the next (Deleuze 1995b).

How might we invent an untimely Image of Thought? To bring into being that which does not exist is extraordinarily difficult, especially where, as Zourabichvili puts it, 'the act of thinking is modeled on puerile and scholarly situations' (2012: 49). Sometimes, when confronted with serially composed combinatorials of images and ideas, it becomes tempting to muse that everything that can be thought under the sun has been thought in advance. Have we exhausted the possible, every possible thought? Is it, finally, that we now find ourselves riffling through a finite and closed set of thought-images, swiping from right to left, or from left to right, in order to serially consume one image after the next while emptying out our capacity to encounter a thinkable?

Thinkables

> Something in the world forces us to think. This something is an object not of recognition but of a fundamental *encounter*.
> Gilles Deleuze, *Difference and Repetition* (1994: 139)

We are habituated to the assumption that we invent or 'have' thoughts that belong to us, that we can secure them with a signature, which then allows us the right to claim them as our intellectual property. The thinkable operates in quite another way. A thinkable, and this will no doubt sound counter-intuitive, is independent of either a given thinker or a fixed object of thought; instead, it circulates between both in the midst of an event, a taking place that takes more or less time. It is less the thought that I have than the thought that strikes me, coming from elsewhere, emerging in the midst of an encounter – not ' "I think" but "something makes me think" ' (Stengers 2015: 131). A thinkable does not belong to me, rather, as Stengers remarks, the situation in which something like thinking erupts transforms thinking into an adventure. If there is a subject who thinks, she explains, 'it is the unfolding of the drama itself, the demands of which turns the thinker into a "larva" or prey' (2014: 189). In this formulation, she is drawing on Gilles Deleuze's discussion in *Difference and Repetition*, where he deliberates on the process of thinking as a process of unfolding the enfolded, embryological, not-quite-yet subjects he calls larvae (1994). Simply, the thinker emerges after thinking has struck. There is always a problem that requires the production of a thinkable, and yet as I have argued in the previous section, problems tend to be constrained by a dominant Image of Thought. The thinkable poses a challenge to the Image of Thought, whereas the Image of Thought stabilizes a status quo. The thinkable is not reassured by what we believe we know, but asks what can we know (Stengers 2014: 191). And, should we hesitate to ask, who thinks? Gilles Deleuze, as though in anticipation, answers: 'The question "*who?*" does not refer to persons, but to forces and wills' (cited in Sauvagnargues 2016: 24). Each new connection with a thinkable is an event, an event of thought. At the same time, we can ask how this thinking situates us in relation to our (architectural) problems amidst our local environment-worlds. But, as becomes evident with the ambivalent role of the Image of Thought: 'There are (at least) two extreme ways in which thought (as well as other modes of experimentation) can fail: it can dissolve into pure chaos, and become a flux without form, or it can solidify into ever more rigid strata' (Beistegui 2010: 70).

In *What Is Philosophy?* Deleuze and Guattari wryly observe that philosophers do not need to reflect, contemplate and communicate; their job description (when they are not occupied with telling the story of the history of philosophy) is to create concepts: 'We can at least see what philosophy is not: it is not contemplation, reflection, or communication', because communication, reflection and contemplation are only 'machines for constituting Universals' (1994: 6). Reflection and contemplation are private affairs that should not be imposed collectively on others; though useful when practised in moderation, perhaps even therapeutic in the face of exhaustion, they remain passive and withdrawn registers of thinking. Contemplations are too focused on circumscribed things in relation to their associated concepts, in that we have a tendency to bracket out the messy relations of environment-worlds. Contemplation contracts a sensory world into the enveloping folds of a phenomenologically secure thinker tucked into a comfortable armchair in the corner of a quiet room. The art of reflection, while no doubt valuable from time to time, is where philosophy 'risks losing everything', Deleuze and Guattari insist, because it operates retrospectively on what has come to pass instead of undertaking the difficult work of concept-construction, which speculatively leaps, usually in an uncoordinated manner, into a future (6).

Communication, no doubt useful in order to make one's way through certain everyday life situations such as asking directions and buying bread, creates consensus, stabilizing opinions, establishing good and common sense. Communication is apt to empty itself out into so many empty signifiers, such as LIKES, emojis and short-cut mass-produced affects designed for ease of circulation and the capturing of protean subjects. Communication, as Brian Massumi explains, assumes an already defined world of things available for mirroring, and straight-jackets our capacity for expression (Massumi 2002b: xv). Deleuze and Guattari warn us that 'the philosophy of communication is exhausted in the search for a universal liberal opinion as consensus, in which we find again the cynical perceptions and affections of the capitalist himself' (Deleuze and Guattari 1994: 146). This is a warning about the usual deployment of devices and techniques of communication to sell us something we do not need.

As I will discuss in the section Concept-tools, the central task for the philosopher is to create concepts, but this is not to say that other disciplines cannot work with concepts too. 'To think is to create – there is no other creation – but to create is first of all to engender "thinking" in thought' (Deleuze 1994: 147). The thinkable though, an agrammatical construct that addles common and good sense, functions differently from a concept. It is what hits you in the face, a blinding flash, a 'green ray', a sudden capacity to see a glimmer of something before it fades away. It challenges you to believe enough in what you witness to do something about it. The thinkable and its subsequent formulation as a concept-tool is not directed at securing universality, but attempts to cope with contingency.

It is the cultural theorist Claire Colebrook who introduces the notion of a 'thinkable' in passing, where she defines noology for the *Deleuze Dictionary*: 'If there are pure noema – or thinkables,' Colebrook writes, 'we can also imagine approaching life, not as grounded in personal consciousness, but as a history of various images of thought, or what counts as thinking' (2005: 194). In the phenomenological philosopher Edmond Husserl's work, *noema* is distinguished from *noiesis*, thereby distinguishing an objective pole from a subjective pole. As Colebrook puts it, the remembered, imagined, desired, perceived *object* is distinguished from the remembering, imagining, desiring perceiving *subject*. Deleuze was instead concerned with liberating a *pure noema* from both, hence the thinkable (Colebrook 2005: 193), and hence the perplexing mobility of affects and percepts as presented previously.

Thinkables are encounters, establishing relations that produce thinkers as conceptual personae, not to be mistaken with fixed sovereign subjects, but as signatures and effects (Sauvagnargues 2016). The signature here is not one that claims ownership, but rather one that makes a concrete mark as a testimonial to a concept in formation. The thinkable arrives in advance of the signed concept-tool that makes thinking durable; it comes less from the privilege of a subjective unity of apperception, what has come to be identified as the correlationist circle binding subject to object, and object to subject (Meillassoux 2008), than as a strange conduit, a meeting place, an encounter, where something in a local environment-world forces us to think, forces a thought to erupt, renders an event thinkable. A thinkable does not arrive pre-packaged from a heaven of forms nor from some overflowing cornucopia where ideas are stored away as goods awaiting discovery. Deleuze offers the following challenge:

> Do not count upon thought to ensure the relative necessity of what it thinks. Rather, count upon the contingency of an encounter with that which forces thought to raise up and educate the absolute necessity of an act of thought or a passion to think. The conditions of a true critique and true creation are

the same: the destruction of an image of thought which presupposes itself and the genesis of the act of thinking in thought itself. (Deleuze 1994: 139)

There is a violence inherent to Deleuze's 'shock to thought' wherein thinking 'depends on forces which take hold of thought'; where thinking is 'an extraordinary event *in* thought itself, *for* thought itself' (1994: 108). The force of an encounter is where creation plays out.

Thought, rather than being the collaboration of minds in agreement, overcomes us with force: 'impressions that force us to look, encounters that force us to interpret, expressions that force us to think' (Deleuze 2000: 95). Expressions are the preferred mode, as distinct from communication, reflection and contemplation, because 'expression is an event', as Massumi simply puts it (2002b: xvii). Affects and percepts amass and circulate, sensation is aroused, thought overwhelms us and this encounter is both inevitable and fortuitous. A thinkable is entangled with a body, and 'a body, fresh in the throes of expression, incarnates not an already-formed system but a modification – a change' (Massumi 2002b: xvii). This is certainly not a matter of pregiven rules, and appropriate methodologies, procedures and propositions determining how thinking should be undertaken. The thinkable is bound up with an 'act of creation' (Deleuze 2000: 96) amidst a material-semiotic encounter: 'The act of thinking does not proceed from a simple natural possibility; on the contrary, it is only true creation. Creation is the genesis of the act of thinking within thought itself' (Deleuze 2000: 97).

Thinking takes place somewhere, and it is localized, taking up various bodies and their relations, human, non-human, admixtures of animate and inanimate things, material and immaterial, a rip-tide, a maelstrom that all the while throws out a speculative gesture towards a future. In taking place thought transforms environment-worlds: 'The same is true for the becoming of thought as for the capacity of thought to transform the world, a world that we are able to act upon precisely because thought has configured it' (Sauvagnargues 2016: 45). Yet it should be promptly added that if thought has configured a world, it has only done so on account of some concrete encounter, some contingent meeting place, some site, some specific geophilosophical situation. 'And the answer – in terms of the plane of immanence to be laid out, conceptual personae to be invented and brought to life and concepts created – makes it felt that philosophy can indeed be destroyed, because the dramatization creates a concept of philosophy that has nothing to do with the general ideals of reflection, contemplation, or communication' (Stengers 2015: 189).

Every mode of life is explored in situ, and the immanent plane of survey, what Deleuze and Guattari famously call the plane of immanence, can be taken quite literally as pertaining to a landscape of encounters composed of ecological relations, amidst which emerges various, differentiated 'environment-worlds'. Deleuze and Guattari's conceptual diagram of the plane of immanence describes 'the image thought gives itself of what it means to think, to make use of thought, to find one's bearings in thought' (Deleuze and Guattari 1994: 37), which requires an affirmation of embodied situation. A difficult terrain must first be explored, concerning what a 'given body seeks out and what it avoids', how it retreats from what harms it, and draws close to what aids it, which also concerns a 'particular being's characteristic relations with its surroundings' (Gatens and Lloyd 1999: 100). Where a 'particular being' begins to experience and experiment with their surroundings, a practical diagram emerges, forging a cartography that pertains to a specific journey, a noourbanography. Moira Gatens and Genevieve Lloyd make an account of such dynamics in terms of ethological bodies, where 'ethology describes the various powers of beings in relational terms by treating an individual as a fully integrated part of the context in which it lives and moves' (1999: 110). It is this question of context and how a mode of life intimately interacts with a context as environmental milieu that is of special importance to creative practitioners.

Responses are local, which is not to say small, or insignificant, nor even detached from the contemporary insidiousness of global networks, but instead situated. 'Concrete learning processes' enable a taste for thinking to emerge (Stengers 2015: 134). Ask then: What is your situation? What problems press in? How can we map the complex relations and encounters we discover ourselves in the midst of? How can we chart our environment-worlds (Frichot 2016)? An active diagnosis, performed as a mapping of composite bodies and their associated affects, percepts and concepts is required, 'an active diagnosis bearing on our milieus' (Stengers 2015: 131). With this emphasis on diagnosis that crops up in Stengers's urgent writings, her form of critique can be found to sit neatly with Deleuze's pairing of the critical and clinical. It is simply not the case that Deleuze's work cannot be used to undertake a critique, but it is a critique of a particular kind that follows the material admixtures of encounters and ethological relations in order to read symptoms. It is an immanent critique. Deleuze himself writes: 'Philosophy is at its most positive as critique, as an enterprise of demystification' (1983: 106). Specifically, as Stengers explains, 'it is a matter of diagnosing the unhealthy character of the milieus in which such experiments will always risk being dismembered, subject to control and scrutiny, and to regulations that are blind to their consequences, summonsed to provide accounts that are not theirs, destroyed' (Stengers 2015: 131). Such are the risks that emerge amidst ecologies of practice, curtailed as they are by disciplinary obligations and requirements.

While I am loath to suggest any kind of progression, there is nevertheless a certain pragmatics that can be associated with the shock to thought that settles, the one we grasp hold of for long enough so that it might be managed as a concept-tool.

Concept-tools

> How did this thinking situate me?
> Isabelle Stengers, *In Catastrophic Times* (2015: 196)

There is no concept-tool if there is not a thinkable that has aroused us, shocked us into thinking for once, or else made us swoon as though in ecstatic realization of our embeddedness in a local environment-world. There is no concept-tool if there is no history of consciousness and a traffic in ideas that is both discipline-specific and at the same time shooting out along transversal trajectories traversing other disciplinary domains. We suffer or enjoy a profound encounter with thought, a thought that has come before us, but which was not ready-made. For a thinkable to survive and propagate it must work, and be able to form allegiances; thoughts 'survive if they work, if they propagate, if they find an appropriate milieu, a welcoming territory … They will only maintain their appeal if they can form some kind of alliance with what we do' (Goodchild quoted in Thrift 1999: 31). Concepts are things for thinking with, they offer aids and prompts to thought, they are like tools, they are what I call: concept-tools (Frichot 2016). Perhaps it is unnecessary to distinguish a concept-tool from a thinkable, except that the concept-tool persists and maintains some durability; where the thinkable, the shock it arouses may never resolve itself into a concept, but can remain something fleeting, often proving impossible to catch hold of. Thinkables are always escaping us, leaking, vanishing and plunging back into the unthinkable. We can rarely grasp hold of a thought.

Isabelle Stengers makes a great deal of the concept as a tool, as does Donna Haraway, with whom Stengers maintains a friendly conversation, stating that Haraway is 'someone who enables us to think about what is happening to us today',[1] with her ecosophical thinking, and her means of producing hope at the brink of the abyss. Unlike the quote from Goodchild I cite earlier, this will sometimes mean trying out concepts that do not easily find alliances, nor welcoming territories, but must challenge the status quo. Together Stengers and Haraway are two aged women of the philosophy of science worth celebrating, and there is much to be learnt from them. Before discussing their respective approaches to the concept-tool, with an emphasis on a feminist ethos amidst what has come to be called the Anthropocene, I will take a detour through another, older, perhaps wearier conversation, one that tends to be privileged when it comes to a toolbox approach to concept construction.

It is primarily from Deleuze and Foucault's dialogue 'Intellectuals and Power', published in Foucault's Language, Counter-Memory, Practice (1977), that I derive this productive thing I call the concept-tool, which I further develop through an engagement in Stengers and Haraway's thinking practices. Thought (or I would stipulate here the 'thinkable') is not passive, nor merely theoretical; it is not something suffered alone, deep within the solipsistic sphere of the stable thinker who thinks and by thinking reassures himself that he exists. Instead, thought wreaks havoc. In his opening statement, in the dialogue in question, Deleuze speaks to what he believes is the shared ground between himself and Foucault, addressing the question of theory, which he explains should never be taken as totalizing, but as partial and fragmentary. This quality of the partial and perhaps even partiality can be amplified by Haraway's framing of 'situated knowledges', wherein thinking and knowing are involved in specific situations and practices including a critical understanding of the semiotic technologies we use for making meaning (1988: 579). Deleuze insists that theory must be located and addressed to a specific and delimited field, something that the architectural historian, theorist and critic Jane Rendell stresses when she reads this conversation (Rendell 2006: 9–10). This is a warning about the risk of empty abstractions or the assumption that theoretical concepts can travel entirely unhindered. When theory hits the wall, another approach must be taken, and Deleuze suggests that where '[p]ractice is a set of relays from one theoretical point to another, theory is a relay from one practice to another', both modes being apt to 'hit the wall' if they are used in isolation (Foucault and Deleuze 1977: 206), as Deleuze stresses elsewhere, 'it's by banging your head on a wall that you find a way through. You have to work on the wall, because without a set of impossibilities, you won't have the line of flight, the exit that is creation, the power of falsity that is the truth (Deleuze 1995c: 133).

When it comes to concepts and their creation, Deleuze argues that the question of representation is of far less importance than action – theoretical action and practical action – operating in relay. Theory, Foucault goes on, does not express, translate or apply practice: 'it is practice' (Foucault and Deleuze 1977: 208). It is at this moment in their dialogue that Deleuze introduces the thought-image of theory as a toolbox. A theory, Deleuze says, 'is exactly like a box of tools ... it must be useful, it must function ... We don't *revise* a theory, but *construct* new ones' (208). We have no choice but to make other theories, and this should be a process of creating transversal links across geopolitical terrain, connecting up with other problematic fields where possible (216).

There is a crucial background to this dialogue, and it concerns the diffuse circulation of power, and struggles of many kinds, of students, of workers, of women, of minorities. Famously, one geophilosophical field is the prison, where both Foucault and Deleuze were involved in an organization Foucault was responsible for convening called GIP (*Groupe d'information sur les prisons*, or Prison Information Group). As Christopher Penfield explains, the prison context gives concrete occasion for the use of Deleuze and Guattari's schizoanalysis, and an opportunity for Foucault to learn first-hand about relations of power, and so develop his analyses (Penfield 2014). This work in prisons places Deleuze and Foucault's dialogue in context, for when they speak of practice it is first and foremost political practice, that is to say, what they can do amidst their environment-worlds understood as socio-political milieux and how from these environment-worlds, intermixed with matters of care and concern, they can extract valuable concepts.

This imperative to 'construct new ones', to construct new theories, will become much clearer when, years later, Deleuze and Guattari write their chapter dedicated to the question: 'What is a concept?' in their final collaborative work, *What Is Philosophy?* (1994). Concepts must be constructed, but that is not to say they arrive out of nowhere: 'Some concepts call for archaisms, and others for neologisms, shot through with almost crazy etymological exercises: etymology is like a specifically philosophical athleticism. In each case there must be a strange necessity for these words and for their choice, like an element of style' (Deleuze and Guattari 1994: 8). Of what use is the creation of concepts? The answer is that the concept must always be directed towards the invention of problems, as a means of drawing an outline around a situation, and determining what is at stake, and what is to be done. To know a concept you must create a concept, not simply trace over a well-known concept. The concept must emerge from an intuition that is specific to it, a thinking-feeling in response to 'a field, a plane, and a ground that must not be confused with them but that shelters their seeds and the personae who cultivate them. Constructivism requires every creation to be a construction on a plane that gives it an autonomous existence. To create concepts is, at the very least, to make something' (Deleuze and Guattari 1994: 7). A landscape of sorts can be witnessed to unfurl, what Deleuze and Guattari call a plane of immanence, including the conceptual personae who tend to seeds of possibility within the problematic fields that concern them. This places those who think (shaping themselves through this exercise) in situations of extreme vulnerability because they think exactly from the midst of things, upon the plane, surveying their immediate problematic field. Philosophy, taken as an activity of concept creation, is a dangerous exercise.

In his recent work on 'general intellects', where he introduces twenty-five thinkers with whom we might think today, including Stengers and Haraway, McKenzie Wark remarks: 'Nobody has all the concepts they need to have. We all work with particular slices of information in particular ways and tend to map the world more or less the same as the bit we know' (Wark 2017a). We all compose our concepts in such a way as to construct a kind of patchwork conceptual landscape, and we rely on other concepts, which we borrow, steal and adapt. Yet, in that concepts can be packaged and transported with relative ease, they are in imminent danger of being abused. There are those who have stolen the work of the concept and put it to nefarious use, the so-called ideas men who sell their concepts on the marketplace (Deleuze and Guattari 1994: 10). The challenge for the intellectual, so activated by a problem that demands a concept, and a concept that operates as a tool, is the constant risk of the recuperation of the concept. The intellectual must struggle amidst relations of power that are always about to transform her into its 'object and instrument' in the domains of knowledge and discourse (Foucault and Deleuze 1977: 208). Architects come perilously close to operating in such a manner because of the ways in which they are obliged to package their ideas, communicate them with enticing graphics that arouse the affects of whatever audience is prepared to receive their message.

The concept emerges amidst contingent geopolitical circumstances, which is not to say it is randomly formulated, or based on some kind of free-for-all. The emergence of a concept is comprehended as an event of creation and construction, insists Anne Sauvagnargues (2016: 31), and as I have argued, the creation of concepts commences its work following a shock to thought, an encounter with a thinkable. Creation, Sauvagnargues goes on to explain, is associated with a clinical exercise, that is to say a diagnostic dedicated to reading signs as they emerge in a body-plus-environment-world composition, keeping in mind the diversity of scales and complex compounds a body can be. There is, furthermore, what can be called a clinic of the exhausted, a 'clinic of thought, a typology of thinkers' (33). As it turns out, my next practice scene discusses such a clinic imagined through queer architectural means. When Sauvagnargues describes a clinic of thought, she is drawing on the Deleuzian series that brings together creation, the critical and the clinical. As I have discussed earlier, what is easily overlooked is the specificity of the critical project that Deleuze developed, attending generously to philosophy, literature, art and film, and many other disciplines besides. This was a critical project that did not presume to judge from the outside, but attempted to think *with* and to read the symptoms of the problems it grappled with without casting judgement. Critical thought, of which Stengers is extremely wary, is usually not critical enough (Stengers 2015: 109–110), by which I understand that critical thought does not think closely enough to the concrete ground and with its companion thinkers.

Daniel Smith, who offers an introduction to Deleuze's *Essays Critical and Clinical*, explains that the critical is a mode of action tied up with the clinical – 'Every literary work implies a way of living, a form of life, and must be evaluated not only critically but clinically' (Smith 1998: xv) – and to literary work, other kinds of creative work can be added too. The critical and the clinical, the creative work and its imbrication in life, present the demand: What do you plan to do about things? Not commentary from the sidelines, not deconstruction, but how a process of subjectivation is individually and collectively taken up by a life, and how the creative is continuous with all that pertains to organic and inorganic life. The clinical draws on a medical analogy, the way in which a doctor maps the symptoms of a patient, what a specific body expresses in the enclosing context of a specific environment-world; the health and activity of a mode of existence, its quantum of exhaustion or exuberance. The critical and the clinical are conjoined at the moment art and life are bundled up in one vast movement, as an impersonal passage of life (Smith 2012: 221). The impersonal concerns this emphasis I have been making repeatedly about how the construction of subjectivity follows after the event in which a subject, an anyone-whatsoever, finds, as well as loses, itself again – the notion of subjects and/or objects emerging from enfolded larvae. To think such a thing is unsettling, because we are so used to positing thought as emerging from a competent, if not a professional, thinker who thinks, who has secured the right to think, thereby excluding those who are not deemed fit, who, unfortunately, have too often been women, children, ethnic, racial, class-bound, non-normative minorities of all kinds.

Finally, what becomes frighteningly clear in this looming-up of life is how creative practice is not something undertaken from a location of safety, but places the creative practitioner ever at risk of decomposition, of exhaustion. Yet we must think and practice. Creative practice is directed towards new compositions of life, especially at the point at which life (of a certain human kind) would appear to be close to extinction.

Concept-tools are sited pertaining to geographies and histories and material entanglements. 'All concepts are connected to problems without which they would have no meaning and which can themselves only be isolated or understood as their solution emerges' (Deleuze and Guattari 1994: 16). Sauvagnargues stresses this geophilosophical emergence of concepts, speaking of 'the contingency of their ethos, the ecology of a territory, which includes the multiple components and the diverse relations it forges with its outside: neighbouring territories or universes of prior or current values, in accordance with an empirical and fluctuating ethology' (2016: 31). Or as Deleuze and Guattari explain: 'Obviously, every concept has a history' (17), which means we can contribute to the unfolding of the drama, as well as map the circulation of concept-tools that form our inheritance.

Creative, critical, clinical, sited, there is also what can be called a pedagogy of the concept, which analyses the conditions in which concepts emerge as always singular occasions (Deleuze and Guattari 1994: 12). Learning from the concept as it presents itself as a means of attending to a problem, attentive to the specific moments of its construction, learning how to deal with the milieu in which you find and lose yourself again. The encyclopedic organization of universally applicable concepts is as dangerous as the commercial application of the concept, what Deleuze and Guattari call a disaster of universal capitalism, and Stengers a disaster of thought. A pedagogy of the concept is located between these tendencies, drawing attention to the practices of caring that attend pedagogical practices. Rather than selfish subjectivities claiming the concept, the concept can be released, remaining sufficiently open and suggestive of ways of learning together, which will become relevant when I venture into the practice scene that follows. For Stengers, teaching philosophy 'involves arousing students' appetite for the free and demanding creation of problems that matter' (2013: 172); the taste for thinking, she adds, is a prerequisite for philosophical thought.

This discussion can be developed by following the feminist philosophers of science, Stengers and Haraway, for they have propelled the creative practices associated with the concept-tool further. The problems Stengers and Haraway address, what Stengers calls the intrusion of Gaia (2015), what Haraway calls the Chthulucene (2016), what yet others name the Capitalocene, and of course the exponential explosion on the marketplace of ideas of the Anthropocene, place us thick in the mess of things and the relations between things. Bound up with environmental disasters, climatic ills, mental degradations and the breakdown of societal structures, we are suffering in Stengers's disaster of thought. Confronted and confounded by this disaster, concepts, Stengers warns, should not be used as a quick fix to colonize or overdetermine the encounters and relations that compose a life (Stengers 2012). Concepts are tools that we share with others and which we are prepared to generously pass on, lest concepts get stuck, turning into unreflective dogma. As Stengers explains:

> Indeed, once 'written down', ideas tempt us to associate them with a definite meaning, generally available to understanding, severing the experience of reading from that of writing. This is all the more so in a world that is now saturated with texts and signs that are addressed to 'anyone' – separating us from the 'more than human' world to which ideas nevertheless belong. (Stengers 2012)

The geopolitical location of the invention and use of concept-tools is stressed yet again in that their application should be in response to the particular shapes our situated problems take.

Haraway continues to develop her long-term project of arguing for situated knowledges where she challenges the conceit of pure objectivity, or the 'God trick', in *Staying with the Trouble*. Here she also turns towards the importance of 'art-design-activist practices' (2016: 133). She is particularly interested in how such practices play out amidst cross-species encounters, for instance, in an engagement with what is said to be the largest living organism on the planet, the Great Barrier Reef, which is a large coral reef system suffering severe degradation off the east coast of Australia. She tells the story of a collective enterprise that mixes the complex geometry of hyperbolic planes with the 'fibre craft' of crochet, and, importantly, an ecological matter of care concerning oceanic environments. From 2005 onwards, two Australian sisters living in Los Angeles – Christine Wertheim, who is a poet, artist and crafter, and Margaret her twin sister, a science writer, mathematician and physicist – created and coordinated an astonishing matrix of connections around urgent matters of care pertaining to imperiled oceanic environments, specifically the bleaching of coral reefs. The sisters initiated a project that has now involved over 10,000 people – mostly women – across 40 cities, who have incrementally crocheted an enormous, distributed coral reef out of yarn, plastic and various discarded things.

This globally distributed handcrafted exercise is based on a geometric model of hyperbolic planes. What is a hyperbolic plane? It is a figure said to have contributed to the inauguration of a non-Euclidean geometry (or geometry *after* Euclid). As the mathematician David Henderson explains:

FIGURE 6.1 *Margaret and Christine Wertheim and the Institute For Figuring*, Crochet Coral Reef, *Museum of Arts and Design, New York, 2016. Photography courtesy MAD.*

One way of understanding it is that it's the geometric opposite of the sphere. On a sphere, the surface curves in on itself and is closed. A hyperbolic plane is a surface in which the space curves *away* from itself at every point. Like a Euclidean plane it is open and infinite, but it has a more complex and counterintuitive geometry. (Wertheim 2004)

Crochet turns out to be a perfect way of modelling such complex geometries, which are likewise expressed in the geometries of coral. Mixing complex geometries with handicraft, with ecological concerns, Haraway suggests that the Wertheim sisters' coral reef undertaking is the world's largest collaborative art project (2016: 78). The aim of this distributed craftwork is to embody material contact with coral reefs via material play performed as a practice of 'intimacy without proximity' (79). Much like Katla Maríudóttir's volcanic coastal planes of southern Iceland, you don't have to go visiting these places to express your support. Instead, Haraway optimistically argues: 'Material play builds caring publics' (89). A material thinking collectively emerges as those who gather together to crochet a massively distributed coral reef out of yarn and debris, thereby forming among themselves a coral-like relation. Thinking together is here expressed by making something together. The concept-tool can be handled through material, collaborative practice.

The concept as tool must be redeployed, and passed from hand to hand because concept-creation includes a collaborative ethos. Each time we take hold of a concept-tool 'the gesture of taking it in hand will be a particular one' (Stengers 2005: 185). What do we address when taking a concept-tool in hand? 'The relevant tools, tools for thinking, are then the ones that address and realize this power of the situation' (185). Power here can be understood as a capacity to act, to make a change, as well as the domineering force of 'power over' where power becomes oppressive, which then means that we must develop concept-tools that enable us to creatively resist. The concept-tool is not deployed to secure recognition; it should not be habitually deployed merely to reaffirm what we already believe we know. When it comes to tools for thinking, Stengers insists, 'habit should be resisted' (185) and if we can change our habits, perhaps we can change our habitats. The invention of concept-tools does not present a general means to a universally acclaimed end, but must be put to particular use.

Thinking is not very respectable, it follows no established methodology, it is indisciplined and wild. Philosophy, furthermore, is a 'dangerous exercise' implying 'a sort of groping experimentation', resorting 'to measures that are not very rational, respectable or reasonable' (Deleuze and Guattari 1994: 41; Stengers 2014: 189). When she reads Whitehead, Stengers describes thinking as a free and wild creation of concepts. As such she draws her inspiration directly from Deleuze and Guattari's final collaborative work *What Is*

Philosophy? within which they write of the 'free and wild' creation of concepts that pertains to a specifically Anglo-American style of literature (1994: 105). The creation in question emerges on account of being constructively constrained. The prepositions that best suit thinking when it is directed at creation are not *about*, or *on*, but *with* and *alongside* – thinking from the midst of things. When we ask the question 'what has happened to us?' says Stengers, this is no reason to go searching for an ultimate explanation but, as she insists, 'a resource for telling our stories in another way, in a way that situates us otherwise – not as defined by the past, but as able, perhaps, to inherit from [the past] another way' (2011c: 14). There is a crucial need to think (2013: 174), Stengers adamantly insists, and with Vinciane Despret she argues 'think we must' in order to venture towards a world that may be habitable. This is a 'modest' as well as 'ambitious' call reiterated by Haraway (2016: 130; Stengers and Despret 2014: 159). What choice have we, lest the world, such as it is, entirely close over us as promised by the Anthropocene thesis? There is no longer even a future to project an imaginary towards, as the potentialities of a future have been exhausted in a past and a present. Stengers's advice: We must go on and do philosophy, which is to say, we must create concepts and Images of Thought (Stengers 2014: 190). We must search for what is better at the same time as refusing to be assigned to a predetermined place, situation or outcome.

Understood as tools, concept-tools suggest practices, and this directs us towards the challenges of an ecology of creative practices. If thinking is an activity, and the thinkable a shock to thought that might or might not be rendered durable through the invention of a concept-tool, then this process is likewise susceptible to exhaustion. In every situation, perhaps we would be wise to ask: What kind of clinic for the exhausted do we inhabit and what are our symptoms? What sheltered sites can we secure so as to share our concept-tools with others?

Practice scene: Michael Spooner's *A Clinic for the Exhausted*

I never really knew what category of patients were destined to visit *A Clinic for Exhausted*, but at the time it did not seem to matter as its entangled stories were compelling and the drawings, models and essays that supported its architecture were a humorous, exquisite cadaver of associative excess, one thing, one reference after the other, a serial combinatorial of images and ideas. As the architect-writer Michael Spooner himself explained to me: *It's like stuffing a lead pipe with as many references as possible, samples, precedents, scraps of images, until it bursts.* This makes his process sound like an instrument of architectural terror, a means by which the common and good-sense assumptions presumed in architecture can be challenged. Yes, *A Clinic for the Exhausted* is the proverbial monstrous offspring and its architecture is explicitly, joyously queer. Even though I followed the project closely, and offered feedback on the manuscript before it was published as a book, I never really understood what was going on inside the clinic. It was enough that somehow it was 'breaking up all the ordered surfaces and all the planes' (Foucault 1970: xvi) by messing with the landmarks of architectural thought, and disrupting the smooth working of things at my previous institution, simply in being an exhaustive excess of discursive production that deployed drawings and models as a medium of argumentation. Through its excessive production it demonstrated that it could *do* theory and practice at the same time, an offence, as it turned out, to those theorists and practitioners eager to purify their sub-disciplinary domains.

I realize now that I was quietly on the lookout for signs of confirmation that it was somehow saying something, or accommodating someone, that the clinic was a place people could arrive at or depart from. My hope was that following convalescence a full recovery could be made. It was Michael Spooner who first introduced me to the theme of exhaustion, and perhaps, after all, I was one of the first unwitting patients to enter the wards of *A Clinic for the Exhausted*.

FIGURE 6.2 *Michael Spooner, The Swimming Pool Library*, A Clinic for the Exhausted, *rendered image, 2010.*

Ostensibly, *A Clinic for the Exhausted* is a long, queer love letter to the incorrigible grandfather of renegade Melbourne architecture, the recently deceased Peter Corrigan, with whom Michael developed a close working relationship. It commences sensibly enough with an account of the procurement process 'for a new building to complete a gap in the Melbourne city campus [of RMIT University] located between Swanston Street and Bowen Lane' (Spooner 2013: 12) designed by Edmond and Corrigan, a practice that had opened its doors in 1975. It then proceeds into a discussion of how RMIT Building 8 'can be read as a collision of citations from various architectural, literary and fine art heritages', a 'brazen sampling' (28) as Spooner puts it. And this is enough to launch the great slow boat that is the book, that is the clinic, that is the project, because the next step is the one that drops us down a rabbit's hole as Michael makes an association between the façade of RMIT University Building 8 and an ocean liner.

Building and boat – it is this deceptively simple association that sets the motor of his work going, specifically because 'the ship is the greatest reserve of the imagination'.[2] It is an associative image he was able to conveniently back up (albeit after the fact of constructing it) by citing a drunken love letter written by one of Peter Corrigan's architectural offspring, Howard Raggatt of ARM (Ashton Raggatt McDougal) addressed to Corrigan and dated 22 December 1993. In the letter, Raggatt explains that he has just suffered something like an ecstatic vision of RMIT University Building 8 as it 'began to lift off as though released from its anchors, or set free from its foundations, now departing like a P&O liner' (Spooner 2013: 31). This composite image of building–boat sets Michael Spooner off on a wild oceanic adventure, 'forever taking leave of a place in place of another' (49), encountering a jewel-encrusted tortoise wandering across an oriental carpet,[3] witnessing the flash of the green ray at the horizon as the sun goes down, escaping in a lifeboat, approaching death's door through a reading of Molière's play *La Malade Imaginaire*, travelling all the while as a troubadour tasked with the telling of tales that are adaptations of associations of images and ideas, aching to express his as the truest love – exacerbating his critics who would from time to time accuse him of wilfully bringing his project to the threshold of failure. *Your boat will go down*, they threaten. He fearlessly, or foolhardily, undertakes a process of exhausting the exhausted.

Exhaustion is a theme I have been tirelessly if sporadically working with on and off since before I edited *Deleuze and Architecture*, which was published in 2013. Our introduction was a lament about the supposed 'exhaustion' of the work of Gilles Deleuze in relation to architectural discourse, a refrain I would reliably hear whenever I was foolish enough to admit that I still enjoyed reading the philosopher's work. But first and foremost, it is Spooner I want to acknowledge, his collected Spoonerisms, his impenetrable, possibly entirely

FIGURE 6.3 *Michael Spooner, The Landscape Room,* A Clinic for the Exhausted, *cross section, 2010.*

and wilfully nonsensical *A Clinic for the Exhausted* that aroused my interest in exhaustion. How do I exhaust the exhausted? It was also Michael who introduced me to a small text by the art critic Jan Verwoert called 'Exhaustion and Exuberance: Ways to Defy the Pressure to Perform' (2007) including Verwoert's speculative gesture towards a community of the exhausted. Reciprocally, I feel quite sure that I introduced Spooner to Deleuze's essay 'The Exhausted'. After all, this is how such intimate critical dialogues proceed and how creative gestures can be shared.

Exhaustion and exuberance can be described as intense affects, and by affect I mean less emotion and feeling than affect as our capacity in a world to affect and to be affected in relation to others (and not all these others need be human others, either). In fact, Michael even describes the journeys undertaken in place within *A Clinic for the Exhausted* as an affective atlas. That is to say, affect is what carries us from one episode to the next, from one material-semiotic encounter towards another, rendering us now capable or else incapable depending on what happens to us, and how we decide to deal with it. How do we make ourselves worthy of what happens to us? How do we make ourselves worthy of the event? How do we creatively resist our present situation when circumstances become intolerable?

I should add that by calling forth the role of affect I am by no means advocating a post-critical turn, one that expresses a commitment to an 'affect-driven, nonoppositional, nonresistant, nondissenting, and therefore nonutopian form of architectural production' that is 'cool' and 'easy' (Speaks 2000, 2002; Whiting and Somol 2002, 2005). This is too often the direction taken when research by creative practice is placed on the table. I am not recommending an architecture that dabbles in the production of affect for the sake of affect, as I suggest Sylvia Lavin is supporting in her little pink book *Kissing Architecture*, where she puckers up to the wonder of a new medium that is specifically 'postfeminist' and suffused with 'intense affect' (2011: 4).[4]

Spooner does not instrumentalize affect, nor does he apply it as a medium; his process is closer to a wayward rambling during which he undertakes the construction of an improbable cartography that draws attention to a queer counter-canon for architectural practice and thinking. Spooner's work places extreme pressure on the exhaustive association of images and ideas, forcing to life another possible world, and this is what he calls *A Clinic for the Exhausted* or, more recently in his pedagogical engagements, an architecture of the unreal. The emphasis Spooner places on the indefinite article, *A Clinic*, means that it is neither possible to exactly locate where the clinic is to be discovered nor to determine what program it accommodates. Instead it constrains the space in which architectural thinking-doing can be made manifest. In fact, it paradoxically offers constraints all the way to infinity through its exhaustive series. When he finds himself up against the wall and obliged to explain himself, Spooner returns to his image of a lead pipe stuffed full of explosive architectural precedents and intertextual references. For instance, there are so many legs, endless legs: The architect Peter Corrigan's legs, which appear in a figurine Spooner has modelled where Corrigan is fitted with a head piece that is a cross between a crown, a Ned Kelly iron mask and a deep sea diver's helmet; Howard Raggatt's drunken legs wandering down Swanston Street one evening; Marilyn Monroe's immortalized cinema-image legs; and Busby Berkeley's dancing legs in choreographed array. The series runs back and forth with more and more speed, refusing to settle in place, producing something like a sea-sick nausea. The legs are subsequently offered respite in the reliquary that is the *Swimming Pool Library*, a wing of *A Clinic for the Exhausted* named for Alan Hollinghurst's 1988 novel of the same name. Where do these legs come from? What do they mean? When a sailor returns from a long voyage at sea, his sea legs make his step uncertain once they hit the ground.

As Building 8 sets sail, Spooner deploys his interminable series of images. He tirelessly riffles and trawls the archives of knowledge, digital and material, to create instructions for his architecture of the unreal. His impossible, seething archive thwarts the idea that an archive is in any way an ordered space. *A Clinic* crams all its worthy and unworthy predecessors into the asylum of its machinic assemblage. It is worth noting here that one

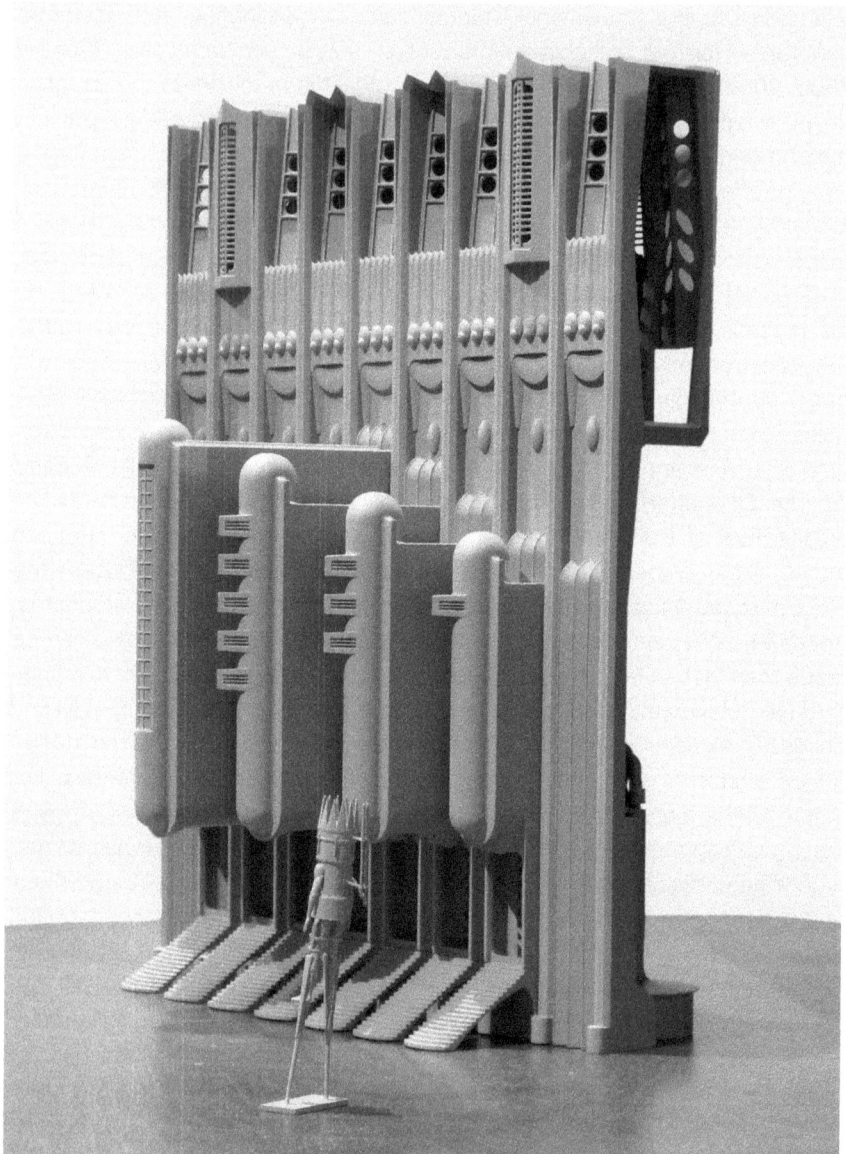

FIGURE 6.4 *Michael Spooner, The Landscape Room,* A Clinic for the Exhausted, *model, 2010.*

of the locations in which Deleuze and Guattari elaborate on this apt-to-be-misinterpreted concept of assemblage (*agencement*) is from inside the boiler room of an ocean liner that has just berthed in the new world. In *Kafka: Toward a Minor Literature*, the definition of assemblage is associated with K's arrival in New York during the opening passages of Kafka's novel, *Amerika*. The first chapter, published separately as 'The Stoker', takes place in a boiler room, the heart of the machine that is the ocean liner. But, as Deleuze and Guattari point out, 'the boiler room is never described in itself (and anyway, the boat is in port), that is because a machine is never simply technical. Quite the contrary, it is technical as a social machine, taking men and women into its gears, or rather, having men and women part of its gears along with things, structures, metals and materials' (Deleuze and Guattari 1986: 81). What's more, you do not stop playing a role amidst such machinic relations, which extend into all modes of life, capturing not just working hours but hours of leisure, placing you inextricably amidst local relations and connecting you up with relations that send you further afield. Sometimes this social machinic involvement wears you down, and sometimes it enables you to do things. A machinic assembly is composed of connections, the kinds of connections that Spooner asks us to concatenate exhaustively.

In the process of constructing his own machinic assemblage, Spooner offers an implicit critique of our architectural fixation on the worthy precedent, aiming to avoid the usual suspects, those references architects and students of architecture are apt to make by drawing on a majoritarian canon of the greats. Spooner searches instead for the minor literature of a wayward architectural history, queering expectations, addling the requirements of good taste and performing a creative resistance to being disciplined. He begins to mess with the disciplinary machine.

A Clinic for the Exhausted takes exhaustion into its title where exhaustion is 'but a vessel without beginning or end' because its connections are interminable. It is the space that emerges between architecture and the imagination. To entertain a methodology of exhaustion inculcated by *A Clinic for the Exhausted*, it is sometimes necessary to construct a lifeboat, and even let loose a life buoy for the wreckage that is left in the wake of a clinic as the productive (if violent) collision between building and boat requires that you find your own line of escape, to say nothing of leakage.

In closing this practice scene it is worth returning to an aside from the art critic Verwoert, who entertains the notion of a community of the exhausted, a community that might be loosely held together by *A Clinic for the Exhausted* such as that composed by Spooner. This community is inoperative in its relation to diagrams of power, that is to say, it addles power where power becomes oppressive. If the community acts together, it does so, according to Verwoert, on account of its 'exuberant politics of dedication' (110). Spooner's exhaustive methods are contagious where the exuberant offerings of the clinic come to be generously shared in what can otherwise be the destructively agonistic pedagogical environment of the architectural design studio. Today, Spooner's *Clinic* is peopled by students of architecture, becoming-architects who are liberated exactly on becoming infected with Spooner's exhaustive, exuberant methodologies.[5] He believes in them, and so they come to believe in themselves and the stories they are able to tell of their local exhaustions. Less the shadows and lies associated with the tall tales of fine forms, Spooner explains to me, the *Clinic* instead supports an 'architecture of the unreal' directed at the emancipation of others. An emancipation from presumed good taste and good design, an emancipation from heteronormative assumptions and an emancipation from institutional norms where the institution casts away in the direction of a neo-liberal enterprise form.

Exhaustion: of the concept

> In this context of theory-fatigue …
> Rosi Braidotti, *The Posthuman* (2013)

It is necessary to return to the importance of investing in theory, feminist, critical, spatial, art and architectural theories, as a means of testing the strength of the relations we explore between the activities of theorizing and practising in architecture and across the creative disciplines from the midst of our environment-worlds. What is at stake in this third pass through exhaustion is how a creative practice can think itself in process, and repel the repeated announcements concerning the end or the death of theory, pronouncements that are pedagogically irresponsible and usually indicate that the subject of enunciation has not been looking in the right places.

One reason we may want to address the exhaustion of concepts and their relation to the cognitive labour of theorizing is that, as we are so often told, theory is in crisis, a crisis that probably emerged when it was first self-consciously posited as an activity for thinkers and practitioners. Everyone knows that theory is in crisis and 'everyone knows' that architectural theory is likely dead, or at least exhausted after its heyday in the 1980s to the 1990s. This is one of the Images of Thought that constrains architectural thinking today – quite simply, the concern that it cannot critically think for itself and must borrow its concepts from elsewhere. Or else, that architecture must content itself with *either* performing theory, *or* engaging in material practice; it must be *either* critical *or* projective. Instead, I want to suggest how architectural theory can participate in a reorientation of thought in engagement with environment-worlds and things. Thinking here is not presumed to originate in a self-secure thinker, but is produced as a shock emerging in the encounter between a subject in the process of unfolding in their environment-world, and enfolding their local environment-world into their specific worldly becomings.

A thinkable strikes the thinker-practitioner in the midst of its environment-world, a thinker who is situated, idiosyncratic, partial and deeply interested.

It is rather tiresome to feel obliged to rehearse, yet again, a discussion that is peculiar to the American architectural discursive scene at the turn of the millennium, and yet which infected global architectural discourse like a pandemic (Crysler, Cairns and Heynen 2012: 4–5; Doucet 2016: 14–15; Rendell 2007: 2–4; Schrijver 2009). I speak of the battle between those who hold firm to a critical position in architecture and those who aim instead for a projective, post-critical approach: as dramatized across Michael Speaks's essays where architectural theory is posited as merely a 'new mode of commodified thought' (2000: 78) or a watered-down version of philosophy; as polemically discussed in Whiting and Somol's co-writings, including a controversial special issue of *Log Magazine* (2002, 2005); as witnessed in a retort from George Baird (2005), a retort subsequently extended by the cautions issued by Reinhold Martin, who insists that a critique of the status quo remains urgent (2005: 2); and not to mention a historical backlog of voices, Sylvia Lavin, Peter Eisenman the student of Colin Rowe, K. Michael Hays a reader of the Italian Manfredo Tafuri and so on, and so forth, whose different positions, as Martin argues, need to be carefully mapped (Martin 2005: 1–2). It is a debate the smell of which lingers, including at conference events such as the inaugural Architectural Humanities Research Association (AHRA) conference in November 2004 at the Bartlett School of Architecture, London, captured in the edited collection *Critical Architecture* (Rendell, Hill, Fraser, Dorrian 2007) and the conference convened by Laura Schrijver at TU Delft in the Netherlands in 2006 called *Projective Landscapes: A Conference on Projective Practice* (Schrijver 2009; Schrijver and Gardner 2006).

At a recent architectural symposium called *Theory's History 196X – 199X: Challenges in the Historiography of Architectural Knowledge*, which took place in Brussels, Belgium, between 8 and 10 February 2017, the disciplinary rigour of architectural history was upheld and architectural theory came out somewhat the worse for wear. In a panel on the Friday morning chaired by Joan Ockman, known for her work on architectural pragmatism, the presenters spoke of 'theory's dead thoughts' and the activity of 'taking apart a cadaver of theory'.[6] It would seem that (architectural) theory has become a relic, an arche-fossil, the remainders of which it is up to the (architectural) historians to distribute, dissect, discuss and judge. There is an implicit prohibition at work here that declares theory ought not be practised, and by no means should it extend a speculative gesture, let alone propose any concept construction. An imperative that needs to be forwarded instead is how (architectural) theory can be reclaimed in its allegiance with practices, and as a practice in its own right.

Even more recently, appearing in the email inboxes of architectural and other practitioners and researchers in the form of an *e-flux journal* update (no doubt simultaneously hitting various social media, circulating, being shared and liked and exuding its noopolitical affects), yet another lament was to be heard, this time from Philip Ursprung, who asks, yet again, that singular question: 'The End of Theory?' (Ursprung 2017). Speaking of the tired old midlife crisis of theory from the comfortable well-funded position of the Institute for the History and Theory of Architecture (gta) ETH Zurich, where he works as a professor, Ursprung suggests that architecture today is in an 'a-theoretical phase' and architectural theory 'is evoked merely as a phantom that haunts us'. He sets up a distinction between a historical past, wherein architectural theory laid out a shared horizon, as contrasted with the situation today, wherein theory is composed of a plethora of statements from architects, of histories of theory, and of discourses appropriated from other disciplines, anthropology, sociology and political philosophy. The flourishing phase of architectural theory petered out in the 1990s, and today it is a mere shadow of itself, he says. Apparently we have outsourced theory to the philosophers and sociologists (the fact that the object-oriented philosopher Graham Harman has recently been appointed an inaugural philosophy chair at the private school of architecture Sci-Arc in Los Angeles would seem to prove Ursprung's point). Today, according to Ursprung, we (architectural theorists) practise malleable forms of argumentation so as not to fix meaning too readily, we gather together murmuring in roundtables and conferences and have dialogues in a culture of 'compromise and agreement', which suggests that nothing is at stake, that we have lost our polemical thrust. Worse still, theory 'remains constantly in flux, ready for adaptation and revision, void of normative functions, and virtually deregulated', which makes it sound like it is politically and ethically vacuous and apt to be co-opted in troubling ways, returning us to Michael Speaks's suggestion that theory has become a mere commodity, a soundbite, a meme.

Ursprung acknowledges that all is not lost, because architectural theory and theorists can still eke out a shadowy existence 'in the academic back seat' on pedagogical and professional design jury panels, on blogs, at biennales and exhibitions. The slowness, the inertia of the institution is what will continue to shelter us, he concludes. What is curiously left out of this picture are many of the other places in which experimental and speculative modes of (critical) theory still thrive, and the question concerning what kind of practices and inventive methodologies are being explored to re-engage a theory–practice relay. There is the ongoing series of events called the AHRA, which celebrates a mix of disciplinary expertise rather than lamenting a lack of autonomy for a sub-discipline called architectural theory. There is the important work that continues to emerge out of the Bartlett School of Architecture mixing practice, theory and history; here too I want to celebrate the work emerging in the Swedish context where I work at KTH (Royal Institute of Technology), with its emphasis on feminist theories and practices. There is the emergence of several new journals and platforms (*Avery Review*, *Ardeth*) and the enduring health of others (*ATR*, *Thresholds MIT*, *Candide*, *Arch+*, the platform *Aggregate* at we-aggregate.org), though no doubt each of these forums suffers its own serial crises, and those concerned must work their way through their fatigue, as Ursprung is evidently doing, including concerns about where the next pot of money will come from. While it may be so that we do not need architectural theorists to reflect, contemplate and communicate in order to offer their disinterested judgement on the 'real' work of architecture, at the same time it is necessary to resist those who claim that the cognitive labour of architectural theorists is now obsolete.

Theory arouses the most profound anxieties, especially in the face of the slipperiness of concepts, and the violence of thinkables. Coming to the close of a wave of theory exuberance in the 1980s and 1990s, what Sylvia Lavin once called a 'theory frenzy' (1990), Fredric Jameson dedicates a chapter of *Postmodernism, or the Cultural Logic of Late Capitalism* to the role of theory (1991). He cites the anxieties of two critical theorists Walter Benn Michaels and Steven Knapp as voiced in their essay 'Against Theory', an essay to which Claire Colebrook more recently returns (2014a: 33–36). Jameson outlines Michaels and Knapp's complaint that theory is 'the name for all the ways people have tried to stand outside practice in order to govern practice from without' (Jameson 1991: 181; Knapp and Michaels 1982: 30). Note ought to be taken here of the span of bibliographical dates, which draws attention to the perennial anxieties over theory, cutting across disciplinary registers from literary to cultural theory to architectural theory.

Theory is supposed to locate us outside a scene, but once the realization dawns that it is not possible to remain outside and disinterested, the immanence of a situation then looms in. We are either too close or too far away, but it is immanence in response to which Jameson raises alarms. Immanence suppresses distance, keeping the mind involved in detail and immediacy, and yet following the performance, which arouses a 'sense of breathlessness', the reader risks coming away with empty hands, 'without ideas and interpretations to carry away with us' (Jameson 1991: 187), and perhaps, I would add, suffering a state of stupor. It is a critique that might be addressed to Deleuze and Guattari's plane of immanence. What is to be done? While Jameson's key target is New Historicism, his general remarks are still cause for hesitation.

Isabelle Stengers herself insists that it is not theory about which she speaks when she calls for a cosmopolitical project (2013: 177). From the top of her aluminium ladder, Maria Reiche archly proclaims to Bruce Chatwin that she is not doing theory (Chatwin 1989). But what kind of theory do Stengers and Reiche reject? It is a specific understanding of theory that they resist, one that assumes that the theorist stands outside at a safe distance from the event that is taking place, in their attempts to 'govern practice from without'. This kind of theory risks imposing a universal Image of Thought, a fixed code, establishing a shared horizon of the type Ursprung seems to allude to nostalgically.

In her recent book Isabelle Doucet asks: 'How can theory better contribute to the formulation of a critical agenda for architecture? Can theory itself operate as a practice?' In answer to her questions she calls on an approach that is 'criticality-from-within' (2015: 5) and suggests that an emphasis on practice does not mean a dismissal of theory. Isabelle Stengers, whom Doucet reads closely, calls criticality-from-within 'immanent critique'. As Jean-Michel Rabaté has put it in conversation with Gregg Lambert, 'even if you drop your studies and become a construction worker, you need a theory or at least an account of why you are doing that' (Frichot 2009b; Rabaté and Lambert 2003: 45). What is it that you are doing, and how are you doing it? This becomes a question of ethico-aesthetics.

Rather than framing an overarching definition of what properly belongs to (architectural) theory, an attention to practices and what we are doing when we theorize needs to be drawn out. The role of ecologies of creative practice, and how they are profoundly entangled with theories, has been a main impetus of this book, alongside the risk of exhaustion we all face as we undertake our practices. These are practices-theories taking place in situ, learning from other theories-practices, proceeding in uncoordinated leaps, feeling about experimentally, making mistakes, retreating, advancing, speeding up and slowing down. There is a great deal that could be said about the weakness of architectural theory as a disciplinary niche, and the way it tends to become the mere supplement to history in programs of architecture. My main complaint would be the way in which it is habitually subsumed by architectural history, a discipline that assumes that it possesses more rigorous methods. No such battle should be proposed, for if each performs within its own ecology of practices, what is required, as Stengers suggests, is a respect for these respective practices.

What if we were to understand the position and practices of the architectural theorist in another way altogether? Another kind of aesthetic figure could be installed who has the impossible task of maintaining a vast survey of current discourse, without presuming she will ever exhaust the field, which leads her to recognize how important it is to enter into collaboration and forums for collective enunciation (Runting 2018).

It is worthwhile retelling the oft-told parable of the (architectural) theorist, found for instance in the *Sage Handbook of Architectural Theory*, where the editors locate the theorist and theory somewhere between a legitimizing role and a capacity to be tactically disruptive (Crysler, Cairns and Heynen 2012: 12). Each time the story is told, it comes out a little differently, which is what happens when stories are passed along.

You too might have heard the story of the etymological origins of the figure of the theorist, who arrives as an ambassador to a strange, far-off land and bears witness to events from a safe distance, returning again to her safe haven with an authoritative report in hand. Here the theorist, and let us say she is an architectural theorist, is assumed to have no impact on what she has come to observe, let us call it the event of architecture, all its rituals and norms, and habits of thought. Instead she is supposed to perform the role of a reliable witness, and like the chronicler or the storyteller of a great saga she makes notes that are as exacting as possible, allowing for the occasional narrative flourish. Her collected documents are to be passed down through posterity, or else simply shared with her colleagues. Now it is true that in many schools of architecture the theorists and the historians too, perhaps deemed too dangerous to be mixed up with the others, are cordoned off and kept well clear of the epicentre of an architect's education, which still privileges the teaching–learning space of the design studio.

What this story overlooks is that the architect-theorist never remains at a distance from the (architectural) event she observes, but gets entangled in its midst, getting her hands dirty, joining in the rituals and feasts and making her own singular contribution to the ongoing construction of the culture and discipline of architecture. In fact, she works alongside the practitioners, 'going native' as they say in ethnographic terms. The architect-theorist arrives from elsewhere, and in witnessing remarkable things is herself transformed by what she encounters, but in observing the symptoms and making critical commentary as well as undertaking creative concept-construction, she likewise transforms what unfolds before her. She has an impact on the architectural event, and she holds the capacity to alter practices. Indra McEwen points out that although the ancient etymology of the term *theoria* suggests the name given to ambassadors, who, arriving from elsewhere and separated from their 'native city', observe an event, these spectators frequently participated by 'offering sacrifices, and by taking part in the dances and games' (1993: 21; Frichot 2009b).

The architectural theorist is susceptible to a kind of stupor when confronted with the seething mass of information she has immediately available to her in this age of information. To conclude this section dedicated to the exhaustion of thinkables, I raise the persistent feeling of the exhaustion of concepts. This is what John Barth in his essay 'The Literature of Exhaustion' once called the 'used-upness of certain forms or the felt exhaustion of certain possibilities' (Barth 1984: 64). Barth originally penned his essay from the midst of the American 'High Sixties' (1965–1973), the Vietnam War, student campus riots, the stirrings of the environmental movement, when things seemed both volatile and possible, and diagrams of power hinted either at future reorganization or else further repression. Looking back at his original essay from the point of view of the early 1980s, he holds to his claim that what artists (and here we can add other creative practitioners) feel about the state of the world and their art is less important than what they do about it. This begs the question: From the midst of a perceived 'theory fatigue' (Braidotti 2013: 5), which we are evidently experiencing today, how do we proceed from exhausted combinatorials of things and ideas, through exhausted voices, through the exhaustion of spaces and images, towards what Deleuze calls 'a movement in the world of the mind' (1998a: 169)? In his essay 'The Exhausted', which has helped me organize my discussion of a methodology of exhaustion, Deleuze's fourth move, I propose, is the one in which he states 'what matters is no longer the any-space-whatever but the mental image to which it leads' (169). Before it seems that what is proposed is some kind of retreat from our environment-worlds and the problems we choose to address, it is important to understand that such movements of the mind do not take place in isolation, and again, that mind must be understood in an expanded sense.

Depending on what direction is taken through the methodology of exhaustion, the point of departure either proceeds from the exhaustive combinatorial of things (including received concepts and images that we are happy to digest and further disseminate by pressing 'LIKE') towards the dissipation of the Image of Thought, or else commences from an encounter with a dogmatic Image of Thought and *what we make of it*, and even the creation of those hopeful images and concepts that assist in the establishment of an affirmative Image of Thought, thence proceeding again towards series of things, concepts and images. This reversibility of the methodology of exhaustion as it pertains to the Image of Thought becomes most clear in Deleuze's books on the cinema where he explains (by way of Artaud) that the image has as its object the functioning of thought, and that the functioning of thought brings us back to images and their powerful organization as an Image of Thought (Deleuze 1989: 165). Again, the methodology of exhaustion can operate in both directions, but notable in Deleuze's presentation where he studies Beckett's television plays is the way the methodology results in the 'iconoclastic' gesture of the dissolution of the power of the Image of Thought (see Hême de Lacotte 2010). Success may well be measured by whether a dogmatic Image of Thought is overturned, installing in its place a new Image of Thought, a paradoxically iconoclastic gesture. Nevertheless, there is no guarantee that the 'new' or 'novel' will not in time also become dogmatic, a restored hegemony.

Exhaustivity and exhaustion together present a working method that enables us to engage in what to do with concepts and images, how concepts can be constructed and how we can struggle to *make* an image, to compose a concept-tool from a thinkable from time to time that could really transform us and our environment-worlds (Deleuze 1998a 158). To make a novel Image of Thought and not recite a ready-made one is difficult work, and there is always the threat of failure, or else corporeal or material exhaustion including the body that is our built environment, and ourselves as social collectives. An Image of Thought enables the capture (more or less fleeting) of sense and sensation, or the powers of affects, percepts and concepts, and this capture or composition either offers a glimmer of liberation or else reinforces repression. We exhaust our concepts and they exhaust us, but we need to be worthy of the uses we discover for our concepts. Deleuze and Guattari explain that the concept 'speaks the event, not the essence or the thing' (1994: 21), but the event is necessarily populated with things, at the threshold between sense-making and states of affairs, some of them pertaining to architectural environments. Take care of your sense, lest it takes care of you. The metaphor must be mobilized, Zoë Sofia (Sofoulis) explained to me in conversation, lest it becomes reified. To this I would add, once reified it settles down as dogma.

Drawing on Franco 'Bifo' Beradi's reflections on exhaustion and depression, Jussi Parikka points out the connection that can be made between 'the slumping global economic regime and the psychosphere' (Parikka 2013), which can be further related to Guattari's ecological thought, whereby ecology must be thought through nature *and* subjectivity *and* social relations. Reading 'Bifo', Parikka comments that 'exhaustion and depression are actually the key moods through which to understand creative and cognitive capitalism and the world economy – the worn-out soul cannot keep up with its digital machines' (2013). You should not be surprised then to discover yourself in the midst of a kind of stupor. What's more, to introduce the question of exhaustion no doubt makes one especially susceptible to its symptoms. The stupor of exhaustion leads me, perhaps ill-advisedly, into the problem of stupidity, a state of beatific stupefaction. Avital Ronell points out that 'once the topic [of stupidity] is broached, one runs the risk of betraying oneself as stupid' (2003: 71). Stupidity, much like exhaustion, is contagious. The voice that cries out in resistance can either become infectious or else dry up the flow of voices.

Broadly speaking, there are two varieties of stupidity according to Ronell, though I am sure these two general areas accommodate a multiplicity of variations on the theme. On the one hand, there is the kind of really pernicious stupidity that Deleuze rails against: 'Great as they are, stupidity and baseness would be still greater if there did not remain some philosophy which always prevents them from going as far as they would wish, which forbids them' (Deleuze 1983: 106). Philosophy, Deleuze argues, is useful 'for harming stupidity, for turning stupidity into something shameful' (106). Here stupidity is set up as the enemy of philosophy. This is a vulgar form of stupidity, and it is where we find the figures of the know-it-all, the loudmouth, those who are really stupid in the worst way exactly because they presume to have some mastery over knowledge that they impose upon others. On the other hand, there is the 'honorable' (Ronell 2003: 78) form of stupidity, marked by a lack of distinction, taste, judgement and determinacy, but in all this lack showing up what we presume to know, destabilizing, even if only marginally, the structures by which we claim to have mastered a world (2003: 73). Deleuze, recognizing the diverse and even divisive forms of stupidity, has recommended a necessary reading of stupidity, asking: What are the conditions of possibility of stupidity? (1994: 151), because stupidity, after all, will continue to haunt philosophy, as well as all the other disciplines that claim to know something, or to love knowledge. And that includes the creative disciplines and architecture.

Stupidity is directly related to exhaustion, and on a number of levels: 'Once you set about to address stupidity, something of a stultifying atmosphere descends on you', making you 'breathless with stupidity' (Ronell 2003: 63). The ineffable lethargy that limits thinking can be called stupidity, or at least, the effects of stupefaction. There is a weariness that can descend upon you while writing, and by extension, in the midst of any creative act. Ronell points out that Emmanuel Levinas describes this sensation as fatigue, while Maurice Blanchot, as he writes in his interminable *Infinite Conversation*, calls it weariness (Ronell 2003: 63–64). Deleuze and Guattari discuss the weariness of thought when it encounters the plane of immanence, and how thought must fall back on relative speeds, and the association of ideas, which may or may not arrive at the construction of concepts (1994). Yet stupor, that which renders us momentarily stupefied, can be enjoyed as something of a brief ecstasy, pulling us out of the presumptuousness of our stable subject-positions.

Here, finally, I conclude by returning yet again to Stengers, who discusses the pernicious ways in which stupidity 'dismembers a concrete situation' (2015: 119), destroying ways of thinking and imagining otherwise. In French this is what is called *bêtise*, with the unfortunate further association of animality (see also Deleuze 1994: 150–151). Stengers's central concern is about those who set themselves up as guardians of knowledge, imposing a distinction between those who *know* and those who *merely* believe (2015: 121). Those who 'know' issue set statements of the kind: 'you should remember that'; 'I am aware but all the same' (119); 'what would you do in our place?' (120); to which can be added the '*Everyone knows, no one can deny*' (Deleuze 1994: 130, emphasis in original) that participates in Deleuze's critique of the orthodoxy of the Image of Thought. They seem to listen, because often that is what is expected of them, but then they go right ahead and impose their more 'appropriate' or 'responsible' way of doing things anyway. Yet here too stupidity of the pernicious kind can be contrasted with stupidity as stupor, which can be further associated with paralysis and impotence, but which may offer something else in terms of 'a movement in the world of the mind'. Moving through paralysis and impotence, this kind of stupefaction can inculcate the necessity of slowing down, even becoming 'slow learners' as a means of creative resistance, that is, not presuming to pre-emptively know what it is that confronts us, not making so many excuses, attempting to think *with*, rather than think *for*. With the greatest caution, and as I now make my way towards a conclusion to this book, I want to venture a connection between stupor and beatitude understood as a form of refuge by passing through the exhaustion of creative practices.

Notes

1. Donna Haraway and Isabelle Stengers took part in an event in Brussels, Belgium, in March 2017 curated by GECo (Groupe d'études constructivistes – Université Libre de Bruxelles), where a documentary film directed by Fabrizio Terranova was also shown called *Donna Haraway: Story Telling for Earthly Survival*. Haraway and Stengers frequently refer to each other in their writings. See http://www.bozar.be/en/activities/124753-donna-haraway
2. Here Foucault's essay dedicated to heterotopias, 'Of Other Spaces', is cited by Spooner. Spooner, *A Clinic for the Exhausted*, p. 28.
3. The scene of the tortoise is taken from Huysman who describes a certain Duc Jean des Esseintes and his 'self-imposed exile away from the grotesque and senseless bourgeois world of the city'. See Joris-Karl Huysman, *A Rebours* (1884) cited in Spooner, *A Clinic for the* Exhausted, p. 204.
4. See Doug Spencer, *The Architecture of Neoliberalism: How Contemporary Architecture Became an Instrument of Control and Compliance*, London: Bloomsbury Academic, 2016, for a critique of the deployment of affect in Lavin, as well as in the discourse of architects such as Farshid Moussavi, Alejandro Zaera-Polo and Lars Spuybroek.
5. Michael Spooner has been leading design studios in the Masters of Architecture, Program of Architecture, RMIT University Melbourne since 2010. Collected examples of his students' work can be found at: https://thexhausted.com.
6. The panel in question was called Educational Settings and included presentations from Guiseppina Scavuzzo, Jasper Cepl, Joseph Bedford and Ole W. Fisher. It took place between 9 am and 11 am on Friday, 10 February 2017.

Conclusion:
Exhaustion and its after-affects

We have a desperate need for other stories, not fairy tales in which everything is possible for the pure of heart, courageous souls, or the reuniting of goodwills, but stories recounting how situations can be transformed when thinking they can be, achieved together by those who undergo them.

ISABELLE STENGERS, *In Catastrophic Times: The Coming Barbarism* (2015: 132)

I must finish up quickly now, because my time is nearly over. I have not exhausted everything there is to say about environment-worlds, things and thinkables at the threshold of architectural exhaustion. What I have offered is an insufficient survey of some collected matters of care and how they can be mapped across a series of creative practice scenes, and how stories can be told that capture fleeting points of view on posthuman landscapes undergoing disturbing changes as well as evincing glimmers of hope. The challenge, Stengers insists, is to work together, think together and to repopulate the 'devastated desert of our imaginations' (2015: 132). I want to close now in search of refuge amidst a sheltered zone, attempting some quietude. This is less to beg a retreat from a local environment-world, which is in any case impossible, than to seek out the means by which to slow down, and how slowing down at the threshold of exhaustion can become an exercise in creative resistance. How, finally, is it possible to secure refuge, or some momentary shelter before moving on?

There are two final practice scenes that I want to describe, each of which expresses a tremulous joy, even an encounter with this uncomfortable term I belatedly introduce, beatitude. Returning to Avital Ronell and the state of stupor with which I closed the third part of this book, she remarks on a connection I want to pursue: 'Replete in itself, immune to criticism, without resistance or the effort of negativity, stupidity contains a sacred element: it is beatitude' (2003: 44). Where stupidity is a condition we imagine best avoided – no one wants to be mistaken for stupid – beatitude is a distinctly uncomfortable concept, especially for a secular audience. For many, it will seem a curious anachronism tied up with blessedness and the passions of spiritual fervour. Stengers admits that part of the reason she chooses the conceptual figure of Gaia is exactly because it is hard to digest, and arouses discomfort (2012); not only that, but Gaia challenges 'those who believed they were at the centre', who turn out to be those who 'desperately mess up what they, and many other earthly critters, depend upon' (2012: 178). For my purposes, beatitude works in much the same way: it is intended to arouse discomfort, it is not meant to be easy and it *is* about intense affect and processes of decentring so as to allow other voices into the practice stories we tell so as to challenge core presumptions, for instance, in a discipline like architecture. Spinoza calls beatitude 'mental liberty' and associates it with the third kind of knowledge wherein body and mind are considered equally at ease, and passivity is transformed into activity (1967: 199). The hope may well be that such concepts are more difficult to exchange on the marketplace of Big Ideas, and the risk is that they will lose themselves in the spiritual and self-help section of the local bookstore. By way of exhaustion, stupor and beatitude, the place I want to arrive at is one that can be called refuge, even asylum. First though, in order to conclude, I return to exhaustion.

If exhaustion as an organizational theme, or a methodology as I have called it, is to be found most intensively discussed in Deleuze's brief study of Samuel Beckett's television plays, it should be no surprise that exhaustion is likewise to be found in Deleuze's two books on cinema. In *Cinema 1* and *Cinema 2*, dedicated respectively to the pre-war movement-image, and the post-war time-image, there is to be found scattered here and there exhausted figures and images, exhausted powers of existence and exhausted spaces (1986, 1989). Exhaustion, a 'side-affect', comes to be historicized according to a logic of cinema and television images, to which Beckett's television plays contribute. Placing exhaustion and beatitude together means bearing witness to the ecstatic passions expressed in what Deleuze calls the affection-image (Deleuze 1986: 70). An exemplary instance of this is to be found in depictions of the ill-fated, subsequently sainted Joan of Arc. No doubt alarm bells of all kinds should begin to go off here, lest we set up the figure of woman as the one who must be sacrificed in order to be saved. Deleuze describes Carl

Theodor Dreyer's cinematographic depiction of the famous warrior-saint in his silent black and white film *The Passion of Joan of Arc* (1928) as an 'affective film par excellence' (1986: 106). Joan of Arc is a figure depicted in close-ups that fill the screen, a figure about whom Deleuze notes that an ecstatic passion passes *through* her face, via its expressed exhaustion, its fears and its joys, its turning away and its encounter with the limit. Benjamin's angel of history and Latour's angel of geohistory can both be called to mind here. Wide staring stupefied eyes. Eyes softened in ecstasy. She has seen more than she can bear, she has experienced too much, yet she witnesses something she then makes available to others.

And so, it is across such affected faces run through with overwhelming percepts, cropped by close-up images, that exhaustion and beatitude come together. Such is the role, furthermore, played by Deleuze's visionaries and mediators, those engaged in creative practices whose speculative gestures feel out what is possible and *through* whom forces, affects and percepts pass. Without a community of mediators (real *and* imaginary), nothing happens (Deleuze 1995c: 125). Chasing the possible: 'We head for the horizon, on the plane of immanence, and we return with bloodshot eyes, yet they are the eyes of the mind ... To think is always to follow the witch's flight' (1994: 41). Here Deleuze and Guattari are making oblique reference to Bernard Malamud's novel *The Fixer*, where the main protagonist happens upon the work of Spinoza in a junkyard sale, curses himself for wasting money on the book, but then gets taken up by the force of its writing, explaining: 'As I say, I didn't understand every word but when you're dealing with such ideas you feel as though you were taking a witch's ride. After that I wasn't the same man' (1966: 71). The witch performs yet another role in Stengers's work. Drawing on the neopagan witch Starhawk, Stengers calls on the figure of the witch and her 'magic rituals' to draw attention to forms of knowledge that sit uncomfortably with the methodologies of scientific knowledge (2012, 2005a: 194).

Who are we who gather around our matters of care and concern amidst an environment-world? I asked in opening this book. I also spoke of the importance of hesitating as we bear witness to our environmental encounters. Stengers's frequent references to the rituals of witches is her way of paying heed to feminist activism, unconventional forms of gathering and the importance she places on 'thinking in the presence of women' (196), a positioning further explored in Stengers and Despret's *Women Who Make a Fuss* (2014). A gathering makes something present, and this is how its magic is expressed, Stengers explains. In the space of gathering, certainties are placed on hold momentarily and we open ourselves up to other modes of practice, in the process 'making present what causes practitioners to think and feel and act' (Stengers 2005a: 195). We pause to listen for a moment rather than immediately casting judgement, and in caring to listen, to hesitate, we open ourselves up to being transformed. In this we create what Donna Haraway calls refuge, spaces for living together, which is the urgent art of reconstitution, recuperation and recomposition, including the 'mourning of irreversible losses' (Haraway 2016: 101).

Practice scene: Margit Brünner's joys

Margit tells me that it is an exhausting exercise attempting to maintain the greatest proportion of active joys, and the least of the sad passions. Over the years, since departing Vienna, Austria, and settling in Adelaide, South Australia, she has ventured farther and farther away from what would conventionally be accepted to be architectural practice. She has probably passed the threshold of (architectural) exhaustion in her pursuit of an aesthetics of joy (Brünner 2015). Having first encountered Margit and her work at a creative research gathering called *Expanded Spatial Practices*, convened by Linda Marie Walker and the late John Barber at the University of South Australia, Adelaide, 10–12 September 2009, I find myself returning to her ephemeral performance-based projects again and again across a series of essays (Frichot 2015, 2016, 2017, 2018a, 2018b). In this I certainly risk exhausting our encounter. Skirting the outer reaches of the properties deemed proper to architecture, Margit opens up ethico-aesthetic 'test-sites' (Brünner 2015) for investigation. Like Katla Maríudóttir she refuses the disciplinary demand to compose a circumscribed, autonomous architectural project organized according to good design and good taste. Unless you have the opportunity to encounter Margit in the midst of a site-based performance, which is unlikely, you must rely instead on documentary evidence in the form of still photography and grainy video clips, as well as her drawings.[1] She comes to us from a great distance, revealing glimpses of landscapes that are near impossible to access, especially in terms of their ancient Australian indigenous lore, to which respect must be extended at every turn. Margit works with pathos and humour: There is an image of a woman standing stock still in a crowded train carriage, on a casino floor, in a car park, surveying a freeway. She is dressed in what looks like white protective gear. There is a woman who handles a large round bat held aloft at the end of a long pole, in post-industrial settings, on a city street. It is as though she is attempting to catch some invisible airborne matter. The woman stands out exactly on account of her beatific stillness and calm. Such images as these belong to Margit's *Cosmethic Space Refinements* (2002) series. Where she enters wilderness scenes, specifically on a station in the Flinders Ranges, South Australia, called Oratunga, she documents her performances on video. *Zwischen Büschel* (*Among Tufts*) (2005) is a video I return to simply to calm myself down. In the video we witness a woman dressed entirely in

FIGURE C.1 *Margit Brünner, Catcher I; Catcher II; Surveyor Metro Melbourne; Surveyor Crown Casino*, Cosmethic Space Refinements, 2002. Photography by Urs Bette.

FIGURE C.1 (continued)

red with a white hat caressing vegetation in gestures that become more and then less frenetic. It seems as though she is attempting to enter into some form of communion with the more-than-human in her encounter with the arid Australian vegetation. Debaise, Stengers and their collaborators' collective account of the intrusion of Gaia is again relevant: 'Gaia's demands constrain us to go back to earthly practices, these alone being able to deal with local, situated and complex configurations. Earthly practices mean due attention to territories, to the various ways all beings, human and non-human, populate and indeed co-produce the Earth through bodily, intra- and interspecific, historical, political, ritual, technical, economical and even mineral practices' (Debaise et al. 2015: 174). Such a practice as this is what I witness Margit performing as she desperately attempts to make contact with the territories in which she finds herself.

Exhaustion, beatitude

It is Margit who has helped me think further about the connection between joy and beatitude, a conundrum that can be sketched out conceptually between Deleuze and his idiosyncratic reading of the seventeenth-century Dutch Jewish philosopher Baruch Spinoza (1632–1677). Deleuze demonstrates that Spinoza's ethics extend a practical philosophy dedicated to the living of a life that strives towards the maximum of adequate ideas and joyful affects (Deleuze 1988b), this maximum being designated with the term beatitude. It seems fitting that Baruch Spinoza, also known as Benedict Spinoza, happens to have a given name that means blessed. Deleuze makes a point of taking the time to explain that Spinoza was not only a philosopher but a craftsperson, a lens grinder (1988b: 7). He died from having inhaled glass dust. What is a life? It is absolute immanence, understood as an infinite survey of the plane of immanence wherein: 'The singularities and the events that constitute *a* life coexist with the accidents of *the* life that corresponds to it' (Deleuze 2001: 29). Absolute immanence, beatitude, pertains to Spinoza's third kind of knowledge, which places the creative practitioner in closest proximity to 'Nature or God' (*deus sive natura*), and despite the seemingly mystical turn this concept takes, Deleuze insists that beatitude remains 'quite concrete' (1978). It is expressed as love of oneself, of Nature or God, and it is composed as a world of pure intensities: God/Nature, Myself, Things (Deleuze 1988b: 74; Spinoza 1967: 222).

Moving too swiftly now in order to summarize: Spinoza's first kind of knowledge accounts for extrinsic encounters between bodies, one body forming a composition with another body or else becoming decomposed following a bad encounter (Deleuze 1992a: 303). Relations between bodies are inseparable from their capacity to be affected and to affect, to be acted upon and to act. This is the domain of inadequate ideas, vaguely formed sensations aroused through encounters, collisions and relations, but also operating on memory and the imagination via the endurance of images. Moira Gatens and Genevieve Lloyd place great importance on the first kind of knowledge and the role of the imagination without which other forms of knowledge would not be possible (1999). The second kind of knowledge pertains to common notions. This is where we work on the agreements to be found between our bodies; for example, the relationship formed between the body of a swimmer and a body of water. We operate on the basis of 'properties common to our body and external bodies' (Deleuze 1992a: 306) and strive to overlay the passive affects and encounters of the first kind of knowledge with active affects of the second kind in order to seek out what we share in common, as well as what distinguishes us. Here adequate ideas emerge upon which we can agree, as well as joys of the second kind. It is worth keeping in mind that passive affects, our fumbling errors, our stupor and even our stupidities, can hold the kernel of what might become an adequate idea (Deleuze 1988b: 60), what I have called a concept-tool in this work and elsewhere. Progressing from the first to the second kind of knowledge involves a great deal of stumbling in the dark, trial and error and happy accidents, until we can make a relation durable and do something about it. Then, should we be so fortunate, and there are no guarantees, we can achieve the third kind of knowledge, which is to achieve an insight into an eternal essence expressed through a passing existence: the two inextricably bound to each other, and essence here should not be mistaken for some a priori universal, but rather designates the peculiar capacities of a mode of life so long as it exists in its relation to 'Essences or Singularities, Percepts' surveyed at absolute speed in eternity (1998c: 148–149). Perplexingly, should we arrive at this third level of knowledge, which collapses two temporal registers, that which is eternal (Aion) and that which is qualified by a specific 'hereness' and 'thisness', *haecceity* (Chronos) we would discover ourselves where we already were: infinite movement expressed as serene immobility. Shelter, refuge.

Deleuze insists that the progression through the three levels of knowledge takes place according to this 'strict order': (1) inadequate ideas come to us and passive affections flow from them; (2) common notions form, but only through an active effort of selection, dependant on the (ethical) choices we make. And what we suggest to be exemplary must be chosen with great care (Deleuze 1992a: 301)! To form a common notion is about being brave, venturing forth from the circle we have drawn around ourselves as a protective barrier. This means that we might suffer a passive affection, but if we select it for a composition and it works, through this effort, this act of selection and extraction 'which is extremely hard, extremely difficult' (Deleuze 1998c: 145),

FIGURE C.2 *Margit Brünner,* Zwischen Büschl *[Among Tufts], 2005. Videostill.*

we make it adequate, and can thereby share it as a common notion with others; (3) When we get to adequate ideas, then we can venture the field of active joys and loves, the third kind of knowledge. All the while, it is a vain hope to imagine that we can achieve and then continue to maintain the greatest proportion of active affects or joys, because 'we will always have passions, and sadness, together with our passive joys', says Deleuze (1992a: 310). It follows then, as Margit demonstrates through her barely durable works, that: 'Existence itself is still conceived as a kind of test. Not, it is true, a moral one, but a physical or chemical test, like that whereby work(wo)men check the quality of some material, of a metal or a vase' (Brünner 2015; Deleuze 1992a: 317). The creative practitioner constantly tests herself in relation to her local environment-world, and the things that gather there. Despite the extreme abstraction of the above-described progression through the levels of knowledge, this account serves to complement Deleuze's methodology of exhaustion and suggests material application in terms of the works, loves, lives and labours of the creative practitioner. Moving in a slow experimental manner amidst things, making surprising discoveries here and there, commencing to formulate what are still inadequate ideas, building on these ideas, for instance, by coming together with others to share concept-tools.

Forming common notions, making something that is sufficiently durable and might be shared, passivity slowly transforms into activity and greater liberty when it comes to one's material and sense-making compositions.

Running as a forceful undercurrent amidst a mounting literature and the associated practices dedicated to 'new materialism', summarized in the demand that we urgently return to our vibrant material relations and acknowledge the ethical challenge of following the material of one's life, one's practices, one's situation, all the while vibrant matter is cut through with immaterial forces, the incorporeal. This is where Elizabeth Grosz ventures in her most recent book, *The Incorporeal* (2017). Grosz warns the reader in her introduction that what she is venturing into is rather abstract. This is no reason to be afraid, or dismissive. Her discussion of the incorporeal is a corrective that she ventures because a world cannot be exhausted amidst a consideration of materials alone, however vibrant or however lacking in life. It is a lesson to be found in Deleuze, especially where he encounters Spinoza and the Stoics (Deleuze 1990), whom Grosz also mentions in her recent book. To follow the material was never about claiming that material relations exhaust all that there is, for the corporeal expression of materials is bound up with incorporeal, virtual potentialities, the reverse and right sides of a surface of affective sensations and conceptual sense-making.

Practice scene: Camilla Damkjaer's handstand

The auditorium was entirely quiet, at least that is how I remember it now. Many of the delegates gathered were exhausted after three intense days of discussions, and for some there had been the week before as well, packed full of seminars and participatory workshops on an island called Utö in Stockholm's outer archipelago. We had barely had a moment to catch our collective breath. Having huddled together to discuss the best way to find a moment of closure, the convenors were now in agreement on how to proceed. Camilla Damkjaer approached the front of the room and set her slideshow in motion. She may have addressed the auditorium, but only to ask them to maintain their silence. With extreme care she placed two black blocks at shoulder-distance apart on the floor. A series of statements were projected onto the wall behind her as she began to position herself, bending over, her gaze concentrated downwards, finding her grip on the blocks. Then slowly, with astonishing bodily strength, she lifted her legs upwards into a handstand. The slides continued to transition from one statement to the next behind her inverted body. Having undertaken such thoroughgoing collective acts of territorializing

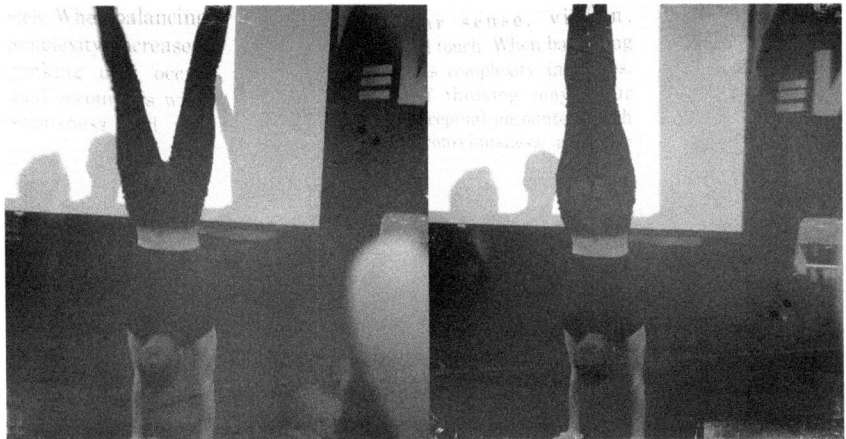

FIGURE C.3 *Camilla Damkjaer's handstand. Conclusion*, Daughters of Chaos: Practice, Discipline, A Life ... *8th International Deleuze Studies Conference, Stockholm, 2015. Photography by Hélène Frichot.*

the earth, deterritorializing its resources as unlimited series of goods, services and experiences to be consumed, she was returning her hands to this earth (albeit one rarefied by an architectural built environment) in a defiant act of reterritorialization.

To place this scene in context, on the first day of the 8th international Deleuze Studies Conference in Stockholm 2015, called *Daughters of Chaos: Practice, Discipline, A Life*, Daniel Smith had offered a concise, materially compelling definition of Deleuze and Guattari's conceptual trinity of territorialization, deterritorialization and reterritorialization as part of his argument concerning technology. The *terre* embedded in these three terms, he pointed out, returns us to the earth, so that to *de*territorialize registers that moment when the human creature lifts his or her hands from the ground in order to manage tools and weapons, and by extension to transform modes of expression into those of an increasingly practised technological species-being, grasping hold of the world in astonishing ways. Without venturing an extended account of how this conceptual trinity has been critically discussed, except to stress that these three concepts or rather actions need to be understood as working in tension through various permutations, sometimes producing troubling compositions amidst environment-worlds, sometimes more promising compositions, Damkjaer's embodied performance expressed its own take on things. She inverts the problem of territorialization, returning her hands to the earth, mounting an embodied structure that will take the greatest effort to maintain.[2] This event belongs to one of her series of lecture-performances where she brings together her embodied skills with her theoretical conceptual dexterity. Sensation and sense-making, corporeal effort and incorporeal force, a material-semiotics.

When Camilla Damkjaer writes her instructional book *Homemade Academic Circus: Idiosyncratically Embodied Explorations in the Arts and Circus*, she describes an adventure in creative artistic research practice that proceeds from sitting very still for way too long in order to finally launch forth into practising a physical art form that is performance based, combining circus clowning with work on a rope, including many encounters with failure, following which the performer must simply get up and start experimenting again, because life proceeds according to trial and error. She explains that, 'the accumulation of stillness will ultimately push you into something else' (2016: 2), and that this, incidentally, reduces the high stress associated with the academic researcher who spends too much time sitting still. Beyond exhaustion, embodied exhilaration is undertaken in collaboration with others from whom new skills can always be learnt.

After-affect: beatitude, joy

Art critic Jan Verwoert argues that beyond exhaustion there is an inkling of something, the potential of convalescence. Between I can (a willingness to be a high performer) and I can't (refusal, I would prefer not to), another disposition arises: I care. I care emerges at that exhausted point at which: 'You begin to care about life again, more than ever' (Verwoert 2007: 110). Maria Puig de la Bellacasa insists that 'thinking care' is a vital affective state, an ethical obligation and a practical labour (2012, 2017). Care, which has been so devalued in our world, is surely a fundamental means of enacting creative resistance at the brink of and beyond our exhaustions. In his *Cartography of Exhaustion*, Pelbart likewise stresses that something must be exhausted so that a different game might be introduced (2015: 53), new and renewed encounters, durable relations. Again, this begs the question: How do we make the best of things from amidst our local environment-worlds?

Maria Reiche spends the greater part of her life on the Pampas, Peru, mapping its ancient lines, immersed in the landscape while maintaining a respect for its material fragility. Agnès Varda follows the murmuring voices that emerge at the threshold of exhaustion, listening in to their stories of making do with what has been left over by others. Zoë Sofia (Sofoulis) addresses the unthinkable, our human extinction, but returns again to the challenge of making the shared infrastructures that support human and more-than-human life work. Tacita Dean depicts scenes of exhaustion, of materials, of lives lived with poetry and dance, of lives lost at sea and of the lives and deaths of industrial materials such as 16mm celluloid film. Katla

Maríudóttir charts landscape, architectural and narrative events that take place in the unstable, apt-to-erupt milieu in which she grew up. She exposes her audience to the landscape-affects of coastal Iceland, but invites us not to visit this place. At the same time, she offers a rebuke to architecture, by using all the architectural skills she has garnered over the five years of her education in becoming an architect so as *not* to forward an architectural project in the conventional sense. Notes that I kept safe from her graduating presentation recall how, less than a standard critique, the critics on her jury instead offered personal reminiscences. They fell silent, then fell to pieces, and could only respond at the level of shared affect by telling their own stories. Chelle Macnaughtan reads messages embedded in the pavement, messages left behind in anticipation of future workers. She takes the time to record these messages in order to produce a suite of creative works, to make meaning out of material signs and relations. Julieanna Preston tirelessly attends to her embodied performative explorations wherein she follows the materials she encounters in order to listen to what stories they have to tell. How very difficult it is to tell such stories when attempting to speak for more-than-human materials and their relations. Architecture may well have exhausted Michelle, but her cure is in her tapestries. She raises herself up from a supine position on the couch, and takes to the road, but what does she find there? One dead end, one wall after the next, but on she goes, one stitch at a time. Margit Brünner, venturing to the end of the world, perilously places herself into vast and foreign territories attempting to commune with environment-worlds within which she tracks signs of life. How will she continue to construct a common notion sufficiently durable to share with us? How will she achieve the greatest ratio of joyful affects and adequate ideas? Camilla Damkjaer discovers the benefits of combining corporeal with incorporeal labour, where and when will she get the time to clown around on her rope some more?

I draw out (that is to say, I exhaust) each practice scene, each of which composes planes of composition, which allows you the reader, or so I hope, to witness these scenes not as the discrete acts of a creative practitioner, but as the way each practitioner maps out a field, *becomes with* a milieu and diagrams an environment-world. The scenes of practice are laid out as distinct intrusions into the flow of parts and chapters because it is important that they are allowed to express themselves according to a different style. The 'writing up' of these encounters is not meant to be received as a report; rather, the writing process itself divulges something; it is my own mode of creative practice. In each instance, the impossible is confronted in order that the possible might emerge, because creation is this process: 'A creator who isn't grabbed around the throat by a set of impossibilities is no creator. A creator is someone who creates their own impossibilities, and thereby creates possibilities' (Deleuze 1995c: 133). Beyond exhaustion, with enough effort, creative practices endure.

Notes

1 See Margit Brünner's website http://margitbruenner.net (accessed 30 November 2017).
2 In *Deleuze and Architecture*, Cameron Duff's 'The Ethological City' presents the achievement of a handstand as one form of engaging with the city as a means of achieving greater health: 'There is no handstand without the cement, the wall, gravity's pull and sway, without the city, without the body. Hands and pavement, weight and movement, motion and rest. An ethology of bodies, cities, affects, relations, encounters and events. A handstand.' Cameron Duff, 'The Ethological City', in *Deleuze and the City*, edited by Hélène Frichot and Stephen Loo (Edinburgh: University of Edinburgh Press, 2013), 215–229. 215.

Bibliography

Agamben, Giorgio (1999), 'Absolute Immanence', in Giorgio Agamben (ed.), *Potentialities: Collected Essays in Philosophy*, 220–42, Stanford: Stanford University Press.

Agamben, Giorgio (2004), *The Open*. Stanford, CA: Stanford University Press.

Agrawal, Arun (2005), *Environmentality: Technologies of Government and the Making of Subjects*, Durham, NC: Duke University Press.

Alaimo, Stacy (2017), 'Your Shell on Acid: Material Immersion, Anthropocene Dissolves', in Richard Grusin (ed.), *Anthropocene Feminism*, 89–120, Minneapolis: University of Minnesota Press, 2017.

Alaimo, Stacy and Susan Hekman, eds (2009), *Material Feminisms*, Bloomington: Indiana University Press.

Allen, Adrien, Hélène Frichot and Bridie Lunney (2011), 'Suspension Test for Three Voices', *UnMagazine*, 5 (2): 82–89.

Allen, Stan (1998), 'From Object to Field', in Greg Lynn (ed.), *AD: Architecture After Geometry*, 24–31, London: Academy Press.

Anderson, Ben (2009), 'Affective Atmospheres', *Emotion, Space and Society*, 2: 77–88.

Andrasek, Alisa (2004), 'Biot(h)ing', in Neil Leach, David Turnbull and Chris Williams (eds), *Digital Tectonics*, 86–87, London: Wiley.

Andrasek, Alisa (2012), 'Open Synthesis// Toward a Resilient Fabric of Architecture', *Log Magazine*, 25: 45–54.

Andrasek, Alisa (2016a), 'Interdeterminacy and Contingency: The Seroussi Pavilion and Bloom', in Leon van Schaik and Fleur Watson (eds), *AD: Pavilions, Pop Ups and Parasols: The Impact of Real and Virtual Meeting on Physical Space*, 107–11, Chichester: Wiley.

Andrasek, Alisa (2016b), 'Xeno-Cells in the Mood for the Unseen', in Matias del Campo (ed.), *AD: Evoking through Design*, 90–95, Chichester: Wiley.

Andrasek, Alisa and David Andreen (2016), 'Activating the Invisible: Data Processing and Parallel Computing in Architectural Design', *Intelligent Buildings International*, 8 (2): 106–17.

Appadurai, Arjun, ed. (1986), *The Social Life of Things: Commodities in Cultural Perspective*, Cambridge: Cambridge University Press.

Appadurai, Arjun (2006), 'The Thing Itself', *Public Culture*, 18 (1): 15–21.

Armiero, Marco and Lise Sedrez (2014), 'Introduction', in Marco Armiero and Lise Sedrez (eds), *A History of Environmentalism: Local Struggles, Global Histories*, 1–19, London: Bloomsbury.

Åsberg, Cecilia, Kathrin Thiele and Iris van der Tuin (2015), 'Speculative before the Turn Reintroducing Feminist Materialist Performativity', *Cultural Studies Review*, 21 (2): 145–72.

Avanessian, Armen and Christian Kerez (2016), 'Xenopolitics', *Arch+ Journal of Architecture and Urbanism, Release Architecture*, edited by Anh-Linh Ngo: 77–79.
Baird, George (2005), 'Criticality and Its Discontents', *Harvard Design Magazine*, 21: 1–6.
Banham, Reyner (1984), *The Architecture of the Well-Tempered Environment*, Chicago: University of Chicago Press.
Barad, Karen (2007), *Meeting the Universe Half Way: Quantum Physics and the Entanglement of Matter and Meaning*, Durham, NC: Duke University Press.
Barber, Daniel (2016), 'Architectural History in the Anthropocene', *Journal of Architecture*, 21 (8): 1165–70.
Barth, John (1984), *Friday Book: Essays and Other Non-Fiction*, Baltimore, MD: John Hopkins University Press.
Barthes, Roland (1975), *The Pleasure of the Text*, New York: Noonday Press.
Bateson, Gregory (2000), *Steps to an Ecology of Mind*, Chicago: University of Chicago Press.
Bateson, Gregory (2002), *Mind and Nature: A Necessary Unity*, Cresskill, NJ: Hampton Press.
Beckett, Samuel (1992), *Quad et autres pièces pour la television*, Paris: les éditions de minuit.
Beistegui, Miguel de (2010), *Immanence: Deleuze and Philosophy*, Edinburgh: Edinburgh University Press.
Benjamin, Walter (1992), 'Theses on the Philosophy of History', in Hannah Arendt (ed.), *Illuminations*, 245–255, London: Fontana Press.
Bennett, Jane (2010), *Vibrant Matter: A Political Ecology of Things*, Durham, NC: Duke University Press.
Bennett, Jane (2015), 'Systems and Things: On Vital Materialism and Object-Oriented Philosophy', in Richard Grusin (ed.), *The Nonhuman Turn*, 223–39, Minneapolis: University of Minnesota Press.
Bennett, Jill (2012), 'Living in the Anthropocene', in *The Book of Books*, Catalog 1/3, dOCUMENTA 13, 344–47.
Berardi, Franco 'Bifo' (2008), *Félix Guattari: Thought, Friendship, and Visionary Cartography*, Basingstoke: Palgrave.
Bloomer, Jennifer (1993), *Architecture and the Text: The (S)crypts of Joyce and Piranesi*, New Haven: Yale University Press.
Bourriaud, Nicolas (2002), *Relational Aesthetics*, Dijon: les presses du réel.
Bradley, Karin, Anna Hult and Göran Cars (2013), 'From Eco-Modernizing to Political Ecologizing: Future Challenges for the Green Capital', in Jonathan Metzger and Amy Rader Olsson (eds), *Sustainable Stockholm: Exploring Urban Sustainability in Europe's Greenest City*, 168–94, New York: Routledge.
Braidotti, Rosi (1994), *Nomadic Subjects*, New York: Columbia University Press.
Braidotti, Rosi (2013), *The Posthuman*, Cambridge: Polity.
Braidotti, Rosi (2017), 'Series Preface: Theory is Back', in Erik Hörl and James Burton (eds), *General Ecology: The New Ecological Paradigm*, xiv–xv, London: Bloomsbury.
Brott, Simone (2013), 'Toward a Theory of the Architectural Subject', in Hélène Frichot and Stephen Loo (eds), *Deleuze and Architecture*, 151–67, Edinburgh: Edinburgh University Press.
Brown, Bill (2001), 'Thing Theory', *Critical Inquiry*, 28 (1): 1–22.

Brown, Lori, ed. (2011), *Feminist Practices: Interdisciplinary Approaches to Women in Architecture*, London: Routledge.

Brünner, Margit (2015), *Constructing Atmospheres: Test-Sites for an Aesthetics of Joy*, Baunach: AADR (Art Architecture Design Research), Spurbuchverlag.

Bryant, Levi (2014), *Onto-Cartography: An Ontology of Machines and Media*, Edinburgh: Edinburgh University Press.

Bryant, Levi, Nick Srnicek and Graham Harman (2011), 'Towards a Speculative Philosophy', in Levi Bryant, Nick Srnicek and Graham Harman (eds), *The Speculative Turn: Continental Materialism and Realism*, 1–18, Melbourne: Re.Press.

Buck-Morss, Susan (1989), *The Dialectics of Seeing: Walter Benjamin and the Arcades Project*, Cambridge, MA: MIT Press.

Burns, Karen (2010), 'Frontier Conflict, Contact, Exchange: Re-Imagining Colonial Architecture', in Michael Chapman and Michael Ostwald (eds), *Imagining … Proceedings of the 27th International SAHANZ Conference*, 70–80, Newcastle, NSW.

Butler, Judith (2014), 'Rethinking Vulnerability and Resistance'. Available online: http://bibacc.org/wp-content/uploads/2016/07/Rethinking-Vulnerability-and-Resistance-Judith-Butler.pdf (accessed 17 February 2017).

Butler, Judith (2015), *Notes toward a Performative Theory of Assembly*, Cambridge, MA: Harvard University Press.

Butler, Judith (2016), 'Vulnerability and Resistance', in Judith Butler, Zeynep Gambetti and Leticia Sabsay (eds), *Vulnerability in Resistance*, 12–27, Durham, NC: Duke University Press.

Butt, Gavin (2005), 'Introduction: The Paradoxes of Criticism', in Gavin Butt (ed.), *After Criticism: New Responses to Art and Performance*, 1–20, Malden, MA: Blackwell.

Carpo, Mario (2004), 'Ten Years of Folding', in Greg Lynn (ed.), *AD: Folding in Architecture*, 14–19, Chichester: Wiley.

Carpo, Mario (2011), *The Alphabet and the Algorithm*, Cambridge, MA: MIT Press.

Carpo, Mario (2016), 'Christian Kerez's Art of the Incidental', *Arch+ Journal of Architecture and Urbanism, Release Architecture*, edited by Anh-Linh Ngo: 70–76.

Carrington, Damian (2017), 'Warning of "Ecological Armageddon" after Dramatic Plunge in Insect Numbers', *The Guardian*, 20 October. Available online: https://www.theguardian.com/environment/2017/oct/18/warning-of-ecological-armageddon-after-dramatic-plunge-in-insect-numbers (accessed 20 October 2017).

Carroll, Lewis ([1871] 1980), *Through the Looking Glass, and What Alice Found There*, London: Macmillan.

Carson, Rachel (2002), *Silent Spring*, Boston: Houghton Mifflin.

Cauter, Lieven De (2004), *The Capsular Civilization: On the City in the Age of Fear*. Rotterdam: NAi Publishers.

Chakrabarty, Dipesh (2009), 'The Climate of History: Four Theses', *Critical Inquiry*, 35: 197–222.

Chatwin, Bruce (1989), 'Maria Reiche: The Riddle of the Pampa', in Bruce Chatwin (ed.), *What am I Doing Here?*, 94–104. London: Penguin.

Clark, Eric (2014), 'Good Urban Governance: Making Rent Gap Theory Not True', *Geografiska Annaler: Series B, Human Geography*, 96 (4): 392–95.
Colebrook, Claire, ed. (2000), *Deleuze and Feminist Theory*, Edinburgh: Edinburgh University Press.
Colebrook, Claire (2005), 'Noology', in Adrian Parr (ed.), *The Deleuze Dictionary*, 193–94, Edinburgh: Edinburgh University Press.
Colebrook, Claire (2007), 'On Not Becoming Man: The Materialist Politics of Unactualized Potential', in Stacy Alaimo and Susan Hekman (eds), *Material Feminisms*, 52–84, Bloomington: Indiana University Press.
Colebrook, Claire (2014a), *Death of the PostHuman: Essays on Extinction*, vol. 1. Ann Arbor: Open Humanities Press, University of Michigan Library.
Colebrook, Claire (2014b), *Sex after Life: Essays on Extinction*, vol. 2. Ann Arbor: Open Humanities Press, University of Michigan Library.
Colebrook, Claire (2017), 'We Have Never Been Post-Anthropocene: The Anthropocene Counterfactual', in Richard Grusin (ed.), *Anthropocene Feminisms*, 1–20, Minneapolis: University of Minnesota Press.
Colomina, Beatriz (1992), 'The Split Wall: Domestic Voyeurism', in Beatriz Colomina and Jennifer Bloomer (eds), *Sexuality & Space*, 73–130, New York: Princeton Architectural Press.
Conley, Verena Andermatt (1993), 'Eco-Subjects', in Verena Andermatt Conley (ed.), *Rethinking Technologies*, 77–91, Minneapolis: University of Minnesota Press.
Coole, Diana and Samantha Frost, eds (2010), *New Materialisms: Ontology, Agency, and Politics*. Durham, NC: Duke University Press.
Crary, Jonathan (2013), *24/7: Late Capitalism and the Ends of Sleep*, London: Verso.
Crutzen, Paul and Eugene Stoermer (2000), 'The "Anthropocene"', *Global Change Newsletter*. International Geosphere-Biosphere Program Newsletter, no. 41 (May 2000): 17–18. http://www.igbp.net/download/18.316f18321323470177580001401/1376383088452/NL41.pdf (accessed 17 March 2017).
Crysler, C. Greig, Stephen Cairns and Hilde Heynen (2012), 'Introduction 1: Architectural Theory in an Expanded Field', in C. Greig Crysler, Stephen Cairns and Hilde Heynen (eds), *The Sage Handbook of Architectural Theory*, 1–22, London: Sage.
Damkjaer, Camilla (2016), Homemade Academic Circus: Idiosyncratically Embodied Explorations in the Arts and Circus, Alresford, Hants: iff books.
Dean, Tacita (2018), *Landscape, Portrait, Still Life*, London: Royal Academy of Arts.
Dean, Tacita and Jeremy Millar (1999), 'Magic World: A Report on a Future Visit to Shepparton', *Afterall: A Journal of Art, Context and Enquiry*, 1: 116–19.
Dean, Tacita and Jean-Christophe Royoux (2005), 'Friday to Saturday: The Millennium Dome Project', in Jean-Christophe Royoux (ed.), *Cosmograms*, New York: Sternberg Press, 249–56.
Debaise, Didier (2017), *Nature as Event: The Lure of the Possible*, Durham, NC: Duke University Press.
Debaise, Didier, Pablo Jensen, M. Pierre Montebello, Nicolas Prignot, Isabelle Stengers and Aline Wiame (2015), 'Reinstituting Nature: A Latourian Workshop', *Environmental Humanities*, 6 (2015). Available online: http://environmentalhumanities.org/arch/vol6/6.8.pdf (accessed 5 May 2017).

Deleuze, Gilles (1978), Spinoza Seminar, 24/1/1978. Available online: https://www.webdeleuze.com/textes/14 (accessed 4 May 2012).
Deleuze, Gilles (1983), *Nietzsche and Philosophy*, London: Athlone Press.
Deleuze, Gilles (1986), *Cinema 1: The Movement-Image*, London: Athlone Press.
Deleuze, Gilles (1988a), *Foucault*, Minneapolis: University of Minnesota Press.
Deleuze, Gilles (1988b), *Spinoza: Practical Philosophy*, San Francisco: City Lights.
Deleuze, Gilles (1989), *Cinema 2: The Time-Image*, London: Athlone Press.
Deleuze, Gilles (1990), *The Logic of Sense*, New York: Columbia University Press.
Deleuze, Gilles (1991), 'A Philosophical Concept...', in Eduardo Cadava, Peter Conner and Jean-Luc Nancy (eds), *Who Comes after the Subject?*, 94–95, London: Routledge.
Deleuze, Gilles (1992a), *Expressionism in Philosophy: Spinoza*, New York: Zone Books.
Deleuze, Gilles (1993), *The Fold: Leibniz and the Baroque*, London: Athlone Press.
Deleuze, Gilles (1994), *Difference and Repetition*, New York: Columbia University Press.
Deleuze, Gilles, ed. (1995a), 'Control and Becoming', in *Negotiations*, 169–76, New York: Columbia University Press.
Deleuze, Gilles, ed. (1995b), 'Postscript on Control Societies', in *Negotiations*, 177–82, New York: Columbia University Press.
Deleuze, Gilles, ed. (1995c), 'Mediators', in *Negotiations*, 121–34, New York: Columbia University Press.
Deleuze, Gilles (1998a), 'The Exhausted', in Gilles Deleuze (ed.), *Essays Critical and Clinical*, 152–74, London: Verso.
Deleuze, Gilles (1998b), 'Literature and Life', in Gilles Deleuze (ed.), *Essays Critical and Clinical*, 1–6, New York: Verso.
Deleuze, Gilles (1998c), 'Spinoza and the Three "Ethics" ', in Gilles Deleuze (ed.), *Essays Critical and Clinical*, 138–51, London: Verso.
Deleuze, Gilles, ed. (2000), 'The Image of Thought', in *Proust and Signs: The Complete Text*, 94–104, Minneapolis: University of Minnesota Press.
Deleuze, Gilles, ed. (2001), 'Immanence: A Life...', in *Pure Immanence: Essays on a Life*, New York: Zone Books, 25–34.
Deleuze, Gilles (2002a), *Desert Islands and Other Texts 1953–1974*, Paris: Semiotext(e).
Deleuze, Gilles (2002b), *Francis Bacon: The Logic of Sensation*, Minneapolis: University of Minnesota Press.
Deleuze, Gilles (2003), 'The Three Kinds of Knowledge', *Pli*, 14: 1–20.
Deleuze, Gilles and Claire Parnet (2007), *Dialogues II*, New York: Columbia University Press.
Deleuze, Gilles and Félix Guattari (1983), *Anti-Oedipus: Capitalism and Schizophrenia*, Minneapolis: University of Minnesota Press.
Deleuze, Gilles and Félix Guattari (1986), *Kafka: Toward a Minor Literature*, Minneapolis: University of Minnesota Press.
Deleuze, Gilles and Félix Guattari (1987), *A Thousand Plateaus: Capitalism and Schizophrenia*, Minneapolis: University of Minnesota Press.
Deleuze, Gilles and Félix Guattari (1994), *What Is Philosophy?* New York: Columbia University Press.
DeLoughrey, Elizabeth (2014), 'Satellite Planetarity and the Ends of the Earth', *Public Culture*, 26: 257–80.

Demos, T. J. (2016), *Decolonising Nature: Contemporary Art and the Politics of Nature*, Berlin: Sternberg Press.
Demos, T. J. (2017) 'Creative Ecologies', *Take Ecology*, 3 (1), June 18: 18–21.
Dolphijn, Rick and Iris van der Tuin, eds (2012), *New Materialism: Interviews and Cartographies*, Ann Arbor, MI: Open Humanities Press, University of Michigan Library.
Dorrian, Mark (2013), 'Utopia on Ice: Climate as Commodity Form', in Etienne Turpin (ed.), *Architecture in the Anthropocene: Encounters Among Design, Deep Time, and Philosophy*, 143–52, Ann Arbor: Open Humanities Press, University of Michigan Library.
Doucet, Isabelle (2015), *The Practice Turn in Architecture: Brussels after 1968*. Farnham, Surrey: Ashgate.
Doucet, Isabelle and Hélène Frichot (2018), 'Introduction: Reclaim, Resist, Speculate: Situated perspectives on architecture and the city', *Architectural Theory Review*, Resist, Reclaim, Speculate, edited by Isabelle Doucet and Hélène Frichot, 22 (1): 1–8.
Doucet, Isabelle, Didier Debaise and Benedikte Zitouni (2018), 'Narrate, Speculate, Fabulate', *Architectural Theory Review*, Resist, Reclaim, Speculate, edited by Isabelle Doucet and Hélène Frichot, 22 (1): 9–23.
Dovey, Kim and Ross King (2012), 'Informal Urbanism and the Taste for Slums', *Tourism Geographies*, 14 (2): 275–93.
Downton, Peter (2003), *Design Research*, Melbourne: RMIT University Press.
Doyle, Shelby and Leslie Forehand (2017), 'Fabricating Architecture: Digital Craft as Feminist Practice', *The Avery Review*. Available online: http://averyreview.com/issues/25/fabricating-architecture (accessed 6 October 2017).
Duff, Cameron (2013), 'The Ethological City', in Hélène Frichot and Stephen Loo (eds), *Deleuze and the City*, 215–29, Edinburgh: University of Edinburgh Press.
Eakin, Emily (2011), 'Celluloid Hero: Tacita Dean's Exhilarating Homage to Film', *The New Yorker*, 31 October. Available online: https://www.newyorker.com/magazine/2011/10/31/celluloid-hero (accessed 5 October 2017).
Elkin, Lauren (2017), 'Agnes Varda's Ecological Conscience', *The Paris Review*, 27 October. Available online: https://www.theparisreview.org/blog/2017/10/20/agnes-vardas-ecological-conscience (accessed 10 November 2017).
Elkin, Lauren (2016), *Flâneuse: Women Walk the City in Paris, New York, Tokyo, Venice and London*, London: Chatto and Windus.
Else, Liz (2010), 'Biosemiotics: Searching for Meanings in a Meadow', *New Scientist*, 18 August. Available online: https://www.newscientist.com/article/mg20727741.200-biosemiotics-searching-for-meanings-in-a-meadow (accessed 5 May 2017).
Fletcher, Robert (2017) 'Environmentality Unbound: Multiple Governmentalities in Environmental Politics', *Geoforum*, 85: 311–15.
Foucault, Michel (1970), *The Order of Things*, London: Routledge.
Foucault, Michel (2000), *Power: Essential Works of Foucault 1954–1984*, Volume 3, London: Penguin.
Foucault, Michel (2003), *'Society Must be Defended': Lectures at the Collège de France, 1975–76*, New York: Picador.
Foucault, Michel (2007), *Security, Territory, Population: Lectures at the Collège de France, 1977–78*, Basingstoke: Palgrave Macmillan.

Foucault, Michel (2008), *The Birth of Biopolitics: Lectures at the Collège de France, 1978–79*. Basingstoke: Palgrave Macmillan.
Foucault, Michel and Gilles Deleuze (1977), 'Intellectuals and Power', in Donald F. Bouchard (ed.), *Language, Counter-Memory, Practice*, 205–17, Ithaca, NY: Cornell University Press.
Frayling, Christopher (1993), 'Research in Art and Design', *Royal College of Art Research Papers*, 1 (1): 1–5.
Frichot, Hélène (2005), 'Stealing into Deleuze's Baroque House', in Ian Buchanan and Greg Lambert (eds), *Deleuze and Space*, 61–79, Edinburgh: University of Edinburgh Press.
Frichot, Hélène (2008), 'The Erasure of the Object that is Architecture', in Rochus Hinkel (ed.), *Notions of Space*, Melbourne: Craft Victoria.
Frichot, Hélène (2009a), 'On Finding Oneself Spinozist: Refuge, Beatitude and the Any-Space-Whatever', in Charles J. Stivale, Eugene W. Holland and Daniel W. Smith (eds), *Gilles Deleuze: Image and Text*, 247–63, London: Continuum.
Frichot, Hélène (2009b), 'On the Death of Architectural Theory and Other Spectres', *Design Principles and Practices: An International Journal*, 3: 1–6.
Frichot, Hélène (2010), 'What Can We Learn from the Bubble Man and His Atmospheric Ecologies?', *IDEA: Interior Ecologies*, 102–13.
Frichot, Hélène (2012), 'Michelle Hamer: One Stitch at a Time', *05401*, 01, edited by Louis Mannie Leoni: 17–19, 25–26.
Frichot, Hélène (2013), 'Deleuze and the Story of the Superfold', in Hélène Frichot and Stephen Loo (eds), *Deleuze and Architecture*, 79–93, Edinburgh: Edinburgh University Press.
Frichot, Hélène (2014), 'Gentri-Fiction and our (E)States of Reality: On the Exhaustion of the Image of Thought and the Fatigued Image of Architecture', in Nadir Lahiji (ed.), *The Missed Encounter of Radical Philosophy with Architecture*, 113–32, London: Bloomsbury.
Frichot, Hélène (2015), 'Five Lessons in a Ficto-Critical Approach to Design Practice Research', *Drawing-On: Journal of Architectural Research By Design*, 01: 19–32. Available online: http://drawingon.org/uploads/papers/IS01-001.pdf (accessed 4 February 2018).
Frichot, Hélène (2016), *How to Make Yourself a Feminist Design Power Tool*, Baunach: AADR Spurbuchverlag.
Frichot, Hélène (2017). 'Local Real(i)ties: A Contemporary Image of Thought', *Artifact*, IV (I). Available online: https://scholarworks.iu.edu/journals/index.php/artifact/index (accessed 23 November 2017).
Frichot, Hélène (2018a), 'Slownesses and Speeds, Latitudes and Longitudes: In the Vicinity of Beatitude', in Beth Lord (ed.), *Spinoza and Proportion*, 141–54, Edinburgh: University of Edinburgh Press.
Frichot, Hélène (2018b), 'From the Exhaustion of the Dogmatic Image of Thought that Circumscribes Architecture toward Feminist Practices of Joy', in Constantin Boundas and Vana Tentokali (eds), *Architectural and Urban Reflections after Deleuze and Guattari*, 267–82, London: Rowman and Littlefield.
Frichot, Hélène and Helen Runting (2015), 'The Promise of a Lack: Responding to (Her) Real-Estate Career', *The Avery Review: Critical Essays on Architecture*, 8. Available online: http://www.averyreview.com/issues/8/the-promise-of-a-lack (accessed 10 February 2017).

Frichot, Hélène and Helen Runting (2018a), 'In Captivity: The Real Estate of Co-Living', in Hélène Frichot, Catharina Gabrielsson and Helen Runting (eds), *Architecture and Feminisms: Ecologies, Economies, Technologies*, 140–50, London: Routledge.
Frichot, Hélène and Helen Runting (2018b), 'The Illusory Autonomy of the Real Estate Interior', in Roemer van Toorn, Gunnar Sandin and Jennifer Mack (eds), *Rethinking the Social in Architecture*, Barcelona: Actar.
Frichot, Hélène and Jonathan Metzger (2016), 'Never Believe that the City will Suffice to Save us! Stockholm Gentri-Fictions', in Hélène Frichot, Catharina Gabrielsson and Jonathan Metzger (eds), *Deleuze and the City*, 79–94, Edinburgh: Edinburgh University Press.
Frichot, Hélène and Stephen Loo (2013), 'Introduction: The Exhaustive and the Exhausted – Deleuze AND Architecture', in Hélène Frichot and Stephen Loo (eds), *Deleuze and Architecture*, 1–14, Edinburgh: Edinburgh University Press.
Frichot, Hélène, Catharina Gabrielsson and Helen Runting (eds), *Architecture and Feminisms: Ecologies, Economies, Technologies*, London: Routledge.
Gabrielsson, Catharina (2017), 'The Critical Potential of Housework', in Hélène Frichot, Catharina Gabrielsson, Helen Runting (eds), *Architecture and Feminisms: Ecologies, Economies, Technologies*, 245–54, London: Routledge.
Gabrielsson, Catharina (2018), 'Staying with the Trouble on the Flats', *Architectural Theory Review*, 22 (1): 83–99.
Gage, Mark Forster (2015), 'Killing Simplicity: Object-Oriented-Philosophy in Architecture', *Log Magazine*, 33: 95–121.
Gannon, Todd, Graham Harman, David Ruy and Tom Wiscombe (2015), 'The Object Turn: A Conversation', *Log Magazine*, 33: 73–94.
Gatens, Moira and Genevieve Lloyd (1999), *Collective Imaginings: Spinoza, Past and Present*, London: Routledge.
Gibbs, Anna (1997), 'Bodies of Words: Feminism and Fictocriticism – Explanation and Demonstration', *Text*, 1 (2). Available online: http://www.textjournal.com.au/oct97/gibbs.htm (accessed 2 August 2016).
Gibson-Graham, J. K. (2011), 'A Feminist Project of Belonging for the Anthropocene', *Gender, Place & Culture*, 18 (1): 1–21.
Gissen, David (2009), *Subnature: Architecture's Other Environments*, New York: Princeton Architectural Press.
Graham, James, Caitlin Blanchfield, Jacob Moore, Jordan Carver and Alissa Anderson, eds. (2016), *Climates: Architecture and the Planetary Imaginary*, Zurich: Lars Müller.
Grosz, Elizabeth, ed. (1999), *Becomings: Explorations in Time, Memory and Futures*, New York: Cornell University.
Grosz, Elizabeth (2001), 'The Thing', in Elizabeth Grosz (ed.), *Architecture from the Outside: Essays on Virtual and Real Space*, 167–83, Cambridge, MA: MIT Press, 2001.
Grosz, Elizabeth (2008), *Chaos, Territory, Art: Deleuze and the Framing of the Earth*. New York: Columbia University Press.
Grosz, Elizabeth (2017), *The Incorporeal: Ontology, Ethics, and the Limits of Materialism*, New York: Columbia University Press.

Grosz, Elizabeth, in conversation with Etienne Turpin and Heather Davis (2013), 'Time Matters: On Temporality in the Anthropocene', in Etienne Turpin (ed.), *Architecture in the Anthropocene: Encounters among Design, Deep Time, and Philosophy*, 129–38, Ann Arbor, MI: Open Humanities Press, Michigan Publishing.

Grusin, Richard (ed.) (2017), *Anthropocene Feminism*, Minneapolis: University of Minnesota Press.

Guattari, Félix (1995), *Chaosmosis: An Ethico-Aesthetic Paradigm*, Sydney: Power Publications.

Guattari, Félix (2000), *The Three Ecologies*, London: Athlone Press.

Haraway, Donna (1988), 'Situated Knowledges: The Science Question in Feminism and the Privilege of Partial Perspective', *Feminist Studies*, 14 (3): 575–99.

Haraway, Donna (1991), *Simians, Cyborgs, and Women: The Reinvention of Nature*, London: Free Association Books.

Haraway, Donna (1997), *Modest_Witness@Second_Millennium. FemaleMan©_Meets_OncoMouse™: Feminism and Technoscience*, New York: Routledge.

Haraway, Donna (2008), *When Species Meet*, Minneapolis: University of Minnesota Press.

Haraway, Donna (2016), *Staying with the Trouble: Making Kin in the Chthulucene*, Durham: Duke University Press.

Harcourt, Wendy and Ingrid Nelson (2015), *Practicing Feminist Political Ecologies: Moving beyond the 'Green Economy'*, London: Zed Books.

Harman, Graham (2002), *Tool-Being: Heidegger and the Metaphysics of Objects*. Chicago: Open Court.

Harman, Graham (2005a), 'Heidegger on Objects and Things', in Bruno Latour and Peter Weibel (eds), *Making Things Public: Atmospheres of Democracy*, 268–271, Cambridge, MA: MIT Press.

Harman, Graham (2005b). *Guerrilla Metaphysics: Phenomenology and the Carpentry of Things*, Chicago: Open Court.

Harman, Graham (2011), *The Quadruple Object*, Alresford, Hants: Zero Books.

Harman, Graham (2016), *Immaterialism*, Cambridge: Polity, 2016.

Harman, Graham (2017), 'Buildings are Not Processes: A Disagreement with Latour and Yaneva', *Ardeth*, 1: 113–24. Available online: http://www.ardeth.eu (accessed 8 December 2017).

Harman, Graham and Slavoj Žižek (2017), 'Duel and Duet: Slavoj Žižek and Graham Harman', public lecture, SCI-Arc School of Architecture, Los Angeles (1 March). Available online: https://sciarc.edu/events/lectures/duel-duet-slavoj-žižek-and-graham-harman (accessed 29 September 2017).

Harrison, Ariane Lourie, ed. (2013), *Architectural Theories of the Environment: Posthuman Territory*, New York: Routledge.

Hauptman, Deborah and Warren Neidich, eds (2010), *Cognitive Architecture. From Biopolitics to Noopolitics. Architecture & Mind in the Age of Communication and Information*, Rotterdam: 010 Publishers.

Hayles, N. Katherine (2003), 'Afterword: The Human in the Posthuman', *Cultural Critique, Posthumanism*, 53: 134–37.

Hays, K. Michael (1990), 'Rebuttal: Theory as Mediating Practice', *Progressive Architecture*, 71 (11): 98–100.

Heidegger, Martin (1993a), 'Building, Dwelling, Thinking', in *Basic Writings*, 343–64, London: Routledge.
Heidegger, Martin (1993b), 'The Origin of the Work of Art', in David Farrell Krell (ed.), *Basic Writings*, 139–212, London: Routledge.
Heidegger, Martin (1995), *The Fundamental Concepts of Metaphysics: World, Finitude, Solitude*, Bloomington: Indiana University Press, 1995.
Heidegger, Martin (2001), 'The Thing', in Martin Heidegger (ed.), *Poetry, Language, Thought*, 161–84, New York: Harper Colophon Books.
Heise, Ursula K. (2017), 'Introduction: Planet, Species, Justice – and the Stories We Tell about Them', in Ursula K. Heise, Jon Christensen and Michelle Niemann (eds), *The Routledge Companion to the Environmental Humanities*, 1–10, Abingdon: Routledge.
Held, Virginia (2006), *The Ethics of Care: Personal Political Global*, Oxford: Oxford University Press.
Hême de Lacotte, Suzanne (2010), 'Iconoclasm of Gilles Deleuze: Deleuze, The Image, the Cinema, the Image of Thought', *Trahir* (2 December): 1–12.
Highmore, Ben (2016), 'Feeling It: Habitat, Taste and the New Middle Class in 1970s Britain', *New Formations*, 88: 105–22.
Hight, Christopher and Chris Perry, eds (2006), *Collective Intelligence in Design*, Architectural Design. London: Wiley, 2006.
Hudek, Antony, ed. (2014), *The Object, Whitechapel Documents of Contemporary Art*, Cambridge, MA: MIT Press.
Hughes, Russell. (2011), *Do It Yourself Future Construction: The Deregulated Self*, PhD thesis, Melbourne: RMIT University. Available online: https://researchbank.rmit.edu.au/eserv/rmit:161361/Hughes.pdf (accessed 5 May 2017).
Hurley, Robert (1988), 'Preface', in Gilles Deleuze (ed.), *Spinoza: Practical Philosophy*, i–iii, San Francisco: City Lights.
Hörl, Erich. (2017), 'Introduction to General Ecology: The Ecologization of Thinking', in Erich Hörl with James Burton (eds), *General Ecology: The New Ecological Paradigm*, 1–74, London: Bloomsbury.
Ingold, Timothy (2000), *The Perception of the Environment: Essays on Livelihood, Dwelling and Skill*, London: Routledge.
Jameson, Fredric. (1991), *Postmodernism, or the Cultural Logic of Late Capitalism*. Durham, NC: Duke University Press.
Janssens, Nel (2012), 'Utopia-Driven Projective Research: A Design Approach to Explore the Theory and Practice of Meta-Urbanism', PhD thesis, Gothenburg: Chalmers University of Technology.
Kafka, Franz (1992), *The Diaries of Franz Kafka*, London: Minerva.
Kaji-O'Grady, Sandra (2007), 'The Dramatisation of "Eco-technologies" in Recent High-rise Towers', in Kristen Orr and Sandra Kaji-O'Grady (eds), *Techniques and Technology, Transfer and Transformation: The Proceedings of the 4th International Conference of the Association of Architecture Schools of Australasia*, 27–29, Sydney.
Kautzleben, Heinz and Axel Müller (2014), 'Vladimir Ivanovich Vernadsky (1863–1945) – From Mineral to Noosphere', *Journal of Geochemical Exploration*, 147: 4–10.
Kepes, Gyorgy (1972), 'Art and Ecological Consciousness', in Gyorgy Kepes (ed.), *Arts of the Environment*, 1–12, New York: George Braziller.

Kohn, Eduardo (2013), *How Forests Think: Toward an Anthropology beyond the Human*, Berkeley: University of California Press.
Knapp, Steven and Walter Benn Michaels (1982), 'Against Theory', *Critical Inquiry*, 8 (4): 723–42.
Kwinter, Sanford (2001), *Architectures of Time: Toward a Theory of the Event in Modernist Culture*, Cambridge, MA: MIT Press.
Kwinter, Sanford (2008), 'Wildness: Prolegomena to a New Urbanism', in *Far from Equilibrium: Essays on Technology and Design Culture*, Barcelona: Actar.
Latour, Bruno (1993), *We Have Never Been Modern*, Cambridge, MA: Harvard University Press.
Latour, Bruno (2004), 'Why Has Critique Run out of Steam? From Matters of Fact to Matters of Concern' *Critical Inquiry* (Winter 2004): 225–48.
Latour, Bruno (2005a), 'From Realpolitik to Dingpolitik, or How to Make Things Public', in Bruno Latour and Peter Weibel (eds), *Making Things Public: Atmospheres of Democracy*, 14–36, Cambridge, MA: MIT Press.
Latour, Bruno (2005b), *Reassembling the Social: An Introduction to Actor Network Theory*, Oxford: Oxford University Press.
Latour, Bruno (2017), *Facing Gaia: Eight Lectures on the New Climatic Regime*, Cambridge: Polity.
Latour, Bruno and Albena Yaneva (2008), ' "Give me a Gun and I will Make All Buildings Move": An ANT's View of Architecture', in Reto Geiser (ed.), *Explorations in Architecture: Teaching Design Research*, 80–89, Basel: Birkhäuser.
Law, John (2004), *After Method: Mess in Social Science Research*, London: Routledge.
Lawrence, D. H. (1987), 'Things', in Ian Serraillier (ed.), *Selected Tales*, London: Heinemann Educational Books.
Lavin, Sylvia (1990), 'Essay: The Uses and Abuses of Theory', *Progressive Architecture*, 71 (8): 113–14, 179.
Lavin, Sylvia (2011), *Kissing Architecture*, Princeton and Oxford: Princeton University Press.
Lazzarato, Maurizio (1996), 'Immaterial Labour', in Paulo Virno and Michael Hardt (eds), *Radical Thought in Italy Today: A Potential Politics*, 133–50, Minneapolis: University of Minnesota Press.
Lazzarato, Maurizio (2002), 'From Biopower to Biopolitics', *Pli: The Warwick Journal of Philosophy*, 13: 99–113.
Lazzarato, Maurizio (2006), 'The Concepts of Life and the Living in the Societies of Control', in Martin Fuglsang and Bent Meier Sorensen (eds), *Deleuze and the Social*, 171–90, Edinburgh: Edinburgh University Press.
Lazzarato, Maurizio (2012), *The Making of the Indebted Man*, Los Angeles: Semiotext(e).
Lazzarato, Maurizio (2014), *Signs and Machines: Capitalism and the Production of Subjectivity*, Los Angeles: Semiotext(e).
Lazzarato, Maurizio (2015), *Governing by Debt*, Los Angeles: Semiotext(e).
Lebovici, Elizabeth (2013), 'This is Not My Body', in Éric Alliez and Peter Osborne (eds), *Spheres of Action: Art and Politics*, 65–77, London: Tate Publishing.
Leland, Mary (2014), ' "South Pres" and the Legacy of Nano Nagle', *The Irish Times*, 8 May 2014. Available online: http://www.irishtimes.com/life-and-style/

homes-and-property/south-pres-and-the-legacy-of-nano-nagle-1.1785518 (accessed 10 February 2017).

LeMenager, Stephanie (2017), 'The Humanities after the Anthropocene', in Ursula K. Heise, Jon Christensen and Michelle Niemann (eds), *The Routledge Companion to the Environmental Humanities*, 473–81, Abingdon: Routledge.

Lewis, Paul (2017), ' "Our Minds Can be Hijacked": The Tech Insiders who Fear a Smartphone Dystopia', *The Guardian*, 6 October. Available online: https://www.theguardian.com/technology/2017/oct/05/smartphone-addiction-silicon-valley-dystopia (accessed 7 October 2017).

Lippard, Lucy (1997), *Six Years: The Dematerialisation of the Art Object from 1966 to 1972*, Berkeley: University of California Press.

Lloyd Thomas, Katie, ed. (2007), *Material Matters: Architecture and Material Practice*, London: Routledge.

Lorimer, Jamie (2015), *Wildlife in the Anthropocene: Conservation after Nature*, Minneapolis: University of Minnesota Press.

Macnaughtan, Chelle (2012), *[De]Bordering Indeterminacy between Architecture and Music*, PhD thesis, Melbourne: RMIT University.

Mairs, Jessica (2016). 'Christian Kerez Creates Cavernous Cloud to Offer "a Pure Encounter with Architecture" ', *Dezeen*, 27 May. Available online: https://www.dezeen.com/2016/05/27/christian-kerez-cavernous-cloud-installation-swiss-pavilion-venice-architecture-biennale-2016 (accessed 17 October 2016).

Malamud, Bernard (1966), *The Fixer*, Harmondsworth: Penguin Books.

Malm, Andreas (2018), *The Progress of this Storm: Nature and Society in a Warming World*, London: Verso.

Maríudóttir, Katla (2014), *Jarðnæði: Tranquil Terra*, Masters of Architecture Thesis booklet, Stockholm: KTH School of Architecture.

Martin, Reinhold (2005), 'Critical of What? Toward a Utopian Realism', *Harvard Design Magazine*, 22: 1–5.

Martin, Reinhold (2006), 'Moment of Truth', *Log Magazine*, 7: 15–20.

Massey, Doreen (1994), *Space, Place, and Gender*, Cambridge: Polity.

Massey, Doreen (2005), *For Space*, London: Sage.

Massumi, Brian (2002a), 'The Autonomy of Affect' in Brian Massumi (ed.) *Parables for the Virtual: Movement, Affect, Sensation*, 23–45, Durham, NC: Duke University Press.

Massumi, Brian (2002b), 'Introduction: Like a Thought', in Brian Massumi (ed.), *A Shock to Thought: Expression after Deleuze and Guattari*, xiii–xxxix, London: Routledge.

Massumi, Brian (2015), *Politics of Affect*, Cambridge: Polity.

McEwen, Indra Kagis (1993), *Socrates' Ancestor: An Essay on Architectural Beginnings*, Cambridge, MA: MIT Press.

Meillassoux, Quentin (2008), *After Finitude: An Essay on the Necessity of Contingency*, London: Continuum.

Metzger, Jonathan and Amy Rader Olsson (2013), 'Introduction: The Greenest City?', in Jonathan Metzger and Amy Rader Olsson (eds), *Sustainable Stockholm: Exploring Urban Sustainability in Europe's Greenest City*, 1–5, New York: Routledge.

Morar, Nicolae, Thomas Nail and Daniel W. Smith, eds. (2016), *Between Deleuze and Foucault*, Edinburgh: Edinburgh University Press.

Morton, Timothy (2007), *Ecology without Nature: Rethinking Environmental Aesthetics*, Cambridge, MA: Harvard University Press.
Morton, Timothy (2011), 'Here Comes Everything: The Promise of Object-Oriented Ontology', *Qui Parle*, 19 (2): 163–90.
Morton, Timothy (2013), *Hyperobjects: Philosophy and Ecology after the End of the World*. Minneapolis: University of Minnesota Press.
Morton, Timothy (2016a), *Dark Ecology: For a Logic of Future Coexistence*, New York: Columbia University Press.
Morton, Timothy (2016b), 'Hyperobjects', *Release Architecture, Arch+ Journal of Architecture and Urbanism*, edited by Anh-Linh Ngo: 94–99.
Mosley, Stephen (2010), *The Environment in World History*, London: Routledge.
Mostafavi, Mohsen and Gareth Doherty, eds. (2010), *Ecological Urbanism*, Zurich: Lars Müller.
Muller, Brook (2014), *Ecology and the Architectural Imagination*, New York: Routledge.
Nancy, Jean-Luc (1997), *The Sense of the World*, Minneapolis: University of Minnesota Press.
Naess, Arne (1973), 'The Shallow and the Deep, Long-Range Ecology Movement: A Summary', *Inquiry*, 16 (1–4): 95–100.
Ngo, Anh-Linh (2016), 'Editorial', *Release Architecture, Arch+ Journal of Architecture and Urbanism*, 3–4.
Obrist, Hans Ulrich and Tacita Dean (2013), *Tacita Dean: The Conversation Series*, Volume 28, Cologne: Walther König.
Oehy, Sandra (2016), 'Incidental Space Inside the Swiss Pavilion', *ArchDaily*, 7 July. Available online: http://www.archdaily.com/790410/incidental-space-inside-the-swiss-pavilion-at-the-2016-venice-biennale (accessed 17 October 2016).
Oehy, Sandra and Christian Kerez (2016), 'Incidental Space', *Release Architecture, Arch+ Journal of Architecture and Urbanism*, edited by Anh-Linh Ngo: 12–15.
Orff, Kate (2016), *Toward an Urban Ecology*, New York: Monacelli Press.
Osborne, Peter (2014), 'The Postconceptual Condition, or the Cultural Logic of High Capitalism Today', *Radical Philosophy*, 184: 19–27.
Parisi, Luciana (2013), *Contagious Architecture: Computation, Aesthetics, and Space* (Technologies of Lived Abstraction), Cambridge, MA: MIT Press.
Parikka, Jussi (2013), 'Dust and Exhaustion: The Labor of Media Materialism', *ctheory.net*. Available online: http://www.ctheory.net/articles.aspx?id=726 (accessed 31 July 2017).
Parr, Adrian (2008), *Deleuze and Memorial Culture: Desire, Singular Memory and the Politics of Trauma*, Edinburgh: Edinburgh University Press.
Parr, Adrian (2009), *Hijacking Sustainability*, Cambridge, MA: MIT Press.
Pelbart, Peter Pàl (2015), *Cartography of Exhaustion: Nihilism Inside Out*, Minneapolis: Univocal Publishing.
Penfield, Christopher (2014), 'Toward a Theory of Transversal Politics: Deleuze and Foucault's Block of Becoming', *Foucault Studies*, 17: 134–72.
Petrescu, Doina, ed. (2007), *Altering Practices: Feminist Politics and Poetics of Space*, London: Routledge.
Preston, Julieanna (2014), *Performing Matter: Interior Surface and Feminist Actions*, Baunach: AADR Spurbuchverlag.

Prigogine, Ilya and Isabelle Stengers (1984), *Order out of Chaos*, New York: Bantam Books.
Puig de la Bellacasa, Maria (2012), 'Nothing Comes without its World: Thinking with Care', *The Sociological Review*, 60: 197–216.
Puig de la Bellacasa, Maria (2017), *Matters of Care: Speculative Ethics in More than Human Worlds*, Minneapolis: University of Minnesota Press.
Rabaté, Jean-Michel (2002), *The Future of Theory*, Oxford: Blackwell.
Rabaté, Jean and Gregg Lambert (2003), 'Conversation on *The Future of Theory*', *Symploke: Theory Trouble*, 11 (1–2): 39–53.
Rawes, Peg, ed. (2013), *Relational Architectural Ecologies*, London: Routledge.
Reisinger, Karin (2018), 'Insomnia Viewing Ecologies of Spatial Becoming-With', in Hélène Frichot with Gunnar Sandin and Bettina Schwalm (eds), *After Effects: Theories and Methodologies in Architectural Research*, Barcelona: Actar.
Rendell, Jane (2006), *Art and Architecture: A Place Between*, London: I. B. Tauris.
Rendell, Jane (2007), 'Introduction: Critical Architecture: Between Criticism and Design', in Jane Rendell, Jonathan Hill, Murray Fraser and Mark Dorrian (eds), *Critical Architecture*, 1–8, London: Routledge.
Rendell, Jane (2010), *Site-Writing: The Architecture of Art Criticism*, London: I. B. Tauris.
Rendell, Jane (2011), 'Critical Spatial Practices: Setting Out a Feminist Approach to Some Modes or What Matters in Architecture', in Lori Brown (ed.), *Feminist Practices: Interdisciplinary Approaches to Women in Architecture*, 17–56, Farnham: Ashgate.
Rendell, Jane (2017), 'From, in and with Anne Tallentire', *Field: A Free Journal for Architecture*, 7 (1): 13–38.
Rendell, Jane, Barbara Penner and Iain Borden, eds. (2000), *Gender Space Architecture: An Interdisciplinary Introduction*, London: Routledge.
Reporting from the Front, La Biennale di Venezia, Biennale Architettura 2016, 15th International Architecture Exhibition. http://www.labiennale.org/en/architecture/2016/biennale-architettura-2016-reporting-front.
Rogoff, Irit (2003), 'What Is a Theorist?', in Katharyna Sykora (ed.), *Was ist ein Künstler*. Available online: http://www.kein.org/node/62 (accessed 9 September 2016).
Ronell, Avital (2003), *Stupidity*, Urbana: University of Illinois Press.
Rossiter, Ned (2016), *Software, Infrastructure, Labor*, New York: Routledge.
Runting, Helen (2018), 'Architectures of the Unbuilt Environment: An Anthology', PhD Thesis, Stockholm: KTH (Royal Institute of Technology).
Runting, Helen and Hélène Frichot (2016), 'White, Wide and Scattered: Picturing (Her) Housing Career', in Teresa Stoppani, Giorgio Ponzo, and George Themistokleous (eds), *This Thing Called Theory*, 231–41, London: Routledge.
Sandin, Gunnar (2015), 'Modes of Transgression in Institutional Critique', in Louis Rice and David Littlefield (eds), *Transgression: Towards an Expanded Field of Architecture, AHRA Critiques: Critical Studies in Architectural Humanities*, 217–29, Abingdon: Routledge.
Saul, Jennifer (2013), 'Implicit Bias, Stereotype Threat, and Women in Philosophy', in Katrina Hutchison and Fiona Jenkins (eds), *Women in Philosophy: What Needs to Change?*, 39–60, Oxford: Oxford University Press.

Sauvagnargues, Anne (2016), *Art Machines: Deleuze, Guattari, Simondon*, Edinburgh: Edinburgh University Press.
Savage, Charles and Mark Mazzetti (2013), 'Cryptic Overtures and a Clandestine Meeting Gave Birth to a Blockbuster Story', *The New York Times*, 10 June. Available online: http://www.nytimes.com/2013/06/11/us/how-edward-j-snowden-orchestrated-a-blockbuster-story.html?hp&_r=0 (accessed 24 April 2014).
Schrijver, Lara (2009), 'Whatever Happened to Projective Architecture? Rethinking the Expertise of the Architect', *Footprint: Agency in Architecture: Reframing Criticality in Theory and Practice*, 4: 123–27.
Schrijver, Lara and Edwin Gardner (2006), 'The Projective Landscape: In Theory, a Step Forward?' in Henco Bekkering (ed.), *The Architecture Annual 2005–2006: Delft University of Technology*, 44–47, Delft: Faculty of Architecture and the Built Environment, TU Delft.
Schweder La, Alex. (2011) 'Performance Architecture', in Rochus Urban Hinkel (ed.), *Urban Interior: Informal Explorations, Interventions and Occupations*, 131–46, Baunach: AADR Spurbuchverlag.
Scott, Felicity (2007), *Architecture or Techno-Utopia: Politics after Modernism*, Cambridge, MA: MIT Press.
Sebald, W. G. (1998), *The Rings of Saturn*, trans. Michael Hulse, London: Harvill Press.
Sebald, W. G. (2002), *After Nature*, trans. Michael Hamburger, London: Penguin.
Seijworth, Greg and Melissa Gregg (2010), 'An Inventory of Shimmers', in Greg Seijworth and Melissa Gregg (eds), *The Affect Theory Reader*, 1–28, Durham, NC: Duke University Press.
Sellbach, Undine and Stephen Loo (2016), 'Mistress O & the Bees: a Whirlwind of Insects Inside the Body of a Girl', in Peg Rawes, Stephen Loo and Timothy Mathews (eds), *Poetic Biopolitics: Political and Ethical Practices in the Arts and Humanities*, 81–106, London: I. B. Tauris.
Sellbach, Undine and Stephen Loo (2015), 'Insects and Other Minute Perceptions in the Baroque House', in Hannah Stark and Jon Roffe (eds), *Deleuze and the Non-human*, 103–21, London: Palgrave Macmillan.
Serres, Michel (2007), *The Parasite*, Minneapolis: University of Minnesota Press.
Serres, Michel (2015), *Statues: Second Book of Foundations*, London: Bloomsbury.
Serres, Michel and Bruno Latour (1995), *Conversations on Science, Culture, and Time*, Ann Arbor: University of Michigan Press.
Schaffner, Anna K. (2016), *Exhaustion: A History*, New York: Columbia University Press.
Shaviro, Steven (2011), 'The Actual Volcano: Whitehead, Harman, and the Problem of Relations', in Levi Bryant, Nick Srnicek and Graham Harman (eds), *The Speculative Turn: Continental Materialism and Realism*, 279–90, Melbourne: Re.Press.
Shaviro, Steven (2014), *The Universe of Things: On Speculative Realism*, Minneapolis: University of Minnesota Press.
Shiva, Vandana (2012), 'The Corporate Control of Life', in Carolyn Christov-Bakargiev (ed.), *Documenta 13: The Book of Books*, 121–24, Berlin: Hatje Cantz.

Shouse, Eric (2005), 'Feeling, Emotion, Affect', *M/C Journal*, 8 (6). Available online: http://journal.media-culture.org.au/0512/03-shouse.php (accessed 30 September 2016).
Simondon, Gilbert (1992), 'The Genesis of the Individual', in Jonathan Crary and Sanford Kwinter (eds), *Incorporations*, 297–319, New York: Zone.
Sloterdijk, Peter (2007a), *Terror from the Air*, Los Angeles: Semiotext(e).
Sloterdijk, Peter (2007b), 'Cell Block, Egospheres, Self-Container', *Log Magazine*, 10: 89–109.
Sloterdijk, Peter (2009), 'Rules for the Human Zoo', *Environment and Planning D: Society and Space*, 27: 12–28.
Sloterdijk, Peter (2014), *Globes: Spheres Volume II: Macrosphereology*, New York: Semiotext(e).
Sloterdijk, Peter (2016), *Foams: Spheres III*, South Pasadena, CA: Semiotext(e).
Smith, Chris and Andrew Ballantyne, eds (2011), *Architecture in the Space of Flows*, London: Routledge.
Smith, Daniel (1998), 'Introduction: "A Life of Pure Immanence": Deleuze's "Critique et Clinique" Project', in Gilles Deleuze, *Essays Critical and Clinical*, xi–liii, London: Verso.
Smith, Daniel (2012), *Essays on Deleuze*, Edinburgh: Edinburgh University Press.
Sofia, Zoë (1984), 'Exterminating Fetuses: Abortion, Disarmament, and the Sexo-Semiotics of Extraterrestrialism', *Diacritics*, 14 (2): 47–59.
Sofia (Sofoulis), Zoë (2000), 'Container Technologies', *Hypatia*, 15 (2): 181–200.
Sofoulis, Zoë (2009), 'Social Construction for the Twenty-first Century: A Co-Evolutionary Makeover', *Australian Humanities Review*, 46: 81–98. Available online: http://australianhumanitiesreview.org/2009/05/01/social-construction-for-the-twenty-first-century-a-co-evolutionary-makeover/ (accessed 5 February 2018).
Solnit, Rebecca (2000) 'Paris, or Botanizing on the Asphalt', *Wanderlust: A History of Walking*, London: Penguin Books, 196–213.
Sörlin, Sverker and Paul Warde (2009), *Nature's End: History and the Environment*, Basingstoke: Palgrave Macmillan.
Speaks, Michael (2000), 'Which Way Avant Garde?' *Assemblage*, 41: 78.
Spencer, Douglas (2016), *The Architecture of Neoliberalism: How Contemporary Architecture Became an Instrument of Control and Compliance*. London: Bloomsbury.
Spinoza, Baruch (1967), *Spinoza's Ethics and on the Correction of the Understanding*, London: Everyman's Library.
Spooner, Michael (2013), *A Clinic for the Exhausted: In Search of an Antipodean Vitality, Edmond and Corrigan and an Itinerant Architecture*, Baunach: Art Architecture Design Research (AADR), Spurbuchverlag.
Spuybroek, Lars (2016), *The Sympathy of Things: Ruskin and the Ecology of Design*, London: Bloomsbury.
Star, Susan and James Griesemer (1989), 'Institutional Ecology, "Translations" and Boundary Objects: Amateurs and Professionals in Berkeley's Museum of Vertebrate Zoology, 1907–39', *Social Studies of Science*, 19 (3): 387–420.
Stead, Naomi (2015), 'Architecture and Memory in W. G. Sebald's "Austerlitz"', *ARQ: Architectural Research Quarterly*, 19 (1): 41–48.
Stengers, Isabelle (2000), *The Invention of Modern Science*, Minneapolis: University of Minnesota Press.

Stengers, Isabelle (2005a), 'Introductory Notes on an Ecology of Practices', *Cultural Studies Review*, 11 (1): 183–96.
Stengers, Isabelle (2005b), 'The Cosmopolitical Proposal', in Bruno Latour and Peter Weibel (eds), *Making Things Public: Atmospheres of Democracy*, 994–1003, Cambridge, MA: MIT Press.
Stengers, Isabelle (2005c), 'Deleuze and Guattari's Last Enigmatic Message', *Angelaki*, 10 (2): 151–67.
Stengers, Isabelle (2010), *Cosmopolitics I*, Minneapolis: University of Minnesota Press.
Stengers, Isabelle (2011a), *Cosmopolitics II*, Minneapolis: University of Minnesota Press.
Stengers, Isabelle (2011b), 'Wondering about Materialism', in Levi R. Bryant, Nick Srnicek and Graham Harman (eds), *The Speculative Turn*, 368–80, Melbourne: Re.Press.
Stengers, Isabelle (2011c), *Thinking with Whitehead: A Free and Wild Creation of Concepts*, Cambridge, MA: Harvard University Press.
Stengers, Isabelle (2012), 'Reclaiming Animism', *e-flux*, 36. Available online: http://www.e-flux.com/journal/36/61245/reclaiming-animism (accessed 2 February 2017).
Stengers, Isabelle, in conversation with Heather Davis and Etienne Turpin (2013), 'Matters of Cosmopolitics: On the Provocations of Gaïa', in Etienne Turpin (ed.), *Architecture in the Anthropocene: Encounters among Design, Deep Time, and Philosophy*, 171–82, Ann Arbor: Open Humanities Press, Michigan Publishing.
Stengers, Isabelle (2014), 'Speculative Philosophy and the Art of Dramatization', in Roland Faber and Andrew Goffrey (eds), *The Allure of Things: Process and Object in Contemporary Philosophy*, 188–217, London: Bloomsbury.
Stengers, Isabelle (2015), *In Catastrophic Times: The Coming Barbarism*, trans. Andrew Goffey, Ann Arbor, MI: Open Humanities Press and Meson Press.
Stengers, Isabelle (2017), Lecture presented at Isabelle Stengers: Thinking with Stengers, Kaaitheatre, Netherlands. Available online: https://livestream.com/kaaitheater/isabellestengers/videos/149358903 (accessed 7 April 2017).
Stengers, Isabelle and Vinciane Despret (2014), *Women Who Make a Fuss: The Unfaithful Daughters of Virginia Woolf*, trans. April Knutson, Minneapolis: University of Minnesota Press.
Stewart, Katherine (2007), *Ordinary Affects*, Durham: Duke University Press.
Stewart, Susan (2001), 'The Coincidence Keeper', in *Tacita Dean*. Catalogue for the Melbourne Festival Australia, Visual Arts Program, Melbourne Australia, curated by Julieanna Engberg, 11 October–3 November 2001.
The Passion of Joan of Arc (1928), [Film] Dir. Carl Theodor Dreyer, France: Société Générale des Films.
Thrift, Nigel (1999), 'The Place of Complexity', *Theory and Culture*, 16 (3): 31–69.
Thrift, Nigel (2006), 'Donna Haraway's Dreams', *Theory, Culture and Society*, 23 (7–8): 189–95.
Thrift, Nigel (2008), *Non-Representational Theory*, London: Routledge.
Thrift, Nigel (2011), 'Lifeworld Inc – and What to Do about It', *Environment and Planning D: Society and Space*, 29: 5–26.
Tilder, Lisa and Beth Blostein, eds (2012), *Design Ecologies: Essays on the Nature of Design*, New York: Princeton Architectural Press.

Trodd, Tamara (2008), 'Tacita Dean, Modernism and the Sculptural Film', in *Art History*, 31 (3): 368–86.
Tsing, Anna, Heather Swanson, Elaine Gan and Nils Bubandt, eds (2017), *Arts of Living on a Damaged Planet*, Minneapolis: University of Minnesota Press.
Tuinen, Sjoerd van (2017), 'Good Sense and Common Sense: A Stengersian Lesson on the PSR'. Available online: https://www.academia.edu/32935808/Good_Sense_and_Common_Sense_A_Stengersian_Lesson_on_the_PSR_2017_my_contribution_to_a_symposium_with_Isabelle_Stengers_ (accessed 20 October 2017).
Turpin, Etienne, ed. (2013), *Architecture in the Anthropocene: Encounters among Design, Deep Time, and Philosophy*, Ann Arbor: Open Humanities Press, Michigan Publishing.
Tyszczuk, Renata and Walker, Stephen (2017), 'Ecology', in Renata Tyszczuk and Stephen Walker (eds), *Ecology, Field*, 4 (1): 1–10.
Tyszczuk, Renata (2017), *Provisional Cities: Cautionary Tales for the Anthropocene*, London: Routledge.
Uexküll, Jakob von (2010), *A Foray into the Worlds of Animals and Humans with a Theory of Meaning*, Minneapolis: University of Minnesota Press.
Ursprung, Philip (2017), 'The End of Theory?' *e-flux*. Available online: http://www.e-flux.com/architecture/history-theory/159230/the-end-of-theory/ (accessed 25 October 2017).
Varda, Agnès (1962), *Cléo from 5 to 7*, Dir. Agnès Varda, France: Ciné Tamaris.
Varda, Agnès (1966), *Les Creatures*, Dir. Agnès Varda, France: Ciné Tamaris.
Varda, Agnès (2000), *The Gleaners and I [Les glaneurs et la glaneuse]* [Film] Dir. Agnès Varda, France: Ciné Tamaris.
Varda, Agnès (2002), *The Gleaners and I: Two Years Later [Les glaneurs et la glaneuse … deux ans après]* [Film] Dir. Agnès Varda, France: C.N.D.P., Canal+, Centre Nationalde la CinEmatographie (CNC).
Verwoert, Jan (2007), 'Exhaustion and Exuberance, Ways to Defy the Pressure to Perform', *Dot Dot Dot* 15, Geneva: Centre d'Art Contemporain.
Vicks, Meghan (2015), *Narratives of Nothing in 20th Century Literature*, London: Bloomsbury.
Walker, Jeremy (2015), 'The Creation to Come: Pre-empting the Bioeconomy', in Jonathan Paul Marshall and Linda H. Conner (eds), *Environmental Change and the World's Futures: Ecologies, Ontologies and Mythologies*, 264–81, London: Routledge.
Wallenstein, Sven-Olov (2010), 'Noopolitics, Life and Architecture', in Deborah Hauptman and Warren Neidich (eds), *Cognitive Architecture. From Biopolitics to Noopolitics. Architecture & Mind in the Age of Communication and Information*, 46–60, Rotterdam: 010 Publishers.
Wambacq, Judith and Sjoerd van Tuinen (2017), 'Interiority in Sloterdijk and Deleuze', *Palgrave Communications*, 3. Available online: http://www.nature.com/articles/palcomms201772 (accessed 5 October 2017).
Weisman, Leslie Kanes (1992), *Discrimination by Design: A Feminist Critique of the Man-Made Environment*, Chicago: University of Illinois Press.
Warde, Paul, Libby Robin and Sverker Sörlin (2018), *The Environment: A History of an Idea*, Baltimore, MD: John Hopkins University Press.
Wertheim, Margaret (2004), 'Crocheting the Hyperbolic Plane: An Interview with David Henderson and Daina Taimina', *Cabinet*, 16. Available

online: http://www.cabinetmagazine.org/issues/16/crocheting.php (accessed 26 April 2017).

Whiting, Sarah and Robert E. Somol (2002), 'Notes around the Doppler Effect and Other Moods of Modernism', *Perspecta*, 33: 72–77.

Whiting, Sarah and Robert E. Somol (2005), 'OK, Here's the Plan', *Log Magazine*, 5: 5–7.

Wulf, Andrea (2016), *The Invention of Nature: Alexander von Humboldt's New World*, New York: Alfred A. Knopf.

Yaneva, Albena (2016), 'Introduction: What Is Cosmopolitical Design?' in Albena Yaneva and Alejandro Zaera-Polo (eds), *What Is Cosmopolitical Design? Design, Nature, and the Built Environment*, 1–20, London: Routledge.

Yaneva, Albena (2017), *Five Ways to Make Architecture Political: An Introduction to the Politics of Design Practice*, London: Bloomsbury.

Yaneva, Albena and Alejandro Zaera-Polo, eds (2016), *What Is Cosmopolitical Design? Design, Nature, and the Built Environment*, London: Routledge.

Yusoff, Kathryn (2016), 'Anthropogenesis: Origins and Endings in the Anthropocene', *Theory, Culture and Society*, 33 (2): 3–28.

Wark, McKenzie (2017a), 'General Intellects', Lecture at the Virtual Futures Salon. Available online: https://www.youtube.com/watch?v=rInfAEHnZXE&feature=youtu.be (accessed 18 September 2017).

Wark, McKenzie (2017b), *General Intellects: Twenty-One Thinkers for the Twenty First Century*, New York: Verso.

Weil, Simone (1952), *Gravity and Grace*, London: Routledge.

Weisman, Leslie Kanes (1994), *Discrimination by Design: A Feminist Critique of the Man-Made Environment*, Chicago, IL: Illini Books.

Weizman, Eyal (2006), 'Lethal Theory', *Log*, 7 (Winter/Spring 2006): 53–79.

Whitehead, Alfred North (1985), *Process and Reality*, New York: The Free Press.

Zourabichvili, François (2012), *Deleuze: A Philosophy of the Event – The Vocabulary of Deleuze*, trans. K. Aarons, Edinburgh: Edinburgh University Press.

Index

Note: Page numbers in *italics* denote figures.

abstraction 44, 109–10, 172–3, 180, 212
actant 103, 113
Actor Network Theory (ANT) 22, 117, 119
actors 10, 103, 104, 121, 122
aesthetic figures 2–3, 11, 199
aesthetics 81, 85, 90, 93, 95, 97, 99, 107, 117, 156, 171, 172, *see also* ethico-aesthetics
affective becomings 134
affects 39–40, 61, 68, 138–9, 151, 154, 166, 177, 178, 191, 201, 207
Agamben, Giorgio 87
Agrawal, Arun 30–1
Ahmed, Sarah 135
Alaimo, Stacy 135
alien other 5, 9
Allen, Adrien 17
Allen, Stan 137
Alþingi (Althing) 118 n.5
Alÿs, Francis 131
Andrasek, Alisa 96–7, 99, 100
Anthropocene 5–6, 9, 21, 38, 42, 45, 94, 95, 179, 184
Anthropocene feminism 26
Anthropogenic landscapes 42–3
Anthropos 5, 21, 94
any-characters-whatever 70
any-space-whatever 70, 72, 74, 161–2, 169, 200
Appadurai, Arjun 86, 137
Aravena, Alejandro 2–3, 88
architectural history 23, 193, 196, 199
Architectural Humanities Research Association (AHRA) 129, 195, 197
architectural space 70, 90, 166
architectural theory 5, 194–200
architectural things 121–4, *see also* thing(s)
Åsberg, Cecilia 23, 105
astronomer 41
Aureli, Pier Vittorio 75
autonomy of all things 98
autre-mondialisation 32
Avanessian, Armen 94

Baird, George 195
Barad, Karen 104, 125
Barber, Daniel 51
Barth, John 200
Bateson, Gregory 12, 20, 25, 30, 55, 56–7, 148
beatitude 206, 207
 after-affect 215–17
 and exhaustion 210–13
Beckett, Samuel 70, 161–2
becoming 11, 44, 85, 95, 103, 120, 122, 125, 133–4, 194, 195
 affective becomings 134
 transformative becomings 44, 172
becoming-imperceptible 115, 145
being for-itself (*être-pour-soi*) 86
being for others (*l' être-pour-autrui*) 86
being in-itself (*être-en-soi*) 86
beings 11, 39, 60, 106, 115, 179, 210
being-there (Dasein) 101–2
Benjamin, Walter 85, 87
Bennett, Jane 27, 86, 113, 114–15, 116–17, 126, 136
Beradi, Franco 'Bifo' 201
Bergson, Henri 123
Berlin, Anita 56

Big Data 153, 158, 167
Biothing 96–7, 100
biothing 96
Blanchot, Maurice 202
Bloom 100, *100*
body 35, 57, 73, 77, 126–7, 157–8, 161, 177, 182, 201, 210–11
Boots 46, 49–51, *50*
boundary conditions 157, 159–60, 161
boundary objects 86
Bourriaud, Nicolas 56
Braidotti, Rosi 56, 114, 135, 149–50
break-flow 124
broken tool 102–3, 120
Brown, Bill 87
Brown, Lori 62
Brünner, Margit 208–10, 216
Bryant, Levi 135
Bubandt, Nils 5
Buck-Morss, Susan 85
built environments 19–21, 73, 201, 214
Butler, Judith 20, 35
Butt, Gavin 46

Cage, John 111, 112
Capability Brown 42
Carpo, Mario 88
Carson, Rachel 22, 25, 27
Cauter, Lieven De 150
Chatwin, Bruce 3, 5, 198
cinécriture 83
citational practices, across disciplines and practices 101
Clark, Eric 170
Cléo from 5 to 7 85
climate change 5, 9, 13, 23, 25, 26, 95, 135, 136, 168
clinical approach 168, 178, 182–3
Clinic for the Exhausted, A 187–94, *188*, *190*, *192*
co-construction 136–7
Colebrook, Claire 35, 45, 115, 146, 154, 176, 197
collective discourses 133
collective intelligence 9, 29, 30, 150, 153, 155
collective thinking 12, 26, 29, 154
Colomina, Beatriz 44
combinatorials
    of concepts 113
    of images 153, 161, 166, 174, 187–8
    of things 34–5, 36, 68, 72–5, 82, 113, 130, 140, 200
commodification
    of environment and their associated goods 24
    of thought 195
    of worlds 165–6, 170
communication 120, 150, 153, 175
communication technology 155
computational ecologies 96
computational technologies of representation 120
computation in architecture 96–100, 106, 113
concepts 12, 61, 178, 181–2, 201, *see also* concept-tools
    combinatorials of 113
    construction of 187, 201
    pedagogy of 183–4
concept-tools 10, 12, 23, 68, 150, 169, 176, 179–87, 201, 211, 212–13
concrete learning processes 178
Conley, Verena Andermatt 31, 56
constructivism 136, 181
    cultural constructivism 103, 134, 135
    social constructivism 103, 132, 134, 135, 149
container technologies 33, 82, 145, 147–8
contemplation 87, 175, 177
Coole, Diana 134, 135
correlationism 106, 176
Corrigan, Peter 189, 192–3
counter-thoughts 151–2
Counter Weight Room Mate 77
creative openness 123
creative practices 6, 7–13, 17–18, 21, 41, 46, 61–4, 70–1, 110, 115, 127, 131, 137, 148, 183, 184, 187, 191, 195, 198, 203, 205, 207, 216–17
creative resistance 13, 83, 131, 168, 194, 203, 205, 215
critical theory 149–50, 168, 197
critical thinking 149–50, 173, 182–3
Crochet Coral Reef 185
Crutzen, Paul 5, 9

cultural constructivism 103, 134, 135
Cunningham, Merce 47

Damkjaer, Camilla 213–15
Dark Ecology 95, 96
Dasein, *see* being-there (Dasein)
Dean, Tacita 46–52, 68, 215
Debaise, Didier 24, 55, 109
decolonization, of nature 8, 25, 63
Deleuze, Gilles 22, 42, 44, 45, 61, 66, 70, 73–4, 99, 107, 110, 121, 123, 141 n.8, 145, 149, 152, 159, 167, 174–5, 176–7, 180, 181, 182, 184, 193, 200–1, 206–7, 210–13
    on chaos 152
    Cinema 1: The Movement Image 74, 77–8, 206
    Cinema 2: The Time-Image 206
    circuit breakers 168
    concept-movement of flows 124
    concept of intensity 172
    creative philosophy 61
    definition of territory 44
    on duration of monument 121–2
    on error 1172
    on ideas 149
    Image of Thought (*see* Image of Thought)
    on landscape perception 43–4
    Logic of Sensation, the 171
    methodology of exhaustion (*see* methodology of exhaustion)
    on philosophy 202
    on philosophy of communication 175–6
    plane of immanence 177–8, 181, 198
    on point of view 44
    on power of indefinite articles 66–7
    on proposition 172–3
    thought-image of theory 180
    transcendental empiricism 123
    on weariness of thought 202
Demos, T. J. 8, 25, 58, 63
Despret, Vinciane 187
deterritorialization 168, 214
diffraction 22, 104
Ding 122
dingpolitik 93, 98, 119
disaster of thought 149, 184

dogmatism 68, 72, 151, 153, 168–9, 200–1
Dorrian, Mark 24
Doucet, Isabelle 110, 117, 198
Doyle, Shelby 82
Dücker, Jasmin 13 n.1
dust 23, 47, 87, 88, 138

ecology(ies) 40, 55–6
    computational ecologies 96
    of creative practices 10, 61–4
    mental ecology 57, 167
    of practices 58–61
    and respect 59–60
    rethinking in architecture 56
    'think by the milieu' 61
    and tools 60
Ecology without Nature 96
ecosophy
    definition of 57
    environmental ecosophy 58
    mental ecosophy 57–8
    social ecosophy 57
eco-subjects 31
Eisenman, Peter 195
Elkin, Lauren 85
Else, Elizabeth 37
emotions 39, 47, 92, 139, 161, 191
entanglement 6, 9, 22, 28, 32, 40, 42, 47, 61, 66, 104, 109, 122, 125–6, 127, 131, 134, 135, 167, 177, 183, 187, 198, 199
environing acts 25, 29, 44
environmental ecosophy 58
environmental humanities 9, 23–4, 27
environmentalism 25, 27
environmentalities 8, 11, 17, 29–31, 36, 56, 61
    and eco-subjects 31
    origin of concept of 30
environment(s) 19–29, 94
    access to 24
    built environments 19–21, 73, 201, 214
    crisis 28–9
    description of 19
    exhaustion 28–9
    flow-through of 23
    intrusions 22–3

as a man-made milieu 26–7
and nature 24, 28
not as a given and stable condition 21–2
and organisms 20, 22–3, 40
support from 19, 20–2
environment-worlds 7–9, 10, 11, 35, 36–45, 58, 60, 77, 108, 110, 111, 154, 169, 177–8, 183, 195, 205, 216 see also worlding; world(s)
   affects 39–40
   Anthropogenic landscapes 42–3
   bubble-worlds 38–9, 40
   definition of 36–7
   exhaustion of 69–78, 74
   extreme perspectivism 40–1
   local environment-world 4, 56, 65, 67, 68, 74, 85, 100, 102, 104, 121, 127, 145, 148, 151, 154, 212, 215
   perspectivism 43–4
   posthumanities paradigm 37–8
   power relations 19, 42, 63
   and storytelling 27, 28
   and subjectivity 57
   territorialization 44–5, 214
ethico-aesthetics 12, 21, 56, 63, 78, 198, 208, see also aesthetics
ethology 37, 178, 183, 217 n.2
event(s) 46, 122–3
   architectural events 66, 67, 67–8
   ethical aspect of 122
   landscape events 65, 66, 67
   narrative events 66, 67
   remembering and misremembering 49
exhaustion 5–6, 8, 10, 12, 18–19, 23, 69, 71, 189, 194–203
   after-affect 215–17
   beatitude 210–13
   methodology of (see methodology of exhaustion)
   process of gleaning 12–13
   of things 137–40
   and tiredness 71
exhaustive combinatorials of images 166
exhaustivity 12, 77, 201
expressions 11, 21, 39, 44, 109, 122, 132, 135, 173, 177
extenuation
   of environment-worlds 73
   of space 70, 72, 73, 74
extinctions 5, 8, 12–13, 19, 26, 42, 47, 48, 51, 69, 71, 115, 146, 183, 215
extinct theory 115, 146
extractions 34, 45, 56, 82, 211
extreme perspectivism 37, 38, 40–1

Fatigue Kills 157
feelings 39, 60, 63, 71, 84, 111, 191
feminism 10–11, 26–7, 35, 72, 101, 105
feminist new materialism 105, 134–5, 147
feminist practices 127, 132–3
feminist situated knowledges 132
fictions/facts, created 29
flâneur, flâneuse 85
Fletcher, Richard 30, 31
Forehand, Leslie 82
Foucault, Michel 22, 30–1, 138, 166, 181
Frost, Samantha 134, 135

Gabrielsson, Catharina 63
Gage, Mark 106
Gaia 25, 184, 206
Gan, Elaine 5
Gannon, Todd 107
gas warfare 30
Gatens, Moira 178
gathering 82, 118 n.5, 119–21, 152, 207
   around thing (see thing(s), gathering of and around)
Gibbs, Anna 46
Gibson-Graham, J. K. 61
Gissen, David 62, 134
glaneurs, glaneuse 83, 85
Gleaners and I, The (Les Glaneurs et la Glaneuse) 81, 84
Gleaners and I, The: Two Years Later 82, 84
gleaning 81–6, 87, 112, 113
globalization
   definition of 31
   and worlding, distinction between 31–2
governmentality 30–1

INDEX

Gregg, Melissa 151
Grosz, Elizabeth 26, 38, 40, 45, 87, 133, 135
Ground Maintenance 128–9
Guattari, Félix 26, 29, 55–6, 57, 61, 110, 121–2, 145, 151–2, 168–9, 181, 183–4, 193, 201, 207
　on chaos 152
　concept-movement of flow 124
　creative philosophy 61
　on duration of monument 121
　on ideas 149
　on Image of Thought, *see* Image of Thought
　on landscape perception 43, 45
　on philosophy of communication 175
　on plane of immanence 123, 177–8, 181, 198
　on subjects 167
　on territorialization 40, 214
　on weariness of thought 202–3
gut, gutter 126

habitat 8, 28, 40, 55, 57–60, 69, 70, 75, 186
habits, reorientation of 25–6
Haeckel, Ernst 55
Ha Ha Wall 42
Hamburger, Michael 47
Hamer, Michelle 156–62
handstand (Camilla Damkjaer) 213–15
Haraway, Donna 10, 20, 21, 24, 27, 179–80, 184, 186, 187, 208
　on autre-mondialisation 32
　on collective discourses 133
　on entanglement 125, 126
　on situated knowledges 132, 146, 184–5
　on worlds and storytelling 34–5
Hardt, Michael 155
Harman, Graham 86, 95, 98–100, 101
Harrison, Ariane Lourie 38, 62
Hauptman, Deborah 154, 155
Hayles, N. Katherine 125, 154
Hays, K. Michael 195
Heidegger, Martin 33, 34, 87, 91, 101
　tool analysis 101–2
Heise, Ursula K. 9
Hekman, Susan 135

Held, Virginia 132
Henderson, David 185–6
Hight, Christopher 155
Hollinghurst, Alan 193
homo oeconomicus 30, 138–9
Homo sapiens 9, 147
housing issues 156, 170
Hughes, Ted 47
human–soil relations 24
human subject 20, 30, 41, 44, 57, 63, 87, 94, 98, 102, 125, 133, 136, 166, 167, 169, *see also* subjectivation; subject(s)
Humboldt, Alexander von 55
Hurley, Robert 42–3
Husserl, Edmond 176
hyperbolic planes 185–6
hyperobjects 28, 33–4, 86, 92, 93–6

ideas 34, 56, 71, 73, 74, 84, 140, 149, 153–4, 174
　adequate 210, 211, 212, 216
　association of 84, 202
　and concepts 179, 182
　and images 153, 174, 187–8, 189, 191
　inadequate 211, 212
　and subject 169
　and things 200
image making 74
Image of Thought 72–3, 74, 75–6, 83–4, 149–54, 165–75, 177, 187, 198, 200–1, 203, *see also* image(s); thinkables; thinking
images, *see also* Image of Thought
　and ideas 153, 174, 187–8, 189, 191
　of real estate (*see* real estate imagery)
immaterialism 6, 11, 104, 122, 127, 132, 134, 153, 177, 213
Incidental Space 88–93, *89*, *91*, 122
incorporeal forces 6, 11, 36, 69, 127, 134, 213, 215, 216
indefinite article, demarcation using 66–7, 191
indeterminacy 111, 112, 116
indiscipline 7, 13 n.1, 62, 186
infrastructures 19–20, 26, 35, 56, 136–7, 139, 215

Ingold, Timothy 37
intelligible things 31, 105
interconnectedness 55–6, 95, 150
Internet of Things 136, 139
intra-actions 104, 121, 135

Jameson, Fredric 197–8
Janssens, Nel 35
joys 71, 73, 206, 208–10, 215–17, 216

Kafka, Franz 86
Kant, Immanuel 86
Kepes, Gyorgy 25, 26
Kerez, Christian 88, 90, 94, 122
Knapp, Steven 197
knowledge 45, 146, 169, 173, 207
   feminist situated knowledges 132
   about knowledges 34
   practical knowledge versus theoretical knowledge 102
   situated knowledge 27, 132–3, 180, 184
   Spinoza's first kind of knowledge 210–11
   Spinoza's second kind of knowledge 211
   Spinoza's third kind of knowledge 206, 210, 212
Kohn, Eduardo 20
Koolhaas, Rem 117

Lambert, Gregg 198
landscape events 65, 66, 67
Latour, Bruno 21–2, 25, 28, 37, 67, 87, 90–3, 98, 103, 119, 120, 122, 149
Lavin, Sylvia 191, 195, 197
La Voix 113
Lawrence, D. H. 137–40
Lazzarato, Maurizio 153
Leach, Neil 97
Lebovici, Elizabeth 141 n.3
LeMenager, Stephanie 23, 27
Les Créatures 84
Les Saisons 113
Levinas, Emmanuel 202
Life in the Fast Lane 158
Lippard, Lucy 137
Litniaski, Bodan 85
Lloyd, Genevieve 178

logistical worlds 136
Lovelock, James 25
Luke, Timothy W. 30

Ma Cabane de l'Échec 84
machinic assemblage 193
machinic servitude 167
Macnaughtan, Chelle 109–16, 117
Maintenance Art Manifesto 129
Mairs, Jessica 90
Malamud, Bernard 207
Malm, Andreas 22
man-made milieu, environment as 26–7
manufactured environments, *see* built environments
Maríudóttir, Katla 64–9, 186
Martin, Reinhold 92, 195
Massey, Doreen 10, 123, 134
Massumi, Brian 29, 59, 151, 175, 177
materialism 103, 134–5
   new 86, 105, 127, 134–5, 213
materialization 123, 133–4
Material Matters 129
Matrix, The 95
McEwen, Indra 200
meditation on things 91
Meillassoux, Quentin
mental ecology 57, 167
mental ecosophy 57–8
mental image 169, 200
mentalities 29–30
   and mind, distinguished 29–30
mental space 168
methodology of exhaustion 71–5, 153, 161–2
   conjoined with exhaustive and exhausted 77
   mathematical and geometrical definition of 73
Metzger, Jonathan 165
Michaels, Walter Benn 197
Millar, Jeremy 52
mind 150
   and mentalities, distinguished 29–30
   and nature 25
Mitchell, W. J. T. 41
mondialisation 31, 32
monument 121–2

more-than-human 6, 27, 32, 37, 40, 44, 63, 69, 94, 139, 210, 215, 216
Morton, Timothy 33, 36, 86, 92, 93–5
Mosley, Stephen 28
Moving Stuff 127–33, *128*, *129*
Muller, Brook 56, 62
Mumford, Lewis 148

Naess, Arne 25
Nancy, Jean-Luc 31, 34, 46, 137
nature 24–5, 28, 94
  bifurcation of 24
  and mind 25
nature/culture schema 21–2
naturescultures 94
Negri, Antonio 155
Neidich, Warren 155
neo-liberalism 30, 153, 170, 194
neologism 5, 30, 98, 181
new materialism 86, 105, 127, 134–5, 213
Ngo, Anh-Linh 88, 92
non-humans 11, 19, 20, 23, 27, 33, 36, 37, 41, 44, 60, 68, 78, 84, 92, 94, 100, 113, 116, 122, 125, 134–7, 177, 210
non-representational theory 117
noology 150–2, 153, 154, 176
noopolitics 30, 74, 150, 151, 152–4
noosensorium 154
noosphere 162 n.2
noourbanography 150, 151, 154–6, 178

object-oriented democracy 98, 119–21
Object Oriented Ontology (OOO) 95, 98, 101–9
Object Oriented Programming (OOP) 98–100
object-oriented things 96–8
object(s) 81, 87–8, 98, 133, *see also* thing(s)
  as anti-political 99
  as arche-fossil 86
  boundary objects 86
  of concern 92–3
  dynamics of 123–4
  exhaustion 107
  hyperobjects 28, 33–4, 86, 92, 93–6
  middle-mining 101

overmining 101, 103, 106
political concerns 103
as real 99
as sensual 99
and things, distinction between 92–3, 104
undermining 101, 103
uniqueness 95
withdrawn and inaccessible 33, 94–6, 98–9, 104, 107, 109
Ockman, Joan 196
Oehy, Sandra 90
online environments 29
onto-stories 27
open future 123
organism and environment, counterpoint between 40, 45
Osborne, Peter 31

Pampas de Jumana 1
Parikka, Jussi 23, 154, 201
Parnet, Claire 66
Passion of Joan of Arc, The 207
Patate Utopia 84
pedagogy, of concepts 10, 183–4
Pelbart, Peter Pàl 56, 70–1, 78, 167, 168
percepts, perceptions 8, 35, 38–9, 43–4, 61, 68, 105, 151, 154, 166, 177, 178, 201, 207, *see also* point of view
Perry, Chris 155
perspectivism 37, 38, 40–1, 43–4
Petrescu, Doina 62
philosophy 61, 95, 99, 107–8, 145, 177, 181, 184, 186, 202
  speculative philosophy 105–6
Piccoli, Michel 84
planetary exhaustion 57
Plato 99, 104–5
point of view 2–3, 11, 20, 21, 22, 28, 33, 37, 42–5, 52, 60, 64, 71, 93, 104, 105–6, 114–15, 117, 120, 126, 159, 165, 170, 200, *see also* percepts, perceptions
political gathering 90, 91–3
politics of things 93, 122
pollen allergy analogy 23
Pons, Louis 85

post-human 6, 10, 19, 37–8, 41, 42, 65, 70, 78, 112, 115, 116, 122, 125–6
power 107
  of existence 40
  of Image of Thought (*see* Image of Thought)
  of naming a architecture 25
  of storytelling 27
  thing-power (*see* thing-power)
power relations 19, 42, 63
practical knowledge and theoretical knowledge, distinction between 102
Preciado, Paul 32
present-at-hand tool 101, 102, 120, 136
presentations 121
Preston, Julieanna 117, 126–33, 127
privileged things 104, 120
Probiotics' Agentware 96
Puig de la Bellacasa, Maria 24, 125

Quad et autres pièces pour la télévision 70, 72, 162
quadruple object 99
quasi-objects 87, 123, 124, 151, 166
quasi-subjects 124, 151, 166

Rabaté, Jean-Michel 198
Raggatt, Howard 189
Rawes, Peg 25, 26, 55, 56, 62–3
ReActor 77
ready-to-hand tool 3, 101, 102, 136
real estate imagery 165, 170–3
recognition 173
Reconciliation of Carboniferous Accretions, A 129, *130*
reflection 17, 87, 92, 93, 96, 175
Reiche, Maria 1–5, 11, 21, 93, 198
Reisinger, Karin 27
relationality 40, 63, 105, 124
  rejection of 106
relationism 33, 106
Rendell, Jane 46, 111, 180
representations 119, 120
responses 178
Roffe, Jon 162 n.3
Rogoff, Irit 46
Ronell, Avital 202, 206
Rossiter, Ned 136, 139

Royoux, Jean-Christophe 32
Runting, Helen 63, 155–6, 165, 170
Ruy, David 107

Sartre, Jean-Paul 86
Sauvagnargues, Anne 45, 182, 183
Schaffner, Anna K. 71
Schweder, Alex 75–7
Science Technology Studies (STS) 22
Scott, Felicity 26
Sebald, W. G. 47, 52
Seijworth, Gregory 151
selection 45, 82, 166, 211
Serres, Michel 87, 120, 123–4, 166
Shaviro, Steven 105–6
Shelley, Ward 77
shock to thought 147, 177, 178–9, 182, 187
signs 11, 36, 38–9
situated knowledges 27, 132–3, 146, 180, 184
situated learning 132
Sloterdijk, Peter 28, 30, 150
Smith, Daniel 124, 182
social constructivism 103, 132, 134, 135–6, 149
social ecosophy 57
social life of things 86
Socrates, cave analogy 104
Sofia, Zoë (Sofoulis) 11, 28, 35, 82, 135–6, 145–8, 201
Solnit, Rebecca 85
Somol, Robert E. 195
sound, spaces of 111, 113
space 26, 41, 62, 69–74, 78, 83, 88–93, 99, 103, 161–2, 200, 206, 207–8
space–time continuums 134
Speaks, Michael 195, 197
speculative facts 27
speculative fictions 27
speculative philosophy 105–6
speculative realism 101, 105–6, 108
Spinoza, Baruch 71, 73
Spooner, Michael 187–94
Spuybroek, Lars 87
Stability 77
Stengers, Isabelle 10–11, 17, 22, 25, 26, 35, 42, 61, 86, 105, 146, 178, 182, 187, 203, 205, 207, 210

on concept-tool 179–80, 184, 186
cosmopolitical approach to design 28, 58–9, 63, 198
ecology of practices 58–60
factishes concept 29
Gaia theory 25, 184, 206
on order and chaos 152
on privatization of resources 24
on teaching philosophy 184
on things 108–9
on thinkables 149, 174
Stewart, Susan 48
Stirring Stillness: Aesthetic Refinement on a Concrete Plane 130
Stoermer, Eugene 5, 9
storytelling approaches
and environment-worlds 27, 28
and worlds 34
Strathern, Marilyn 34
stupidity 202, 203, 206
and exhaustion 202
subjectivation 151, 167, 183
subjectivity, subjectification 43–4, 57, 63, 166, 167, see also subject(s)
subject(s) 167
dynamics of 123–4
human subject (*see* human subject)
non-human subject 41
unstable and constrained 167
Susan, Starr 86
Suspension Test 18
sustainability discourse 9
Swanson, Heather 5

Tarde, Gabriel 154
technological infrastructures 19–21
technological objects 120
territory, territorialization 7, 8, 18, 23, 24, 26, 28, 38, 39–40, 42, 44–5, 69, 70, 76, 152, 154, 179, 183, 210, 213–14, 216
Thiele, Kathrin 23, 105
thing-feeling 87
thingness of things 23, 102, 104, 108, 117
thing-power 86, 116–18
architectural things 121–4
entanglement of things 125–6
object-oriented democracy 119–21

thing(s) 10, 11–12, 81, 86–7, 91, 133–7, see also object(s)
accumulation of 140
boundary objects 86
gathering of and around 87, 90, 93, 118 n.5, 135, 140
hyperobjects 93–6
as hyperobjects 86
intelligible things 31, 105
object-oriented things 96–8
political gathering 90, 91–3
politics of 93, 122
quasi-objects 87
social gathering 90, 93
social life of 86
thingness of 23, 102, 104, 108, 117
Things (short story) 137–40
things for us (phenomena) 86
things-in-themselves (noumena) 86
thing theory 87
thinkables 10, 12, 149–50, 174–9, see also Image of Thought; unthinkables
thinking 108–9, 168, see also Image of Thought
weariness of thought 107, 202
Thomas, Katie Lloyd 129
Thrift, Nigel 32, 125, 135, 154
tool and broken tool 102–3, 120, see also concept-tools
Trottoirs 109–16
Tsing, Anna 5, 41–2, 147
Tuin, Iris van der 105
Turnbull, David 97
Turpin, Etienne 9
Twombly, Cy 51
Tyszczuk, Renata 56

Uexküll, Jacob von 36–7, 38, 39, 40–1, 45, 55, 60, 76, 114
Ukeles, Mierle Laderman 114, 128
Umwelt, Umwelten 11, 17, 37–8, 41, 45, 55, 75, see also environment-worlds
unthinkables 11, 115, 145–8, 149, 172, 179, 215, see also thinkables
urban gleaners 82, 84, 85
urban problem 30, 112, 117, see also noourbanography
Ursprung, Philip 196–7

van der Tuin, Iris 23
Varda, Agnès 11, 81–6, 148, 159
Vernadsky, Vladimir 162, 162 n.2
Verwoert, Jan 71, 194
vibrant matter 116, 131, 133
visual representation 119–20
vitalism 71, 134

Walker, Stephen 56
Wark, McKenzie 181
'we,' enunciation of 20, 73
Weibel, Peter 92, 103
Weisman, Leslie Kane 26
Weizman, Eyal 168
Wertheim, Christine 185
Wertheim, Margaret 185
When War Is Over 160
Whitehead, A. N. 24, 105, 107–8, 123
Whiting, Sarah 195
Williams, Chris 97
Wiscombe, Tom 107
Wolfe, Cary 37
worlding 31, 34, 35, 36
and globalization, distinction between 31–2
world(s) 31–5, 94, *see also* environment-worlds; worlding
as an exhausted concept 33
bubble-worlds 38–9, 40
as container 33
and creatures 37, 41
definition of 33
forming of 34
logistical worlds 136
sensual 34, 44
and storytelling 34
world worlds 34–5

Yaneva, Albena 28, 60–1, 117, 122
Your Turn 75, 75–6
Yusoff, Kathryn 9

Zitouni, Benedikte 110
Žižek, Slavoj 98
Zourabichvili, François 171, 174
Zwischen Büschl 212

www.ingramcontent.com/pod-product-compliance
Ingram Content Group UK Ltd.
Pitfield, Milton Keynes, MK11 3LW, UK
UKHW021838220426
470268UK00007B/241